The Theological Papers
of
John Henry Newman

The Theological Papers of John Henry Newman

on

Faith and Certainty

partly prepared for publication by
Hugo M. de Achaval, S.J.

selected and edited by
J. Derek Holmes

with a note of introduction by
Charles Stephen Dessain

CLARENDON PRESS · OXFORD
1976

Oxford University Press, Ely House, London W.1

GLASGOW   NEW YORK   TORONTO   MELBOURNE   WELLINGTON
CAPE TOWN   IBADAN   NAIROBI   DAR ES SALAAM   LUSAKA   ADDIS ABABA
DELHI   BOMBAY   CALCUTTA   MADRAS   KARACHI   LAHORE   DACCA
KUALA LUMPUR   SINGAPORE   HONG KONG   TOKYO

ISBN 0 19 920071 8

© *The Birmingham Oratory 1976*

Printed in Great Britain by
Cox & Wyman Ltd
London, Fakenham and Reading

Contents

Introduction

WHEN Cardinal Newman died on 11 August 1890 he left behind at the Birmingham Oratory various writings of his own, some of them background material for his biographer, some of them preparatory work for one or other of his books, none actually meant to be published. He had expounded authoritatively his views and his history in a long series of publications, which he revised and included, with only minor omissions, in the forty or so volumes of a uniform edition. Nevertheless, from the time he died there has been a demand that some of the hidden riches should be made available. From the middle of the twentieth century the number of those consulting his papers has steadily grown. Quite apart from their historical value, these papers make it possible to see how Newman wrestled with problems, and they sometimes supplement his published work or expound it more vividly. A certain amount, chiefly writings on spiritual subjects, has already appeared in print. In 1893 William Neville brought out *Meditations and Devotions*, which has often been reprinted; in 1913 the volume of *Sermon Notes . . . 1849–1878* was edited by the Fathers of the Birmingham Oratory. In 1956 appeared *Autobiographical Writings*, and in 1957 *Catholic Sermons*. In 1969 Placid Murray was responsible for *Newman the Oratorian*, which contained Newman's papers on the Oratory and on the religious life in community. In the same year came Edward Sillem's study of Newman's philosophy, introductory to *The Philosophical Notebook*, edited by Sillem and revised by A. J. Boekraad in 1970. There remain to be published some 250 Anglican sermons and the various papers on philosophical and theological subjects, of which the present volume is the first instalment. It is hoped to publish eventually two further volumes of Newman's papers on doctrinal subjects, one containing those written as an Anglican, and the other those on the inspiration of Scripture and on papal infallibility. Hugo M. de Achaval, S. J. began to collect the material and to annotate it for these three volumes until his return to his native Argentina in 1970. This present volume of Newman's papers on faith and certainty has been selected and edited by J. Derek Holmes, lecturer in Church History at Ushaw College, Durham.

These papers are quite separate from and independent of *The Philosophical Notebook*, which was a kind of commonplace book, to the first part of which Newman gave the title 'Discursive Enquiries on Metaphysical Subjects' and to the second 'Sundries'. The problems of faith and certainty were ones with which Newman had long been grappling. At the end of his life, in the final paper in this volume, Newman wrote: 'From the time that I began to occupy my mind with theological subjects I have been troubled at the prospect, which

I considered to lie before us, of an intellectual movement against religion, so special as to have a claim upon the attention of all educated Christians.' When he returned from Rome to England in 1847 he lectured to the students at the Oratory and there are papers which show him describing his own views on faith and certainty in the language of traditional Catholic theology.[1] From 1853 the papers on this subject become more his own, and he himself has described the nature of most of those included in this present volume and what makes them into a unified whole. On 30 October 1870, some six months after the publication of *A Grammar of Assent*, he noted in his Journal: 'The book itself I have aimed at writing this twenty years; — and now that it is written I do not quite recognize it for what it was meant to be, though I suppose it is such. I have made more attempts at writing it than I can enumerate.' Then after drawing up a list, Newman added: 'These attempts, though some of them close upon others, were, I think, all distinct. They were like attempts to get into a labyrinth, or to find the weak point in the defences of a fortified place. I could not get on, and found myself turned back, utterly baffled.'[2] The papers in this present volume give an idea of other shapes which *A Grammar of Assent* might have taken, and other books on faith and certainty which Newman might have written. They also enable the reader to follow Newman's efforts to solve his problem, now stressing the part played by the will in the act of faith, now qualifying this and emphasizing the role of the faculty of imagination. In view of what has been said of the importance of Newman's published works these papers in no way supersede *Sermons preached before the University of Oxford* or *A Grammar of Assent*, but they serve to illuminate and even to complement those works.

At the beginning of this volume will be found a list of Newman's theological papers from 1846 until 1886, many of which will take their place in the volume on inspiration and infallibility. Those included here are marked with an asterisk. Not every paper that he wrote on faith and certainty will be found here. Earlier ones have been omitted as not being sufficiently representative of his own thinking, others as being repetitive, a few because, as the list shows, they have already been published. All are available for consultation. The papers printed here were written between 1853 and 1869, excepting the two last, 'Assent of Faith' 1877, and 'Revelation in its Relation to Faith' 1885, which represents Newman's final apologia for this part of his life's work, and rebuts the accusation of scepticism.

The papers are arranged in chronological order. Some passages which Newman erased have been included because of their interest. These are noted as they occur, but it should not be forgotten that nearly all the papers are

---

[1] Some parts of these 1846–8 documents are quoted in David A. Pailin, *The Way to Faith*, London 1969, pp. 205–10.

[2] John Henry Newman, *Autobiographical Writings*, pp. 269–70. This list is supplemented in Pailin, op. cit., pp. 202–4.

The actual manuscript and drafts of *A Grammar of Assent* will be utilized in the projected critical edition of that work.

tentative, unrevised, and unprepared for publication. Newman's alternative readings are inserted in angle brackets, and his marginal notes and corrections are also in angle brackets and are placed where they appear to belong. Newman's own brackets are always printed as round ones, square brackets being reserved for editorial additions. Newman's paragraphs and punctuations are reproduced, except that single quotation marks are printed throughout, and double ones for quotations within them. Further, a parenthesis or quotation which he began with the proper mark but failed to complete, or completed but failed to begin, are supplied. All other punctuation marks supplied by the editor are enclosed in square brackets. Newman's abbreviations, except in the case of proper names, are printed out in full.

CHARLES STEPHEN DESSAIN

The Oratory Birmingham,
Easter 1974

A List of theological papers 1846-1886[1]

17 June 1846	The Assent of Faith	B.9.11 [Birmingham Oratory Archives]
1847?	De Deo	A.18.11
1847	De Catholici Dogmatis Evolutione. Printed in *Gregorianum*, vol. XVI (1935), pp. 402–47	B.7.5
1847	On the Nature of Faith	B.9.11
1847	Several drafts Theses de Fide. Fair copy dated 7 April 1877	B.7.5
1847	Rough draft for Preface to *University Sermons* later written in Latin for J. D. Dalgairns's French translation. Printed in *Gregorianum*, vol. XVIII (1937), pp. 219–60. *The Letters and Diaries of John Henry Newman*, XII, p. 5	B.9.11
1847	Newman's Latin text of the Preface to the French edition of *University Sermons*. Dalgairns's draft with Newman's notes	B.7.5 A.23.1
21 May 1847	On the Church written for R. A. Coffin	B.9.10
1848	On the Church and the Pope. Partly quoted by G. Biemer, *Newman on Tradition*, London 1967, pp. 177–9	A.18.20
18 Feb. 1848	Paper for a lecture on the Pope	A.18.11
1848	On the Certainty of Faith; a final and fuller paper drawn up after lecturing Easter, 1848	B.9.11
1848	De Gratia	B.9.10 A.18.11
1848	De Trinitate	B.9.10

[1] Documents reprinted in this volume are indicated by an asterisk.

*July 1857	Modern Astronomy and the existence of God	A.18.11 A.18.20
*10 August 1857	Preface – Egoism is modesty. Also on 2 September 1857	A.18.11
*August 1857	Imagination	A.18.20
*2 September 1857	The argument for Christianity and the existence of God	A.18.20
*25 September 1857	Arguments for Catholicism	A.30.11
17 October 1857	Our Lord's Age	A.23.1
15 February 1858	On the development of Doctrine. Printed in the *Journal of Theological Studies*, vol. IX 2, October 1958, pp. 329–35, and in *Gregorianum*, vol. XXXIX. 2, July 1958, pp. 589–96	A.43.12
*January or February 1859	Lecture on Logic and Philosophy	A.18.11
*1859	On Mysteries	A.30.11
31 October 1859	Pope Hippolytus	A.23.7
*December 1859	Letter on Economy and Reserve.	See Appendix
*1860	Assent and Intuition. Introduction on Phenomena, Sensation, etc.	A.18.11
1860	On Intuitions	A.30.11
*5 January 1860	On the Evidence for Revelation	A.30.11
*12 January 1860	The Evidences of Religion	A.30.11
*26 January 1860	The Reasoning of the Religious Mind	A.30.11
*12, 13, 14, 27 March 1860	On Certainty and Personal Reasoning	A.18.11 A.23.1 A.30.11
3 April 1860	Personality and Corollary	A.18.11
23, 26 January and 7 March 1861	The Trinity and the belief of the early Church	A.28.8
1861–3	The papers on the Canon and Inspiration of Scripture to be published in a later volume. Printed in J. Seynaeve,[1] *Cardinal Newman's Doctrine on Holy Scripture*, Louvain and Oxford, 1953, pp. 60*ff.	A.11.1 A.11.2 A.11.3 A.11.11 A.13.4 A.23.1 A.35.1 A.35.5 A.43.14
1 September 1861	Letter on Matter and Spirit. Printed	A.46.3

[1] But see also J. H. Newman, *On the Inspiration of Scripture*, London 1967, p. 19, fn.

1882	Newman on Design for Ogle	A.23.8
1886	Rough Drafts of an answer to Principal Fairbairn	B.8.17
*1890	'Revelation in its Relation to Faith', the third of the *Stray Essays on Controversial Points, variously illustrated*, privately printed.	

The Theological Papers
of
John Henry Newman

I Papers of 1853 on the Certainty of Faith

[An elaboration of notes on the Catholic doctrine of the Certainty of Faith written during April 1853].

Such is the Protestant notion of our duty towards our religious sentiments. A man is bound to have his reasons so in hand, if not before him, as to believe only when he can tell over his reasons, if called upon to do so, and in proportion as he can do so. But since he is not to be called candid, unless he professes a willingness to give them up, if they fail him, it follows that he must be contemplating the possibility of their failing him, ⟨their failing him as a thing (to say the least) not impossible,⟩ if his profession be not nugatory, and can never be said to have closed the ⟨his⟩ inquiry.

If this be a correct account of his view, it will follow, that a Protestant disclaims the notion of religious certainty, in any proper sense of the word; for moral certainty, as a Catholic considers implies two things, at least the absence of all doubt on the point of which there is certainty, and, if it be really certainty, not only the absence of doubt, but of fear also. Thus (illustration) He is certain who has neither doubt at present nor fear for the future. Now when a Protestant professes to keep his mind open to change on a point if evidence comes or fails him, he therefore implies that the thing in question may perhaps turn out in the event not true. And, when he considers that his personal acceptance of it as true must even be firmer or weaker with the evidence, he implies it is a question of the greater or lesser probability, that is, of lesser or greater doubt. And the anxiety of Butler to fly off to the consideration of what is *safer*, as I have said, implies this.[1]

The next question is, does the Protestant apply this principle of doubt or certainty to all questions or to some.[2] If to some, he has to draw the line, between those which are certain, those which are not; if, as the language of the foregoing writers seems to imply, he means all, then he is saying that we are not certain, for instance, of the Being of a God. It seems a tremendous statement that we are all uncertain whether there be a God or no; yet, if not, then, here is at least one point on which inquiry is to be closed; we are not to believe in proportion to the proof we have at hand; we are not to profess ourselves open to objections, and to bind ourselves to answer them. On one point at least the passages I have quoted from Protestants do not apply. Why do they not apply? But we heard the reasons. On first starting, the very first religious point which

[1] See below, p. 35.
[2] The rest of this paragraph was deleted.

3

takes us, is in direct opposition to their theory, as they admit. We must have good reasons to satisfy us here. But if they are forthcoming, then we shall have to look sharp that they do not apply to other points of religious belief. Perhaps we may in like manner be certain of the divinity of Christ. Else, they will be exceptions too, and we shall be in the way to destroy ⟨break down⟩ the principle of rational Protestantism altogether. Here there is an apparent dilemma of very serious character; either all religious points are necessarily uncertain; or none are necessarily so.

Let us look at the principle more closely still. We ought to be able to show our reasons, if questioned; who can show his reasons? Who in the whole world on questions ⟨subjects⟩ not mathematical, can give *the* reasons ⟨full and just [reasons]⟩ on which he holds a truth. Why do you believe Louis Napoleon is on the French Throne? The plainer and more obvious a thing is, the more difficult often is it to give reasons. You say a thing is 'too plain to reason about' — is *this* pondering your reasons? If any one asks me so I should laugh in his face.

Certainty is a state where not only doubt but fear is absent.

NB. Since the foregoing remarks are in answer to the Protestant principle 'There is no such thing as speculative certainty in religion, it is really prejudice etc.' The answer should have been

(b) i 1. Is there no such thing as security? (without *fear*?)
    2. Apply it to the Being of a God, etc.
    3. If some where you will draw the line? How far will this series descend? You will say that at least it cannot include historical facts or the Incarnation.
  ii. Explain *how* it can be — latent reasons, which though not brought out avail, and make it a moral certainty they will not all fail.

April 14.

Now we turn to consider the Catholic side of the question; and first, by certainty I suppose is meant a firm reception ⟨simple acceptance⟩ of a fact or truth as existing; and it has two degrees — First by the very word, is implied the absence of doubt; if a person doubts ever so little, he is not certain; and if he does not doubt, he may be called, and is truly called, certain. But there is a question still unanswered, which, if removed, makes way for a higher degree of certainty. A man may doubt, not the result of his arguments and researches, but he may doubt whether there is not some faulty principle at the bottom of this, which invalidates the whole process; as, for instance, that he has not sought in the right direction, or in the right spirit; or that he has omitted some cardinal considerations, or some fields of inquiry, though he is not conscious of having done so. He may be perplexed in fact by an appeal to his ignorance; and be confounded by objections, and by what is known in the matter of his inquiries, but what may be unknown. When he has determined that it would be irrational to enter[tain] any such supposition, or, in other words, *not only concludes from particular grounds, but is clear that these grounds can never substantially fail him,* he is said to be certain without *fear*. Such then are the two stages of certainty: certainty without doubt, and certainty without fear.

Thus, for instance, (the laws of motion are grounded on a vast infinity of observations — so is the proof of the Newtonian doctrine. We cannot have any apprehension that the mass of those proofs will fail us in any great quantity; i.e. we have the higher degree of certainty, viz, that which is without fear).

[The following passages are deleted].

Again ⟨On the other hand⟩, we should trust implicitly to the statements of some eminent man of science who declared that a deluge was coming on the world. We might have no doubt at all, by reason of his proved and wonderful sagacity, in predicting *physical phenomena*. We should say he never has been mistaken, and we have no doubt that he is right now. Still the fact will remain, that the greatest minds may go astray, and this will generate not a doubt, but an apprehension that possibly he may just in this instance exhibit the infirmity of human nature. When however we find that it was not any mere man of science who had reckoned on the prophecy, but God Himself speaking through man, we should have brought the question beyond that of doubt into the province of the domain of fear; for when God Himself speaks a thing, there is no chance of mistake or deceit — the underlying suspicion is cut [?] away, and certainty is without fear. I may have no doubt whatever, that Saint Mark the Evangelist and John Mark were different persons, or that a certain Creed assigned to the Second or Third century was spurious, yet, on hearing of the discovery of some primitive documents which settled the matter ⟨point⟩, I might feel some anxiety as to the result, if I had committed myself in public to my own view; whereas I not only am quite clear beyond doubt that Saint Paul would have considered Protestantism a great heresy, but so far from feeling nervous on the subject, did I hear he had come again on earth and could tell ıs from his own lips, I should hail the news, as my best triumph.

Now this higher state of moral certainty, which is both without doubt and without fear, is a state of mind very familiar to us, and of usual occurrence. No one has any doubt that Louis Napoleon is Emperor of the French, any misgiving that, were he to go to France, he might find it otherwise. You will say that it is just *possible*, no one can say that it is impossible. That is, possible in *idea*, or supposable, but it is not possible in fact. It is impossible that, with such evidence as I have on the subject, it should be otherwise than I believe; moreover it is impossible that that evidence can fail me. It is not impossible to *fancy* Louis Philippe still on the throne or Charles X, as I can *fancy* myself that (I once was Pythagoras or Euphorbus, or that) I shall one day be the Emperor of the French myself. But natural good sense puts aside with a smile such imaginations, and knows very well that Louis Napoleon is on the imperial throne of France. And if some officious philosopher came, and told me that I must be prepared to give up my belief as soon as my grounds for believing

5

went, that I must not believe beyond my grounds, and that I must beware of enthusiasm or prejudice or party spirit, and that it would be safer to take it as practically certain than speculatively, I should laugh in his face, and tell him that certainly I would renounce my belief in Louis Napoleon's sovereignty directly that any ground for believing failed me, but not till then.

Now Protestants mean to say, if they mean anything, that no religious truth or fact can have a certainty of this kind. Catholics say such facts and truths can;[1] and here is the difference between them. Protestants, who deny baptismal regeneration, would have some unpleasant feeling (on their own admission, for they have no certainty on the point) did they hear Saint Paul had come on earth to tell them vivâ voce, for they would feel there was the chance of his giving it against them. Catholics would have no such fear at all lest he should not give it for themselves, and would stake the matter upon that issue. Protestants on their own showing would rather Saint Peter was not here to expound Our Lord's words to him, 'Thou are Peter etc.' Catholics would hail his presence. I am not saying at the moment which view is right or which is wrong, I am prescinding the question of revealed doctrine; I am but illustrating the difference between the Catholic view and the Protestant.[2] I am but drawing out the Catholic line of idea or theory, as such, and it is enough for me, if I do not come across some great improbability or paradox or untruth, which (almost physically) would prevent a reader's mind ⟨intellect⟩ from following me.

(NB. These two sections — viz the Protestant view and the Catholic view, should be blended together in one).[3]

Plan of the work

Statement. I suppose it granted that there are strong and good arguments for Catholicism — but it is objected

1. That there is no such thing as *certainty* — that certainty is *impossible* — that is the point — not to prove that we are certain of this or that.

2. That there are great *objections* to Catholicism

3. That reason generally is against it — whereas it is imagination.

4. That it is obsolete — good in its time. It was quite as much opposed, and on the same grounds, to the early heathen.

On whether a person has a right to be certain — or is certainty without fear according to right reason

Objection — error is always *possible* foreknowledge

answer — not *supposable*. *When* not supposable no definite criterion can be granted any more than about mind's duty. περιωδευομένη [carefully considered]

Objection 2

The *underlying* suspicion, which brings in fear necessarily. I once was not certain of the certainty. Differences of opinion.

[1] These two sentences were not deleted.
[2] See also *Certain Difficulties felt by Anglicans*, London 1901, I, p. 269; *Letters and Diaries*, XVIII, pp. 471–2.
[3] This sentence was not deleted.

Hence about its not subserving the well being of States. This the *early* objection. I can fancy it enter into the bitter, contemptuous spirit of the Pagans.

The young. The otiose.

Objection 3

Then why do you forbid embracing doubts? because they are on false grounds, and so great a tendency in the mind to wish a thing untrue.

April 30, 1853[1]

Opinion   is the belief that an alleged fact is a fact or alleged truth is a truth, without the belief that it cannot be otherwise ⟨must be so⟩.

Doubt   is the absence of belief either that such alleged fact or truth is really such or that it is not. ⟨[absence of belief] that it is such, without the belief that it is not such⟩.

Certainty   is the belief that a fact is a fact or truth is really such, or a truth is a truth, with the belief that it cannot be otherwise.

Persuasion   is an opinion or the belief about an alleged fact or truth (that an alleged fact or truth is really such) with a determination ⟨maintenance/belief⟩ that it can not be otherwise ⟨never to think otherwise/ that that belief will continue⟩.

An argument against an alleged fact or truth is called objection, an argument for it is called a probability and a conclusion against it is called a proof.

Opinion then implies belief when there are probabilities and objections arising out . . .

Doubt implies the absence of belief arising out of ⟨implying⟩ probabilities and objections.

Certainty implies proof.

Persuasion is belief implying probabilities and the absence of objections.

Persuasion is destroyed by objections.

Doubt is destroyed by proof. Opinion is destroyed by proof. Persuasion is destroyed by objections — certainty is not destroyed by objections.

Persuasion is destroyed without an act of the will, and is preserved by an act of the will.

Certainty is destroyed by an act of the will and is preserved without an act of the will.

When a man is 'open to conviction' he means he has a *strong opinion* the other way, *so* strong that nothing but a counter *proof* can overcome it.

An *argument* is an inducement, made to the reason, to (recognize an alleged fact or truth to be such) judge [a fact] as true or false.

An argument, which induces the reason to judge, is called a *proof* for or against it.

---

[1] This paper was erased until the passage beginning 'an argument is an inducement'.

An argument, which tends to induce the reason for or against, is called a *probability* or *objection*.

An *inference* is the judgment for or against made upon that inducement. An inference, which is made upon a proof, is called *conviction*.

An inference, which is made upon a probability or objection, is called *opinion* for or against ⟨favourable or adverse⟩.

Belief is the mental recognition of a judgment for an alleged fact or truth to be such, after an inference.

Disbelief is the rejection ⟨Distrust discount judgment against⟩ of an alleged fact or truth as not such, after an inference.

Belief and disbelief follow, either upon an inference or upon an act of the will.

Belief, following upon an inference, is *belief proper*, if the inference is a favourable opinion for *certainty*, if the inference is a conviction.

[Belief] (following upon an act of the will, is *persuasion*).

Distrust, following upon an inference is *doubt*, if the inference is an opinion against ⟨adverse⟩, *disbelief*, if the inference is a conviction.

[Distrust] (following upon an act of the will, is *prejudice*).

(An act of the) The will can command ⟨effect/create⟩, an act or state of belief or distrust, without or contrary to this previous process of reason.

[Fragment on Scepticism]
April 30. 1853

It is the tendency of a thinking age, viewed apart from the influence of religion, to fall into a state of scepticism, as it is the tendency of an ignorant age, apart from these tendencies, to fall into superstitition. Stagnation and activity of thought ⟨mind⟩ have each in matter of fact, and historically considered, been both of them, hostile to divine truth; not indeed from anything in themselves, for religion is really benefitted by free inquiry, though it can do without it, but because there are deeper and more subtle principles ⟨agents⟩ of our nature really in operation, which, in that warfare against religion which is peculiarly theirs, make use of free inquiry or of unreasoning obstinacy as their instruments. Pride, sensuality, selfishness, worldliness, distrust of God, and similar bad principles are the real enemies of religion, and as these are the ruling spirit in every age of the world, the form which their hostility to it takes in an ignorant age, is superstition, in an inquiring age is scepticism.

We start with what we have received as children; we accept, we prize, we defend, what we have been taught; we may see difficulties in it, which we may not be able to answer, which may tease us, but they do not shake our confidence in it. We try how to answer the objections, which we feel, and we manage to go on without any great trouble of mind. At length as our mind grows, as our information accumulates, as we see more of the world, and exercise more freely our minds, questions occur which really require an answer, and, if we are external to the Catholic Church, begin to impair the implicit trust which we have hitherto cherished in the creed which we have received whether from our parents or our revered instructors. We gradually lose altogether that trust, which once was so simple, with or without the power of attaching ourselves to some other profession. Sometimes perhaps we think we have done so; though, generally speaking, our minds have opened far more *truly* to the hollowness of what we once believed than to the truth of anything else. However, for a time we profess some other creed, and keep steadfastly to it. But the same process recurs, the mind goes on acting, it is filled with objections it cannot answer. It sees the bottomless depth which lies before it, and is unwilling to give up what though only a second, it feels to be virtually a last attempt to gain a hold upon the truth. It attempts to modify, and patch up its theory as it best can; it becomes eclectic, or it tries to throw itself upon authority. One attempt or another it makes to retain itself in its position; but in proportion to the activity, clearness, honesty, and boldness of its intellect, it finds the attempt hopeless; and as time goes on it slowly and calmly is floated upon the open bosom of an ocean without a shore, the dead profound of interminable, hopeless, scepticism, in which nothing is believed, nothing professed, nothing perhaps even guessed at.

Even scepticism cannot be content without some positive theory or view to express and then justify its determinations, and the view which it takes of religious truth and man's duty is such as this:- that in religion we cannot get beyond opinion, that opinions are always in course both of formation, and of destruction, as so many bubbles which are bright and promise well, and then break. Or like the waves of the sea, which diversify its monotonous surface, and seem to be mounting up and forming into something of substance and permanent shape, but which subside and disappear as quickly as they rose. In every country, in every active mind (they will go on to say) these creations are ever coming into being, according to the accident of the time; and, while they are commonly evanescent, yet circumstances may give them a temporary consistency and an appearance of durability. The power of government, the influence of the great, the interests of class, the popular fancy, the national character may conspire to fix and fossilize the ephemeral life, and to hand it down to generations unborn. Then education, habit, association, political expedience may be enlisted in its favour; it may be changed from a religious dogma into a social and civil institution; it may be developed into an establishment; and may be intertwined with the laws of the country. In this way a happy lie ⟨fraud⟩ or dream may become the brightest jewel in a monarch's crown, the palladium of the liberties of a country, or the corner-stone of its philosophy; till the political and social fabric breaks up, and the religious opinion flits away with it. Or it may be surrounded or combined, with sanctions of an awful nature, with anathemas on its denial, with benedictions on its supporters, with the voice of a large religious party, and thus be perpetuated in the world. And so necessary is a fixed faith for temporal and national welfare, so desirable it is to be rid of controversy, so expedient to have a religious and moral sense implanted in a people, so hard to imprint upon a population, that thoughtful and philanthropic minds, which have not a particle of belief in its truth, may yet rejoice that it is successful, and look both with dismay and hatred at those who would overturn it, though it seems to them false, and tolerate a pious fraud better than an irreligious truth. Hence they encourage it, and support it, do anything but in their secret hearts acknowledge it themselves, and this from pure benevolence, since religion supplies a want in human nature, a man is not ⟨perfect and entire⟩ in the perfection and integrity of his powers without it (Vid. Carlyle's lament over the folly of the French Revolution).[1]

If asked, as to their belief in God, or whether they are content to carry out their scepticism to the full extent, some of these persons ⟨men⟩ will go the length of owning that they are sure about nothing; others will have no seriousness enough to answer the question at all, others will be happily inconsistent and will admit the truth; and these have found a moral or a use in the melancholy uncertainty to which they confess. They will say that the search after truth is of greater moral benefit to us than its possession; that we do not ever possess it, but we ought ever to be seeking it; that we shall never be condemned for [not] having it, because we cannot have it, or because there is no such thing as religious truth, or because one religious truth is not truer than another, but we shall be altogether condemned if we do not seek it properly; — that candour, impartiality, honesty, and perseverance are the virtues which will bring us safe to heaven, not faith. Others go further and say that the search after knowledge is far more pleasurable and better than knowledge itself — and some of them accordingly, discarding the Catholic notion of the future reward of the good consisting in the beatific vision ⟨vision of God⟩, consider it consists in a life like this, busy, inquisitive ⟨acquisitive⟩, and various. I am giving a generic account of the school in question, which belongs as a whole to no individual, but in a fuller or scantier ⟨partial⟩ measure to this or that person.

May 13, 1853

Propositions are either true or false: I shall consider them here, however, only as true, because false propositions are but the contradictories of true ones, and thus we may always convert them and view them under their equivalents. It will be more simple and manageable for my line of thought, to view propositions, since we can do so, under one head than under two. ⟨Again they are true either from intuition or from proof. I dismiss the first.⟩
I set off then thus:-

1. An *argument* is an inducement made to the reason to judge a certain proposition to be true.

[1] *The French Revolution,* final chapter.

An argument, which induces the reason to judge it true, is a *proof*.

An argument, which tends to induce the reason to judge it true, is a *probability*.

An argument, which proposes to induce the reason to judge it true, is a likelihood.

2. An *inference* is the judgment following on that inducement. An inference, which follows on a proof, is a *conviction*. An inference, which follows on a probability, is an *opinion*. An inference, which follows on a possibility, is a *view* ⟨an *anticipation* a *presumption*⟩.

3. *Assent* is the acceptance of a proposition as true. Assent is either *absolute* or *conditional* ⟨and in the particular case is always a reflex act⟩.

Absolute assent ⟨or assent without fear⟩ is such as certainty, persuasion, prejudice, unbelief.

Conditional assent is such as belief, doubt, conjecture, suspicion, scruple, etc.

4. Assent follows on inference, and that *by an act of the will*, which determines whether it shall be absolute, or conditional, whether it should ⟨shall⟩ be withheld, or whether it should ⟨shall⟩ be given to the contradictory.

There is, however, a natural sequence and direct correspondence between the kinds of Assent and the kinds of Inference.

5. Absolute Assent naturally follows on a conviction, and is then called *certainty*.

Conditional Assent naturally follows on an Opinion, and is then called *Belief*; and on a View ⟨Presumption⟩, and is then called *Surmise*.

6. Absolute Assent, by a mere act of the will, follows on an Opinion or on a View ⟨Presumption⟩, and is then called *Persuasion*.

Conditional Assent,[1] by a mere act of the will, follows on a Conviction, and is then called *Doubt* ⟨What is above called opinion is often popularly called doubt. Here doubt is always wrong⟩.

7. Since every proposition, which, as being true, admits of proof, a fortiori admits also of probability and of possibility ⟨likelihood⟩, that is, may be held as an Opinion or a View ⟨Persuasion⟩ with the Conditional Assent of Belief, of Surmise, or of Persuasion ⟨the Absolute? Assent⟩, though in its own nature claiming Conviction and Absolute Assent; and since Probability and Opinion, Possibility and View ⟨Presumption⟩, as the words imply, are compatible with ⟨or imply⟩ probability and opinion, possibility and view ⟨presumption⟩, in behalf of the contrary or false proposition, and in consequence with a Conditional Assent, that is, Belief, Surmise, and Persuasion of the false proposition, therefore let us call such assent to the false proposition *Dissent* to the true; such Belief, Surmise, and

---

[1] In later years, Newman would not speak of 'conditional assent', lest it be regarded as conditional in the same sense as inference; assent is absolute and unconditional – we assent *absolutely* to the *probability* of what is only probable.

Persuasion, of the false, *Disbelief, Suspicion,* and *Prejudice* towards the true; and such probabilities in behalf of the false, *objections* to the true.

8. Furthermore, it may happen, that in the absence of proof and of consequent conviction of a true proposition, there may be probabilities and objections producible of equal weight, so that no inference is possible. The state of mind *naturally* following upon this is an absence of Assent, and is called *Suspence,* being the limit? between Belief and Disbelief.

This absence of Assent, when determined by a *mere* act of the will, is called *Ignoring,* whether the inference upon which it comes be a Conviction, Opinion, or Surmise.

9. And thus we have ten intellectual feelings, or postures of mind towards, or modes of receiving, a true proposition; of which six are the natural and legitimate correspondents of certain reasoning processes respectively, under ⟨not without⟩ the determination of the will; and four are the creation solely of that determination; — viz

Certainty, Belief, Surmise, Disbelief, Suspicion, Suspence.
Persuasion, Doubt, Prejudice, Ignoring.

Of these 1. Certainty is the mental posture of Philosophy

2. Belief .... of Conduct ⟨Experimental science?⟩ action.

3. Surmise .... of Inquiry, Curiosity, Inquisitiveness, Discovery.

4. Disbelief .... of Error.

5. Suspicion .... of Scrupulousness.

6. Suspence .... of Ignorance.

7. Persuasion .... of Enthusiasm.

8. Doubt ⟨Hesitation⟩ .... of Scepticism ⟨Doubt⟩.

9. Prejudice................. of Bigotry ⟨the bigot⟩.

10. Ignoring .... of Indifference ⟨the ignorer⟩.

10. For one or other reason, viz because the proposition, or the inference, or the assent is different, these ten mental postures are severally distinct from each other.

11. As to the question, whether any two or more of these mental frames or postures can exist together at the same time in the same mind, it may be replied that it is impossible in any case as regards those frames themselves; but as regards the inference on which they follow, it is possible, when they are such as to assert the same proposition, or not to assert its contradictory. Thus Conviction, Opinion, and Presumption of the contradictory, may all exist at once in the same mind (as drawn severally from distinct arguments) the resulting frame of mind being Certainty. In like manner there may be Opinion, and Opinion of the contradictory, which will result in Belief, or Disbelief, or Suspence. Or Belief may be the

resulting frame of mind of Opinion and View of the contradictory, weakened in proportion to the strength of the contradictory View.

12. Since every natural appointment is right, the former six are right, which are according to nature, and the latter four wrong, which are against nature; — and morally right and wrong respectively, according and so far forth as, in each particular case, the will acts as a moral agent.

§ On the relation of the 10 postures of mind to each other.

1. As each of these ten postures of mind really depends on the will, each can be lost or reversed by the will.

2. As each presupposes as a sine qua non an antecedent act of reason of a definite kind, none of them is simply created by an act of the will.

3. Persuasion and Doubt, Prejudice and Ignoring, are the results of a stronger act of will, than the six natural or rational postures.

4. Persuasion is materially the same as Certainty, and Doubt as Belief, as being respectively an absolute or conditional assent to the same proposition.

5. Persuasion, remaining materially the same, becomes Certainty, and Belief, remaining the same materially, becomes Doubt, when Opinion becomes Conviction.

6. Persuasion becomes ⟨is succeeded by⟩ Doubt, and Belief becomes ⟨by⟩ Certainty when Opinion becomes Conviction.

7. Persuasion is succeeded by Belief, and Belief by Persuasion, simply by an act of the will, for both follow upon Opinion.

8. Certainty is succeeded by Doubt, and Doubt by Certainty, simply by an act of the will, for both follow upon Conviction.

9. Certainty can never be succeeded by any posture of mind but Doubt, nor Doubt by any but Certainty, for Conviction never can become Opinion.

10. What has been said of Belief, may be said mutatis mutandis of Surmise, which is of the nature of Belief.

11. What is said of Persuasion, Belief, and Surmise intra se, may be said of Prejudice, Disbelief, and Suspicion intra, which are the same postures of mind directed to a different subject.

12. Suspence and Ignoring are materially the same; but Ignoring cannot become Suspence, though Suspence can become Ignoring, as soon as there is a View ⟨Presumption⟩, an Opinion, or a Conviction.

Perhaps best to make this chapter
[§ 3] 'Analysis of Religious Inquiry according to the foregoing Rules'
It may be necessary before proceeding to illustrate and interpret some of the statements which have been ⟨are⟩ contained in the foregoing chapter. Nay, even to apply them; for as in pure mathematics truths are stated in the abstract in a way in which they are never found on earth, and then are accommodated in its mixed branches to things as they are, so here we have first

viewed truths ⟨principles⟩ scientifically in their very idea, and shall afterwards have to adapt them and embody them in a concrete form for our use in conduct and controversy.

Now whether or not there be such a thing as conviction in fact, as it has been above defined, which must not be assumed of course without inquiry, so far is plain that, being what it is in idea, it must have certain characteristics as a matter of necessity. If we suppose that there are any objective facts or truths at all, and again that they can be revealed as existing to our minds, it stands to reason that nothing but the loss of our mental powers can hide them again from us.

When I say that a conviction is indestructible, I mean, supposing that the logical platform, premises and inferences, remain (just as a conclusion from sense is indestructible while the impressions on the senses remain and are active.) I mean that the premises which have at one time brought conviction to the mind, will always do so; and that certainty implies the presence of that conviction, acting from the presence to the mind, at least *in confuso*, of those premises. And when I say that the will can obstruct and stifle certainty, I mean conviction remaining. The question then is, can the will, conviction remaining, withdraw the mind from any impression, or, if not, what will it substitute for it?

If, for instance, our senses convey it to us infallibly the fact that a living thinking being is with us in the house, is our companion, converses with us, advises, comforts, and supports us, does us continual good offices, nothing can obliterate from our mind this fact, while our mind is itself. Now conviction is the logical determination of this or any other fact. It is a decisive judgment formed on sufficient proof; and this account of it being taken for granted it is irreversible. Once convinced always convinced. The mind cannot unlearn its own knowledge ⟨intelligence⟩. That it is attainable, I shall show by and bye: here I assume it in the way of science, as I assume there is such a thing as length or breadth, or that from the idea of a line, two lines cannot enclose a space. Before I proceed, this irreversibility of conviction must be clearly entered into, mastered, and allowed.

Next I assume, what I suppose I need not prove, that upon an inference of whatever kind there is a natural spontaneous act of the mind towards it of acceptance or the reverse, which I have above expressed under the word Assent, and said to be under the jurisdiction of the will. E.g. when we believe another's statement, we make it our own, and re-affirm it as if with our lips. So when the reason has drawn an inference, the mind at once takes it up and adopts it, and enters it on its catalogue of knowledge, and that according to its claims for reception, absolute or conditional. And if the inference be (demonstrated or) really proved, or a conviction, then a very special acceptance or recognition of it will take place, sui generis and different from anything else, as a conviction is different from anything else, which acceptance is called certainty. The objective fact then which, viewed as a subject of conviction, is relative to premises, and in the luminousness of its proof, or what is called evidence, when viewed as a subject of certainty, stands absolute and as a first principle and a starting point, as if with an axiomatic force; thus changed indeed in the order of viewing it ⟨its aspect⟩, but the same in this, that it is simply perceived by the mind.

This is one distinction between conviction and certainty, the former is an ending ⟨conclusion⟩, the latter a commencement; the former reasons, the latter ⟨feels⟩ perceives ⟨?⟩ But there is another, at which I have just hinted. This certainty, which though it naturally follows upon conviction, is a making up the mind that a thing is true which is proved, and therefore is under the control of the will; that is, the will may suppress, extinguish the feeling. I do not know whether I shall be called upon to prove this, or may assume it; at all events I shall assume it now, when I am but drawing out a scientific system. The will cannot absolutely create it, for it is the natural and direct result of conviction, but the will can hinder that direct result taking place. The will cannot hinder an inference from premises, when the premises are clearly perceived, for that inference is of a necessary? character, but it can interfere between the perception of the conclusion, the judgment whether it be of opinion or conviction, and the legitimate impression they make upon the mind, if left to themselves. The will then, though it cannot create ⟨force⟩ certainty, can stifle it.

Now here, without limiting the power of the will, I will observe that it is a great principle of the human mind that it cannot proceed in any course without at least a recognition of reason. The brutes are incapable of giving a reason for their movements; man not only can, but is irresistibly impelled to do so; he is restless till he can. What then is the will to do, when a clear conviction is before the mind of a certain fact, which it does not wish to recognise? E g as near to the case of the senses. I am perfectly convinced that I have seen a spirit, but it told me I should die, and this I do not like, and therefore I will reject the fact of its appearance, or will not allow myself to be certain of it. On the other hand, I must offend reason and evidence as little as possible; what then is the wisest course for me? Of course, not to deny it, not to say 'there is nothing in it', not to affect suspence and put it aside, but to say 'I am not certain of it', 'I have nothing to say against it, but I want more evidence'. 'Objections may be argued against it — I don't see how this or that is answered. A case, that is, a view may be made out against it. I cannot argue on the subject, it is incomprehensible, but it does not convince me'. I use the word 'convince', but I mean 'I am not impressed by my conviction'. I cannot refute the arguments that there is an opinion for it, that a view may be taken against it, and therefore I refuse to be certain. I give it a conditional assent, not an absolute assent, but an assent as far as it goes. (I do not mean to say that an abandoned man would not hide his convictions and his fears, under a reckless mockery and denial of the whole occurrence; but I am not treating for madmen; I am describing the posture of mind of men in their senses, of the ordinary mind.)

This conditional assent I have above called Doubt. Doubt is used both by religious and secular writers in a great many distinct senses, and I have applied it to that which it seems to suit best. Sometimes it stands for the ⟨frame⟩ posture into which the mind is thrown ⟨finds itself⟩, when it has no evidence ⟨argument⟩ at all on either side of a question; sometimes it denotes the result of an equivalent weight of evidence on either side; here called suspence — sometimes of a refusal to weigh conflicting evidence when offered — which I have called ignoring; sometimes the result of a difficulty or impossibility to digest and compare antagonist considerations differing from each other in kind; sometimes the result of a view against an alleged fact or doctrine, which is here called suspicion. Sometimes the resulting feeling of an opinion as professed in its favour, embarrassed by a suspicion against it. — In all cases it implies an avowal of evidence for a proposition, but not enough for its acceptance; but still these various frames of mind are so distinct from one another that they claim a distinct ⟨separate⟩ recognition, and the word 'Doubt' must be confined to one of them. I have thought best to make it denote conditional belief in a case of conviction; for doubt is a positive something, which *suspence* and *ignoring* [are not] and something distinctly and necessarily culpable, which is not the case with *suspicion*. ⟨This treatise should not bring in revelation here? Or at least anything more than *human* faith?⟩

Doubt then being the state ⟨frame⟩of mind I have described, is not a natural feeling; it will not exist in the mind, if left to the operation of its own laws: it never can so exist; but is the creation of the will and hence it is that in Revelation it is necessarily a sin. It may follow three other frames of mind; certainty, as when the mind, after certainty, begins with certainty, and go[es] on to resolve to doubt; this is the case of infidelity succeeding faith. Next, belief; viz when sufficient evidence is given to change opinion into conviction and the mind does not choose to go on to believe. Thus it is that men may often live in a kind of assent to Catholicism for a time, and be gaining light and advancing towards it; but as soon as the necessary light comes for conviction, may refuse to advance on from belief to certainty, but remain in the conditional assent in which they were, which though it seems the same henceforth is not longer belief but doubt. This accordingly is not an unfrequent course in the history of inquiry; a mind starts with *prejudices* or *disbelief* of the truth; a number of possibilities of the truth dawn upon him sufficient to create a view and to lead to *surmise* of the truth. This *surmise* grows into an opinion; and then *prejudice* or *disbelief* is gradually exchanged for *suspence*. The opinion goes on growing, and the opinion against gradually shrinks into a *suspicion*; that is there is a growing demand for an act of *belief*. Then perhaps the mind fails under the trial, refuses to *believe* ⟨make it⟩ and the suspence becomes *ignoring*, and so it is left for life. But supposing it goes on to *believe*; this is a great step, but another must be made, the evidence increases, and *conviction* is near at hand; at length it comes. Here again there is the chance of the mind refusing to change its frame, and then it is abandoned to its wilful conditional assent, which instead of *belief* has become *doubt*. One case more remains; Doubt may follow upon Persuasion, and in this way.

December 16, 1853.

On the Certainty of Faith

§ 1. On the two modes of apprehending or holding truth, the Evidentia Veritatis, and the Evidentia Credibilitatis. ⟨I may consider the matter without introducing certainty – take a person with a good ear, or who *only* knew mathematical truth, the question of certainty would not come in at all.⟩ We may

    1. *see* that a proposition is true,

or 2. *feel* that it is true.

These two words, 'see' and 'feel' are words of sense, and convey at once the essential meaning and mutual contrast, of the two modes I am going to speak of. Sight is an immediate, direct, and complete informant, and touch has no breadth, complexity, correlativeness or wholeness in its information, or what is meant by the expression "coup d'oeil". Or to take another metaphor, to see a proposition true, is to have its truth actually before us; to feel it to be true is to have a presentiment or anticipation of its truth. In the first case, we say the thing *is*; in the latter, it *must be*.

2.   1. An instance of *seeing*.

'Tis absolutely impossible, that, the whole view and intention, the original and the final design of God's creating such rational beings as men are, with such noble faculties, and so necessarily conscious of the eternal and unchangeable differences of good and evil; 'tis absolutely impossible (I say) that the whole design of an infinitely wise and just and good God in all this should be nothing more than to keep up eternally a succession of new generations of men, and those in such a corrupt, confused, and disorderly state of things as we see the present world is in; without any due and regular observation of the eternal rules of good and evil, without any clear or remarkable effect, of the great and most necessary differences of things, without any sufficient discrimination of virtue and vice by their proper and respective fruits, and without any first vindication of the honour and laws of God, in the proportionate reward of the best or punishment of the worst of men. And consequently 'tis certain and necessary (even as certain as the moral attributes of God before demonstrated) that, instead of the continuing and eternal succession of new generations in the present form and state of things; there must at some time or other be such a revolution and renovation of things, such a future state of existence of the same persons, as that by an exact distribution of rewards and punishments therein, all the present disorders and inequalities may be set right . . .' Clarke vol. ii. p 646.

2. An instance of *feeling*

'Rumour speaks uniformly and clearly enough in attributing it to the pen of a particular individual. Nor, although a cursory reader might well skim the book without finding in it anything to suggest, etc., will it appear improbable to the more attentive student of its internal evidence; and the improbability will decrease more and more, in proportion as the reader is capable of judging and appreciating the delicate, and at first invisible touches, which limit, to those who understand them, the individuals who can have written it to a very small number indeed. The utmost scepticism as to its authorship, (*which we do not feel ourselves*), cannot remove it further from him than to that of some one among his most intimate friends; so that, leaving others to *discuss antecedent probabilities*, etc'[1]

Here a writer holds a proposition as true on a sort of presentiment, or that it must be.

3. 1. When we *see* a proposition to be true, we say it is clear, or to be surrounded with a certain light, which theologians call 'evidentia'. But we must now drop metaphors, and say plainly what this seeing, this clearness or evidentia is ⟨NB. In *intuition* the light is in the proposition itself —in *demonstration* the light is thrown upon the proposition from surrounding already known truths.⟩ — First, however, I will use another metaphor or illustration which will serve to introduce the literal meaning of the words. Take a child's dissected map; you have put all the parts together but one — you then take that one, and dovetail and snap it into the gap left for it. That last one certainly belongs to that gap — because it just fits it. The other parts or pieces already in their places, testify to its being the right piece, by their just wanting it. In like manner, supposing I know nine propositions to be true, and a tenth proposition just completes or fits into them, that tenth is true too, *because* it and none but it fits — or the existing located nine bear witness to the tenth as true, or surround it with their support, that is, their evidentia. By evidentia then is meant the witness of existing or ascertained truths, to a certain further proposition that it is their correlative, or hangs together with them.

⟨Negative. If I do not love some one in the room, and it is not yourself, or your brother, or myself, and there are only four persons in the room, why, it must be grandmother.

Positive. If a man of great ideas is not therefore a great man — nor a man of great deeds — but if it is a word only used when there is some moral greatness — and if Napoleon, etc. Put some better instance. Give an evidence in fact, viz a number of principles.⟩

I prefer to put it in this way, as being the nearest explication of the idea contained in the word 'evidentia'; but of course the more common account of it, and that which we should always use in practice as being most natural and intelligible, is to call these previous truths and their separate and joint relations to the proposition in question, *proofs*. We see a proposition to be true, when

---

[1] See also *A Grammar of Assent*, London 1906, pp. 328–9; *Letters and Diaries*, XV, p. 459˙

we can make it dovetail closely into our existing knowledge, and when nothing else but it will so dovetail, that is, when we have proofs of it; for a proof is a necessary inference from facts, such that it just fits the proposition they are said to prove. This is exactly expressed in the negative formula so common in Euclid; 'for, if it is not true, then its contradictory is true, and then, etc. etc'.

This is then what is meant by saying that a proposition is true as having evidentia, or being clear. Evidentia is the lumen rationis.

2. Now secondly what is meant by *feeling* a proposition to be true? This is meant; that though we cannot see that it fits or snaps into existing recognised ⟨known⟩ truths, yet we have reason for anticipating that did we know those existing truths more fully, we should see they did presuppose or require it; in other words, that, though we cannot prove it, we perceive it or can prove it to be *congruous*, to known facts, and that we have sufficient grounds in reason for thinking that it is only by an accident that we cannot prove it, and that under other circumstances, we *should be able* to prove it.

Passage in Wood's Mechanics about the laws of motion illustrative of this, quoted in Development p 142[1]

4. 1. Under the head of truths which we *see*, fall, (putting aside the objects of intuition and of sense,) all subject matter of science, as the mathematics, theology, metaphysics, which are in what is called *necessary* matter, and are *syllogized*, or have *logical* proof.

2 Under the head of truths which we feel, are those which are in *contingent* matter, and are recommended to us on what is called *moral* ⟨probable⟩ grounds; those which are gained, not by syllogism, but by *induction*, those which are reached, not by one direct simple and sufficient proof but by a complex argument consisting of accumulating and converging probabilities. ⟨Enlarge 1. on converging probabilities — question — whether they can make up a proof sufficient for *feeling*. I have no doubt of it. 2. on induction — enlarge on the views in the works specified in this text (Quote Wood's Mechanics).⟩ Here I hold the analysis of the process of induction, as I have laid it down in my third University Discourse, and not as it is described by Whewell or by Mill,[2] viz I do not think that induction is a necessary proof or demonstration.

---

[1] 'Thus a writer on Mechanics, after treating of the laws of motion, observes, "These laws are the simplest principles to which motion can be reduced, and upon them the whole theory depends. They are not indeed self-evident, nor do they admit of accurate proof by experiment, on account of the great nicety required in adjusting the instruments and making the experiments; and on account of the effects of friction, and the air's resistance, which cannot entirely be removed. They are, however, constantly, and invariably, suggested to our senses, and they agree with experiment as far as experiment can go; and the more accurately the experiments are made, and the greater care we take to remove all those impediments which tend to render the conclusions erroneous, the more nearly do the experiments coincide with these laws." (Wood's *Mechanics*, p. 31). And thus a converging evidence for facts or doctrines through a certain period may, under circumstances, be as cogent a proof of their presence throughout that period, as the *Quod semper, quod ubique, quod ab omnibus.' An Essay on the Development of Christian Doctrine*, London 1845, p. 142; London 1906, p. 123. See also A. D. Culler, *The Imperial Intellect*, New Haven, Conn., 1955, p. 16.

[2] See below, p. 45. Newmans Discourse is 'The Usurpations, of Reason', now the fourth of *Oxford University Sermons*.

5. 1. The first class of truths, then, are those which are *demonstrable*, that is, which can be *made sure* ⟨proved⟩, are the subject matter of proof, i.e. can be proved true, or which are *known*. To *see* and to *feel* are to know and to *believe*.

2. The second class of truths are those which are *credible* or rather *credificative*, that is, which can be proved believable, or have credentials, and are then subject-matter of faith, or which are *believed*. Where, observe, we have no word to mark the *process*, answering to demonstration, but we call this class of truths (credible) from the quality of our apprehension of the conclusion. (If we ask what is the process or medium or formal cause of faith, as demonstration or proof is of knowledge, I should call it *judgment*. Judgment is here used, not for a faculty, but a process.)

However, it is usual, with the sense I have been setting down, to contrast the two truths as *demonstrable* and *credible*, instead of demonstrable and judgeable.

6. It follows, as a corollary, from what I have said, or rather has been already said, that, whereas in truths which we see, the truth is evident, so in truths which we feel, though their truth is not evident, yet the grounds for thinking them true, that is, for believing them, are evident. That is, the one has the *evidentia veritatis*, the other, the *evidentia credibilitatis*.

7. The proof that a proposition is credible may be ⟨is⟩ as complete and sufficient as the proof that it is true; or, referring to our original language, we are as rational when we feel as when we see a truth. A person says 'I cannot prove it, but I firmly believe it', does he mean that he is believing without proof? No — he means 'I cannot prove its truth, but I can prove I ought to believe it ⟨it ought to be accepted as true⟩.'

That the proof of the latter is more elaborate, circuitous, and trying to the patience and attention I grant — but the question is, whether it is as real a proof. Take e.g. the proof that all men die, or that Great Britain is an island. If anyone argued against it, you would say 'It is absurd, it is impossible to doubt it,' which put into other words is 'It is necessary to believe it'. This expresses that belief or feeling may be necessary in reason.

Let us look into this instance more attentively. I deny that we have *proof* of the *truth* of the proposition 'All men die'. First we do not obtain it by deductive or syllogistic reasoning. Next (even granting that you can come to a demonstration by means of an induction) yet A or B has not and cannot make an induction. Yet, I repeat, who can doubt it? The conclusion is, that we may have a demonstration that a proposition is to be 'felt' or 'believed', which is not demonstrated to be true. ⟨Though feeling is inferior in *proof*, to seeing, no one will say that in particular cases (e.g. of a blind man used to it, answering to judgment as opposed to mathematics) it may not be quite as sure.⟩

The sort of reasons, cumulating or convergent, on which we believe, are such as these:-

⟨First, the major is What all men say is true. Death is what all men say Ergo.⟩
1. Men are under circumstances to be trusted.
2. I never heard anyone doubt that all men die.
3. All men I ever heard affirm it.
4. I never saw a dead man, but I never saw one alive who was commonly ⟨distinctly⟩ said to be dead.
5. What becomes of men, if they do not die and disappear?
6. Are funerals solemn mockeries?
7. Whose interest is it to tell lies, or enact mockeries, here?
8. Could a plot be carried on without failing?
9. The grief of people, it must be sincere.

§ 2. On the contrast in the process of apprehension between the Evidentia Veritatis and the Evidentia Credibilitatis in the two modes above set down.

Since in propositions known and seen, we have the evidentia veritatis, and in propositions believed or felt we have the evidentia credibilitatis, and since by evidentia is meant demonstrative proof, it would seem to follow that either on the one hand there is a *science* of credibility, or on the other that evidentia does not mean the same thing in the one phrase and in the other. But the latter alternative is plainly very harsh, whereas the former, if true, leads us to ask whether such a science is recognised and where it is to be found, as mathematics or theology are sciences both recognised and attained.

On this subject then I lay down the following dicta.

1. Whereas evidentia exists or not according as the previous truths (or premisses) which create it are known, and whereas what is known to one man need not be known to another, what is evidentia (of a truth) to one man is not evidentia to another, or a truth may be evidens, and known, to one and not to another.

Thus, if Archimedes had been the only man in the world who knew that the three angles of a triangle are equal to two right angles, he would have been the only man in the world who had evidentia of Proposition xlvii, that the square of the hypothenuse of a triangle is equal to the squares together of the sides.

2. The principles or existing truths or premisses in one subject matter are not the same as those in another; so that two men A and B may possess evidentia of the propositions respectively in one of two subject matters a and b, and not in the other b and a.

3. One set of existing truths or premisses may be ⟨is⟩ easier of apprehension to the human mind than another.

Mathematics — theology — morals — metaphysics.

4. Those families of principles or existing truths, which are easier, are more widely attained — and those which are more difficult, are less.

5. Since whether they be difficult or not, the logical process is always the

same, they are to be discriminated in point of easiness or difficulty, popularity or reconditeness, not by the logical process, but by the principles or premises.

6. Principles at first sight difficult, and therefore recondite, become easier, the more they are dwelt on and tried.

7. It follows that in difficult and recondite subject matters, those who have studied them are more likely to attain the conclusion which they exhibit ⟨possess⟩. Cuique in art suâ credendum.

8. In proportion as the premises are easy and popular, and the subject matter drawn out of the hands of the few, or of particular classes of men, into public and popular apprehension, is a study called a science. Thus geology is not yet a science.[1]

9. Scientific proof then is not merely logical proof, but logical proof from generally ascertained and received principles.

10. Therefore since evidentia is synonymous with logical proof, it need not be the same as scientific proof, and will not be so, unless its principles are generally received.

11. It follows that the evidentia credibilitatis need not admit of scientific proof, unless its premises are simple and generally admitted; and therefore the absence of any scientific exhibition of that evidentia if it be wanting, will only prove its principles recondite, not its proof wanting in logical perfection.

12. Hence, recurring to the original objection, I accept neither horn of the dilemma; as to the first, distinguo — evidentia has two meanings *accidentaliter*, not *essentialiter*; in each case there is a logical process from known premisses, but in the evidentia veritatis those premisses are known and received by *all*, in the evidentia credibilitatis by the *individual*. As to the second horn, it follows from this distinction, that since one of the conditions of a science is that its premisses are generally received, and this is not the case with the evidentia credibilitatis, there is not science of the latter.

Another condition of a science is, that its premisses should be few, whereas in the evidentia credibilitatis, there are so many as not to admit of convenient exhibition; ⟨Think how many propositions it has taken to arrive even at number 12. immediately above!⟩ for this reason again the evidentia credibilitatis does not admit of a scientific treatment.

On the whole then it differs from the evidentia veritatis, first in its proving the truth apprehended, not true, but credible or to be held as really true; next that it proves its credibility, not by any scientific process resting on generally received principles and drawn out in exact syllogisms, but on the action of the individual mind, which knows what others may or may not know, and acts, not necessarily by rule, but by practical expertness. The proof of evidentia is called the motivum of its object — e.g. motivum credibilitatis.

[1] See also Anne Mozley, *The Letters and Correspondence of John Henry Newman*, London 1891, I, pp. 41, 61. *John Henry Newman, Autobiographical Writings*, pp. 44, 54-5.

To take an instance in point:-

Quaestio.

A. B. wrote a certain book.

Reasons against:-

1. It is not likely he should have time.
2. It is not likely that he should have the will.
3. It is not likely that he should have the power.

Reasons for:-

1. It is commonly ascribed to him.
2. It is ascribed to no one else.
3. He has not denied it, as he did of another volume in a former case.
4. Very few but he could have written it, from the necessary position of the author, whoever he is.
5. There are many things in it like his writing.
6. The closer it is examined, the more things are to be found in it, in favour of his being the author.
7. The better his writings are known, the more this book will seem like his, etc. etc.

Hence there are a number of probabilities for, a certain number against. But no proof of the quaestio. ⟨N.B. That the premisses were recondite was one of the very reasons why they did not prove the point ⟨quaestio⟩ — they do not cease to be recondite because they are directed towards its credibility not its truth.⟩

If a person maintains the negative, how will you answer him? where is your syllogism? He will dispute your seven or more probabilities — he will deny they coalesce into a proof, if admitted — he will urge his own probabilities the other way, which you have not answered.

Then suppose you go back to prove your seven probabilities. Take the fourth, 'Very few but he could have, from his position, written it'. This may be most true and undeniable, and your opponent would be forced to admit it, could you give him all your grounds — but that one probability branches out, on being pursued back, into a multiform argument; and so of others.

You cannot then prove your point to another.

Nay you must confess it is not a *proof* at all. For what does it say that [at?] the utmost than that, the *more* you examine it, the more it is *like* a proof?

It comes short, then, of a proof of the fact — but does it prove nothing? Syllogism.

1. That which comes to me through a definite and sufficient course of investigation with the arguments in its favour ever increasing, and the arguments against it ever diminishing, has claims on me to be held as true. ⟨This is the principle of belief in deduction also⟩.

2. This quaestio is such. Ergo I am bound to hold it true. But to hold true without proof is to believe.

§ 3. On the Office of the Judgment or Prudentia (as the arbiter of) in determining the Evidentia Credibilitatis.

It appears that the difference of the proof in the Evidentia Credibilitatis, and of the Evidentia Veritatis, is that in the latter the premisses are generally received, and the logical process short; whereas in the Evidentia Credibilitatis the premisses are recondite and personal, and the process intricate and indefinitely long.

It follows that the Evidentia Veritatis admits of scientific treatment and external exhibition, and the Evidentia Credibilitatis is lodged more or less in the minds of the individuals possessing it, and if it admits of science at all, it admits it but partially.

The mental faculty which sees, furnishes, uses, dispenses and applies the premisses of the Evidentia Credibilitatis is called Prudentia or Judgment.[1] ⟨E.g. the phenomena of the case appear to the common mind as the wrong side of a carpet or as the object of sight to one born blind first seeing, but prudentia *groups* them and tells their value. Thus, the Tablet from the first said there would be war with Russia — or Canning might say that the next war would be a war not of nations, but of opinions.⟩

Thus it is Prudentia which detects the arguments for referring a book to a certain author, which weighs their worth, which combines them, which disposes of them and of objections each in its right place, and presents the collection of arguments as one mass sufficient to take their place as the minor in the syllogism above set down.

This Prudentia is partly a natural endowment common to all, or a special gift to certain persons, partly the result of experience; and it varies in its worth and preciousness, and its rarity, with the subject matter on which it is employed. Accordingly it has different names, and kinds; sometimes it is sagacity, sometimes common sense, strong sense, shrewdness, acuteness, penetration, are all terms denoting it in different subject matters; so are instinctive perception, the tact of experience, the sensitiveness of innocence or saintliness. ⟨In Newton and Napoleon it is genius. Vid. A. overleaf⟩

Moreover the possession of this Prudentia in one subject matter is no guarantee for a person's possessing it in another; as very sagacious men are often wanting in common sense. On the other hand, there are persons, like the late Duke of Wellington, who possess common sense so consistently in various provinces of thought, that we do not know whether to praise them for sagacity ⟨genius⟩ or for strong straight forward sense. In *his own* subject matter, he always saw just what one ought to believe, say, or act upon, though he would not be able to prove his point scientifically in one case in 100. Again, when you speak of an ingenious man, you mean a man who cannot take things in a direct natural way, but proves, as he thinks, matters credible, which are not so; and on the other hand when you speak of a dry hard headed man, you mean a man who, from misplaced demand for scientific truth, will not admit

[1] See also *Philosophical Notebook*, II, p. 163.

matters to be credible which are. When it is said that mathematics spoil the judgment, it is meant that those who are accustomed to prove things true, do not relish proofs which only prove things credible. They pretend 'they have not proof enough', that is, not a scientific process proving the point true.

⟨(Prudentia also decides between its own way ⟨method⟩ or science — *which* is to be used; empiricism and the rule of thumb, or the rule of Laputa.)[1]

Further than this prudentia is a sovereign judge what subject matters or cases admit of proof, of truth, and what do not, and how many and what arguments are necessary in each varying case to prove credibility. πεπαιδευμένου γαρ ἐστιν etc.,[2] and of the difference between credibilitas and probabilitas.

Prudentia *really* extends to ⟨may be found in⟩ any subject matter — thus Newton in mathematics — calculating boys in arithmetic — but some subject matters *can* be reduced to science — hence it is left in possession of those provinces which are not so reducible.

A. (Newton had ascertained his great discoveries, before he had *proved* them true; and he had great difficulty in proving them. He was obliged to invent a calculus in order to prove them, and people found fault with the calculus, as clumsy, if not sophistical. He had a sort of presentiment of their truth, the result of his genius, and believed them before he knew them. It was his prudentia which made them credible to him, presenting to him a proof of their credibility, which he could not communicate to another. So he went about to invent a scientific proof of their truth.

Napoleon said that in 50⟨?⟩ years that Europe would be republican or Cossack. He could not prove it to another, nay not to himself; but he felt it. He had sufficient reasons for believing it. He had a prudentia which others had not. At this moment, strange to say, the two powers exciting Europe are just the Socialists and the Russians. Should he be right, the event will be the proof of the fact. He had no proof of the fact, for it was future, but he had proof of its credibility).

§ 4. On the propagation of truths apprehended on the Evidentia Credibilitatis.

⟨Evidentia $\begin{cases} \text{veritatis} \\ \text{credibilitatis} \end{cases}$ is a proof of a fact which *terminates*

in $\begin{cases} \text{truth of it,} \\ \text{credibility of it,} \end{cases}$

$\begin{cases} \text{which proves the truth of it} \\ \text{which proves the credibility of it} \end{cases}$⟩

In the case of truths which admit of proof, or are apprehended on the Evidentia Veritatis, not only the method, but the process of propagation is easy. In this Evidentia, the premisses are few and generally received, or received as

[1] A flying island in Swift's *Gulliver's Travels* whose inhabitants indulged in absurd or visionary projects.
[2] 'It is the mark of a well educated man.' See *A Grammar of Assent*, pp. 414–15, and below, p. 38.

soon as stated, and the argument is concise — and you can compel assent. All then you have to do is to set down your premises, to draw your argument, and lo and behold your conclusion! Such are the propositions of Euclid.

But, though the method is the same as this in the Evidentia Credibilitatis, the process is neither easy nor short; because, though it be demonstrative, yet the premises cannot be taken for granted, nor are they few, nor is the argument brief ⟨neat⟩, but elaborate, circuitous, and perplexed. ⟨Where are you then when you would convince another?⟩ This is why Prudentia is required to come at the true conclusion, instead of a scientific treatise.

How then are we to propagate truth, that is, to cause its reception by others as well as ourselves, when it is apprehended on the evidentia credibilitatis?

I answer, we give ⟨offer⟩ others two ways of gaining it:- either

1. by gaining that Prudentia, (in the particular subject matter in which the Quaestio lies,) which discerns, seizes, and applies the premises or principles.

or

2. by using the Prudentia of those who are already versed in that particular subject matter.

Of these two modes the latter is the more common, on the principle Cuique in suâ [arte credendum] etc., Life is not long enough to obtain prudentia in every subject matter. When table turning is concerned, we trust Faraday. He showed us his experiments, but it was more satisfactory to trust *him* than his arguments.[1] When we want to know a truth in Political Economy, or Medicine, or Civil Engineering, we feel that we cannot do better than take the word of those who know better than we do, from having studied those respective subjects. If we want to know a point of law, we do not attempt to decide it for ourselves, we consult our lawyer; if we would make an investment of property, we consult our banker, or our man of business, if we know nothing of the matter ourselves. What these informants say may startle us. We say 'It is very strange, but all the lawyers, all the medical men, or all the experimentalists, or all the metaphysicians, or all the theologians say so —' etc. etc.

On the other hand, if we really wish to have a view of our own, and to accept the truth in the matter in question on our own judgment, we never think we can enter into it at once, but we know it will take time, and we give ourselves to the study. If we were tempted by the offer of some high priced picture, which was on sale, we should either go by the judgment of connoisseurs, or, if not, we should set about gaining a real taste and judgment in the art, which would not be the work of a day. Did we wish to know the difference of good and bad music, we should set about educating ourselves for the knowledge. Nor could we gain the prudentia necessary for a great commander, without going on active service.

I know no other way of enabling ourselves to apprehend truth which we cannot prove than these two ways; viz either mastering the principles of the

[1] Cf. *Letters and Diaries*, XIX, p. 285.

subject matter in which the Quaestio lies, which is a work of time, or availing oneself of the decisions of those who have mastered them. The second way really falls under the first, for the duty of going by the decisions of others who are skilled in the matter in question, is one of the very principles which the Evidentia Credibilitatis requires and which Prudentia dictates. But we may fairly consider them as two; and so considering them, we see them both in strong contrast to the process by which the Evidentia Veritatis is attained, for the Evidentia Credibilitatis depends on obvious, natural, and generally received principles, and discards authority altogether.

§ 5. Application of the foregoing doctrine to the instance of religious ⟨revealed⟩ truth.

1. Since we are saved, not by knowledge, but by faith, Revealed Religion has the evidentia credibilitatis, not veritatis.

2. And since that evidentia is level to the intellect of children and of the illiterate, as well as others, it must be gained, not in the way of science, but by the exercise of prudentia. (At the same time, since it must be a real evidentia, it must imply a rational proof.)

3. Moreover, since it is intended for very various classes of persons, for all ages and stations, the Evidentia must be variously gained; that is, it must appeal to a variety of grounds, reasons, or motiva, each of which is capable of creating it. (The reasons constituting or producing the evidentia are called the *motivum*.)

4. At the same time, since it is a real Evidentia, it must imply a rational proof or combination of *motiva*. It always implies demonstration; however, we must be sure what we mean by the word, for it has several significations. If then by demonstration is meant a valid proof, the word certainly has a place here. If the word means that certain portions of the integral proof can be represented ⟨drawn out⟩ scientifically, in this sense too it is admissible. If it means that any one whatever will find the proof irresistible, who fairly studies its premisses, here too the proof is a demonstration; but, if it means that the Evidentia can be forced on the mind of anyone whatever who understands argument by a process of logical formulas such as that which forces us to admit a demonstration of Euclid, I cannot follow such a statement.

I conceive that in every case, of man, woman, and child, the credibilitas (and therefore faith) is based upon reason, and that, when the subject is too young to have reason, he is too young to have faith. By reason, of course, I mean right reason, reason exercising itself in legitimate proof. (This exercise of reason, or proof, is called the motivum credibilitatis.)

Let me take some instances in point:- and that in order to show two things

1. That there is no faith without a sufficient motivum; 2. next that prudentia forms and shapes the motivum.

I. (1) A child is taught there is one God, and believes. This is an instance of real reason and of faith. His sufficient motivum is the word of his teacher (because supported by the inward sense)

(2) A child is taught there are two Gods, and believes. This is not an instance of real reason or of faith. Here the word of his teacher is not a sufficient motivum (for he contradicts his inward sense).

(3) A child is taught there are two Gods, and does not believe. Here reason does not act, or rather he has motiva contradictory with ⟨to⟩ each other, and has not faith, but doubt.

(4) A child is taught there are two Gods, and believes there is one. Here is an act of real reason and of faith. He has a sufficient motivum (for the denial *brings out* the secret sense, as heresy truth.)

(5) A child is taught that 'Christ' is a mere man and believes — here there are not data enough for belief or disbelief, for we cannot assent or dissent to a proposition in itself, till we know something of the *terms* — e.g. 'A is B'.

(6) A child reads the Gospels and is taught that Christ is a mere man, and believes. Here is no real reason or sufficient motivum, because the Gospel contradicts the teacher.

(7) A child is taught that Mahomet is the Apostle of God. Of course Mahomet is a mere name, and no judgment is formed.

(8) A youth, who knows the life of Mahomet, is taught the same. The impurities of the Impostor are so shocking (he sanctified impure thoughts of his own daughter — he reeked of impurity) I am not alluding to mere polygamy, and the instinct of the excellence of purity is so strong and natural to us, that one might as well worship Mylitta or Venus. He has a sufficient motivum against the teaching.

(9) A youth is taught by a Protestant the doctrine of justification by faith only, and he believes it, i.e. he really holds it as true. I think this may be an instance of a sufficient motivum. He has nothing to put against the word of a religious man whom he loves and reveres; but then, when you look into the matter, he does not believe the doctrine as Luther held it, but as Melanchthon, viz that we can do nothing of ourselves, that Christ is our sole Saviour, that we are simply dependent on him, etc etc.

(10) A person is taught by his Priest that the Third Person of the Blessed Trinity was incarnate for us. If he knows nothing of his religion, then 'The Third Person', as 'Christ' above, or 'Mahomet', is a word without an idea — but, if he does know anything of his religion from Catechism, Prayers, Mass, and the various ways in which the broad outlines of Christian Truth penetrate the rudest minds, so that they be not simply stolid and brutish, (when they cannot assent *or* dissent) he will have sufficient reasons the other way to invalidate his apparent motivum.

I think then, on the whole, that the case is scarcely conceivable, of a soul making a rational act of faith in a lie — and if there be such cases, then the extraordinary intervention of God may be supposed to meet it.

I suppose the ordinary motiva credibilitatis of an illiterate person in England who is converted are such as these taken together —

1. There must be some way of reconciling oneself to God.
2. That way must be a *religion*
3. The Catholic religion is the only one which even professes to be such a way.
4. Catholics always speak the same, as a Prophet of God should.
5. I can trust none but Catholics for telling me how to please God.
6. There is something so holy in the Catholic Religion — all is holy about it.
7. It is the only religion which sets itself to conquer sensuality.
8. I feel it to be so soothing.
9. I feel its rites so awful. They seem heaven upon earth.
10. Catholics are persecuted etc etc.

Next, take the case of educated men. I suppose, while they may attain a much higher assemblage ⟨force⟩ of motiva, yet they are open to the force of many more objections, which confuse and obstruct the evidentia, and make them much longer in coming to a clear view of the case. To overcome this difficulty (intellectually speaking), requires a prudentia (so far from its being superseded by science) far greater than that which unlearned persons require, for it must be vigorous enough to override technicalities and formalities, or, what is called in politics, red-tapism. Learning is like Saul's armour, which David put off. It requires great intellectual strength to walk in such learning; or simple faith and spiritual perception to supersede the intellect. Hence Our Lord's words, 'I thank ⟨confess to⟩ Thee, O Father, Lord, etc.[1]

Take the common way in which Anglicans are at this minute perplexed. They do not attempt to deny the Catholic arguments, but they bring others on their own side. We want then prudentia to determine the relative worth of arguments, and of apparent proofs, the argument sufficient for this or that point etc etc.

The case occurs every day. 'I see that, if the Church is a visible body, it must be visibly one — I see that it cannot be visibly one without inter-communion — I see the Established Church is not in communion with the rest of Christendom. If this were the whole of the case, I should be determined what to do at once — *but*

(1) on the other hand, I find strong negative evidence in all antiquity, and some strong positive evidence against the existing Catholic cultus B.M.V. [of the Blessed Virgin Mary]. I cannot find anything about the Sacrament of penance for three centuries from Christ, and St. Augustine takes the Gallican view of the Pope's Supremacy.'

or

(2) on the other hand, I have a tangible proof of the sanctity to which

---

[1] 'because thou hast hid these things from the wise and prudent and hast revealed them to little ones.' *Matthew* 11: 25.

members of the Establishment may arrive, and a shrinking from the bold and free talking common among Catholics, such, as to constitute an argument for remaining where I am, considering Establishmentism is in my case in possession, so very real and vivid, that I am inclined to think that the argument for Catholicism, which I have been candidly conceding is but a paper argument, I mean, a cut and dried red-tapism, an ingenuity which I cannot indeed answer, but which might be answered were I more acute and more learned than I am.

or

(3) All those I know best all around me warn me that I am under a delusion. Why should I feel the argument and they not? They point at the delusions all around of those who nevertheless profess to go by reason, and whose delusion is really one of reason or a sophism. Directly you leave the port of the Establishment, in which you were brought up, to get upon the open sea, and the winds may hurry you to infidelity as well as to Catholicism. I am not denying that reason is the gift of God, I am only questioning whether I am under a legitimate or a perverse exercise of the gift. Till I can answer this question, I must remain where I am.

Thus the mind gets perplexed with the multiplicity of arguments, and runs the risk of never attaining to truth.

The want is prudentia. Therefore either

1. It must be increased intellectually.

2. or it must be stimulated in energy by grace and spiritual earnestness.

3. or the event must be left to time, which becomes a sort of arbiter between truth and falsehood by a natural proof — e.g. 'if it is a delusion, it will in time blow off etc etc.'

N.B. The last has in matter of fact been the common case with intellectual converts.

Next of seceding.

1. A child is urged by its parents, who are apostates, to secede. What argument can they give against the Catholic Religion, say 'superstitions', 'corruption', 'the Pope is a bad man', 'you must read your Bible, and the priest will not let you', which is a sufficient motivum to overcome its various experience of the divinity of the Church?

2. An Irish peasant is souperized[1], question: the motivum?

3. An educated person becomes a Catholic; he finds himself in a new world, a fish out of water; no one sympathizes with him; he had difficulties when he was converted, e.g. about the Blessed Virgin Mary, he has never got over them — he is disappointed in the lives of Catholics; he finds he took a romantic view of them etc. Such is his sort of ground.

Now either he came over to the Church on a sufficient motivum or not.

(1) If not, he never had faith at all — but came on a fancy — and has been playing with sacred things — and (putting aside the unseen supra-rational

---

[1] A 'Souper' was either a Protestant clergyman seeking to proselytize by dispensing soup or one who was converted to Protestantism by receiving soup or other charity.

power of grace) commits no illogicality in going back, because he exercised no logicality in coming over.

(2) If on a sufficient motive; then I ask, is the above objection *sufficient* to overcome a sufficient motivum?

§ 6.   On certainty

Certainty is an act (or habit) of the intellect reflecting on, recognising, and ratifying its existing apprehension of a truth, whether known or believed. Since, according to this definition, certainty is a judgment, and a judgment is the assent of the intellect, and again an apprehension of a truth is a judgment and assent, therefore certainty is the judgment of a judgment or an assent of the intellect to an assent.

E.g. proposition enunciated by the *apprehension* — 'C is A'
proposition enunciated by the certainty — 'I apprehend C is A.'

2. This account of certainty implies that it is a natural and ordinary, but not a necessary consequence of apprehension. For instance, I am intent on what I am reading. I hear the clock strike, but do not observe it. Presently I look at my watch, and cry out 'Dear me, it is past the hour!' Then I recollect I had heard the clock strike. This will illustrate the process I wish to point out. Again, I say to a friend that I met so-and-so today — it does not occur to me to doubt the fact. He says 'It is impossible, for he is out of the country'. Then I begin to think about my own apprehension whether it be real or not, and about the motiva (look, gait, etc.) which gave me the impression; and I say 'After all, I *did* notice something unlike him', or 'Well, it was but a passing sight I had of the man, I had not opportunity enough to be positive,' or 'I am quite positive it was he'. Again, let us suppose a world in which there could be no difference of opinion, or, supposing all things were known by strict science. The word 'certain' would not be known — every thing would be taken for granted. Brutes cannot have certainty — for they have not even apprehension. Saints and Angels probably have apprehension without certainty.

3. Hence it appears that certainty implies two things besides itself, first a difference of opinion, a questioning, or a doubt about the apprehension, — and next a certain reference to the motiva on which the apprehension is founded.

4. From the second of these implications an important consideration follows. Certainty, it seems, is an assent of the mind to an apprehension of a truth accompanied with a reference to the grounds or motiva of that apprehension, e.g. first whether it is a truth known or believed, next what the reasons are, etc. That is, it is a recognition, not simply of an apprehension, but at least improperly and accidentally of the motiva and consequently the evidentia of that apprehension. ⟨That is, it contemplates and recognises the truth *in* its formal proof.⟩

5. If certainty is a recognition of an apprehension of a truth, it is a recognition

of a truth; for we cannot apprehend falsehood. Hence (from its very definition) certitudini non potest subesse falsum. If it is not a truth, we do not call it certainty.

6. Since an assent does not admit of degrees, neither does certainty; but since it is a recognition, not only of the apprehension itself, which is also an assent, but of the motiva and consequent evidentia which does admit of more or less, it follows that though we cannot be more or less *certain* of a truth, we can be certain of it with more vigour, keenness, and directness according to the quality of the evidentia ⟨motiva⟩ in the particular case. ⟨As apprehension views the object in its evidentia, so the certainty recognises the apprehension in its motiva.⟩

7. Thus, for instance:

(1) We are certain that cruelty or impurity is sin, with a directness and completeness correspondent to the luminousness of the evidentia and its inherence in the truth which we recognise.

(2) We are certain we took a walk yesterday, from the overpowering luminousness which our memory sheds over the fact. ⟨Question: is this intuition or what?⟩

(3) We are certain that three angles of a triangle equal two right angles, from no internal luminousness — and 1. the luminousness of the proof, when we come to think over it — which is not of the first order, but 2. without perception of that luminousness, from the luminousness of our memory that we *have* before now proved it.

(4) We are certain that we are sitting in our room, talking to others etc. from the overpowering evidentia of sense, which under circumstances is brighter than that which is produced by acts of reason.

(5) We are certain, not more, but still more vividly that fire has the power of paining us.

(6) We are certain that all stones, left to themselves, will fall to the earth or that all men die (1) because it is impossible to doubt it — (2) next and more commonly because we are habituated to the notion that it is so. ⟨N.B. *habit may be without any basis of proof*. Thus people talk themselves into believing. This is prejudice, fanaticism, etc etc.⟩

(7) We are certain that Richard iii was an unscrupulous usurper, but we are obliged to think over the proof for believing it before we make our act of certainty, and we relapse into our state of slumber on the subject, as soon as we put it aside.

(8) We are certain of the loyalty to us of a friend, against whom presumptive proofs ⟨arguments⟩ lie after examining them; but the arguments come up again and again before our minds, though directly we rouse ourselves they disappear, but they rise and flit about us and haunt us, when our mind is passive, and thus blunt the vigour and promptness of our certainty.

(9) We are certain of the loyalty to us of a friend, against whom there are appearances; and with great vigour in spite of their coming up again and again

before us, because we so love him that we are indignant at ourselves, and *will* does what habit or memory might do.[1]

§ 7. On certainty in conclusions from trains of logical arguments.

1. Since there are no degrees in certainty, properly so called, and the only aspect of the act, which may [be] said to admit of degrees, is its accidental and improper extension to a recognition of the evidentia, and since the evidentia is not the same to one as another, the same certainty may vary in its evidentia and consequent vigour in the same person from time to time, or in two persons at the same time. ⟨ *What I have been saying last is that there is,* (in the definition of certainty as an act of reflexion,) *a certainty proper, and a certainty improper or accidental,* like 'accidental glory' — and the latter is the evidentia of the certainty arising from the momentum, and though *legitimately* particular evidentia have their own legitimate and correspondent evidentia, yet that in matter of fact it depends very much in a particular case on the will of the individual. However, there is one law, though I cannot analyse it, that we go by the evidentia of the last certainty.⟩

E. g. Newton might be certain of his own conclusions, not more so than any disciple who followed him, but with an evidentia which made him speak far more authoritatively, and enabled him to take them as first principles for future discoveries.

2. Evidentia then being an accident, and varying with the individual's knowledge, recollection etc; it follows that in trains of reasonings it will vary with the collection of separate evidentias for each successive step in the train which are remembered and brought together.

3. In train of reasonings then, it depends very much upon the habit, will etc., of the individual, as he takes this evidentia and not that.

4. It is more common to go by the final evidentia, caring little about the preceding, E.g. instance scratched out overleaf.[2]

5. And on this principle, because the final conclusion is the important one, and if we are to believe this or that, we must not believe it on halves — but must be consistent.

Thus in the affections, if a person is proved to have benefitted us, we do not limit our gratitude to the evidentia — but we let the object of our gratitude act freely on our heart.

So again in a matter of conduct, we very long debate whether we shall go to war with Russia or not — but, if we once make up our minds, we say, we

---

[1] The first formulation of § 6. No. 9, read: '9. Some cases are complex. I am certain though with faint evidentia that X.Y. is either an impostor or a person of remarkable gifts and graces – there is no medium. In proportion then as I assent to the former, my dissent grows from the latter — and when I have utterly proved the former, I am certain with great evidentia against the latter. I mean that the indignation which accompanies my disproof of his extraordinary sanction [sanctity?], is measured by that disproof, and not by the original hypothetical syllogism.'

[2] Alongside Nos. 2, 3, and 4, in the margin, is written: 'This is not satisfactorily analysed.'

must go to war in earnestness, not by halves'. Or languid and only barely sufficient reasons for ⟨evidentia of the expediences of⟩ going to war, are no measure of our exertions when at war.

Again, if a certain libel is brought home to an individual, a judge sentences him, not according to the evidentia of the proof, but according to the virulence, his position in society etc., etc.

Again, when we have once proved, (gained evidentia) that a certain work is Saint Augustine's or Saint Thomas's, we throw ourselves upon it with a fulness of confidence quite independent of the evidentia of the proof.

§ 7. [sic] On the kinds of certainty so called.
1. Certainty of impression ⟨imagination⟩.

I suppose a great portion of our professed certainty is only certainty of imagination or impression without intellectual, i.e. rational, ground at all. We say 'I am certain he has this or that object in view;' — 'I am certain he meant me;' 'I am certain he said those words', 'I am certain it rained yesterday'; when we do not reflect on an assent and the motiva for it at all, when we notoriously and undeniably speak without any deliberation whatever, but merely recognize and bear witness to our vivid impression of the occurrence of a fact. ⟨Certainty in this case is a reflex action or recognition, not of an assent, but of an impression.⟩
2. Certainty of the affections, passions etc.

We form an acquaintance with a man — he is amiable, engaging, clever; he has a number of good points; he does us services; he becomes useful to us; we love him, we confide in him, we throw ourselves upon him unreservedly. Then we say 'I will stake my life he is honest and faithful to me'. Suspicions arise about him; we lay down the proposition categorically 'I am certain that he is most true to me'. What reflection, recognition, ratification, has there been of an assent founded on motiva (motiva credibilitatis) leading to the conclusion — 'I must believe he is true'.

And so of prejudices, prepossessions, suspicions, presumptions, and of hope, self-interest, etc. ('The wish was father to the thought') etc etc.
3. Certainty of memory.

Memory is a safe medium of an assent, when it has relation to matters that cannot change. But that I made a rational assent a year ago is not logical ground for assuming I can make it now, in circumstances which may vary. If I proved yesterday that the radius of a circle is equal to the side of a hexagon inscribed in it and assented to it, I may rationally assent to it to-day, and recognise that assent. If I proved a year ago that I could not but believe that all matter gravitated to matter inversely as the square of the interval, I might believe it rationally to-day, but it is but assuming that the Creator of the world has not since last year changed the laws of the physical world. But if I had the strongest proof and an evidentia that A. B. was my devoted friend five years ago, I could not therefore say, on the memory of the assent and its motiva of that date, that I was certain he was my devoted friend now.

4. Practical certainty.

Most things in the course of human life of which we say we are certain, we are but certain of on practical certainty. What we call certainty is but an opinion which it is safe and wise to take as true. We are in fact only practically certain of much, about which we easily might have speculative certainty. The sun will rise to-morrow morning; I do not mean to say we may not be speculatively certain of it; but we do not take the trouble to consider whether we have given a rational assent to the proposition, but we act as if it were certain. It is only when we are deeply interested in a matter, and when there is not exact safety in any view, but dangers on both sides, that we hunt after speculative certainty. There is a report that our bankers are breaking; if we could do it without any inconvenience, we should think it safest at once to draw out our money. But to do so would make a talk; we are ashamed of doing so; it would [be] unfair to them, and this would be both unkind and look unkind; it would be much to our pecuniary disadvantage, if we did so, and the report was a mistake; — so, we try to find what the truth really is, or to arrive at a speculative certainty. If we can, well; if not, we then act as is safest as a balance of inconveniences.

We never have recourse to speculative certainty (to speak generally) if practical will do. This is especially the case with the English people, a race so practical, so impatient of questions of truth and falsehood. They waive every question they need not entertain. Their greatest book in defence of revealed religion, dispenses with truth, as such, as far as ever it can.[1]

Again, a jury is instructed to let off a prisoner — *it is the safer course* — here is but practical certainty of his innocence. A vast proportion of judicial decisions are made on no higher certainty.

Again, the certainty on which the priest administers the Sacraments, considers men fit recipients etc etc. is practical.

5. Speculative certainty.

All these kinds being considered, it would seem as if there were (comparatively speaking) but little real certainty in the world.

Speculative certainty implies —

    1. an earnestness about the subject matter of it.

    2. a reflex assent to our possessing a rational assent.

    3. hence a deliberation, however rapid.

---

[1] See also Newman's comment on the publication of *Essays and Reviews*:
'It was serious enough, in spite of what I have said, a century ago. Bishop Butler stopped the evil, only by lowering by many pegs the pretensions of Christianity — for, without wishing to speak disrespectfully of a writer to whom I owe so much, as many others do, still it does seem as if the practical effect of his work was to make faith a mere *practical certainty* — i.e. a taking certain statements of doctrine, not as true, but as safest to act upon. The Anglican defenders of Christianity have all along been fighting and retreating. Paley half gave up the Old Testament — And there is every reason to anticipate that the antagonists of these seven Essayists, if such there shall be, will give up still more.' *Letters and Diaries* XIX, p. 480. See also XV, pp. 456ff., XXI, p. 270; *Philosophical Notebook*, I, pp. 176ff; above, p. 3.

After cutting off all these apparent certainties, real speculative certainty would seem to be uncommon; — i.e. in the world, for I suppose (as I have said) it is ever possible in the case of religious faith, in consequence of the imperium voluntatis, to be hereafter explained.

The certainty that is possible is a recognition of an assent, that there are sufficient rational grounds for wishing to believe.

I conceive a great multitude of persons may have that assent *without* the recognition of it which we call certainty — but I do not think anyone *need* become a Catholic on merely practical certainty, none ought and I think very few do.

§ 8. On the criterion of certainty.

From the nature of the case certainty is its own criterion, for it is a mere ascertainment of and testimony to a fact, viz. to our apprehension. It is an act of consciousness.

The objection to this statement obviously is, that many men say they are certain of opposite things etc.

Now I would have a person consider that certainty, in the above view, requires a deliberate act of reflexion etc.

§ 9. On the process of supernatural faith, and the portion of it which is supernatural.

Every step of the process, from the very first up to the assent to the credibilitas of the supernatural revelation *inclusive* is natural.

Every step then of that process, including the judgment of the prudentia declaring the credibilitas of the revelation may be mastered by a mind destitute of the grace of Christ.

Every step then of that process may be made a matter of natural consideration and reason, and may be taught the natural man, in the same way medicine or farming is taught him.

The process is as follows:-

A body of proof exists for the credibilitas of Revelation which make that credibilitas evidens, and which viewed as one is the motivum credibilitatis to the individual.

This body of proof is substantially the same to all men, but it is variously represented, with various relative prominences of its portions to various minds.

This body of proof is the formal cause of the conclusion, or the shape in which the conclusion comes to us.

It consists of all the facts and truths of the case, each in its right place as the prudentia sees and arranges them, conspiring to the conclusion of the credibilitas of Revelation.

It exists and is present to the mind of every one who has prudentia; it is not present to those who have not.

This prudentia is simply a natural acquisition, in the subject-matter of revelation, as well as in the subject matter of medicine and farming.

This prudentia, not only arranges and forms the body of proof, or motiva of the credibilitas of Revelation, but carries on the mind to a distinct judgment of, or assent to, that credibilitas, ⟨but only an assent with *fear*.⟩

And this assent to, or speculative evident judgment of, the credibilitas of Revelation is followed by the act of reflexion upon, or recognition of, that assent, which I have called certainty.

The whole of this is within the powers of natural reason. An infidel may get as far as this. A mind which gets as far as this does not yet believe. It only sees that Revelation is credibile. ⟨Though theologians speak as if, *when* the mind goes on to divine faith, this illumination of the intellect which precedes the pia voluntas is supernatural. Vide Suarez, Perrone p. 515.[1]

But again on the other hand, supposing *no* grace, can the unaided mind go *further* than the judicium speculativum? Yes, it can go on to a *human faith*, which does not exclude fear etc. 'Res credibilis etc.' Bellarmine.

(Digression — on grace generally as a stimulus enabling, not superseding, the intellect. Thus opium in natural things. Coleridge said wonderful things under its influence, but still *natural*. Again look at the First Book of Kings, or Saint Luke's Gospel — how *intellectually* beautiful, from the stimulus of *theological* ⟨religious⟩ inspiration).⟩

The steps which follow are all rational, according to human reason, but supernatural also, or require grace. They consist of

1. A practical judgment, as it is called, accompanying the speculative — viz an assent to the proposition that it is right and fitting and excellent to believe what is credible.

2. A pia affectio, or voluntas credendi, determining and commanding the intellect to believe.

3. The act of faith, in the intellect, thus commanded; the object being at once Revelation and the Res Revelata, viz. that God has spoken, and that he has spoken thus.

Hence there are three supernatural habits involved in the act of faith, 1. the assent to the fitness of believing, 2. the wish to believe. 3. the act ⟨habit⟩ of faith distinctly embracing and holding as true, the fact of the Revelation, and the thing revealed.

I will speak of these three separately.

First the practical judgment.

This is held by Suarez, Tanner, Viva — not by de Lugo.

It is held more commonly.

---

[1] G. Perrone *Praelectiones Theologicae*, II. ii, Rome 1842, *De Locis Theologicis*, p. 515, quotes Suarez on how the Holy Spirit moves the will 'ad actum fidei eliciendum circa illud ipsum objectum quod erat naturaliter cognitum ut quis credere possit *sicut oportet*', and how 'supernaturalis illa superveniens illustratio intellectus quae praecedit voluntatem credendi, non est necessaria ad judicium credibilitatis efformandum, sed solum praerequiritur propter supernaturalem actum.'

It does not immediately lead to faith, or is the ratio credendi — but it is the ratio volendi credere. ⟨here Coleridge's question⟩[1]

Since it is a judgment of the *honestas* credendi *hic et nunc* — I suppost it implies an additional act of reflexion on the whole state of the case; e.g. on the impossibility of obtaining the knowledge of God in any other way but faith, on the necessary nature of the proof etc., etc. Here Aristotle's words come in, πεπαιδευμένου γαρ ἐστι — And that if God has appointed the end, He has appointed sufficient means, but His means are these — and the famous saying of Richard de Saint Victor, 'Domine, si error est, etc'.[2]

2. The pia affectio or voluntas.

If this pia affectio acts without a sufficient ratio volendi or *motivum* credibilitatis, it is not supernatural.

It is analogous to a philosopher believing in a certain geological theory sufficient data for setting his voluntas credendi in motion. ⟨Question — unless you say that a human fides may follow on the judicium speculativum without the voluntas.⟩

The ratio (or motiva) which is sufficient for the voluntas credendi is not sufficient ad credendum, except with a human faith which has doubt or fear.

This voluntas exerts an imperium, obliging of itself the mind to believe without doubt or fear

The pia motio voluntatis belongs to a specific virtue, not charitas, but studiositas (Valentia), complacentia quaedam erga summam Dei veritatem — (Billuart)

3. Fides divina.

It is sometimes considered that an *act* of fides humana or acquisita precedes the *habit* of fides divina — humana and acquisita, yet aided by grace, — but it is difficult to understand this — for the *imperium* voluntatis goes before, and excludes doubt and fear.

The object of divine faith is both the revelatio and the res revelata.

Neither of them have evidentia — or they are what is called *obscura*. Fides divina, I suppose, has this difference from Fides humana, not only in its quality, but that fides, in the latter phrase, has something of a vague sense, and does not *necessarily* suppose a speaker — and hence is applicable to belief in our experimental conclusions in science. (But question — is not all doubt and fear excluded in our faith in the laws of nature?).

---

[1] According to Coleridge, faith is an act of the will and therefore of the practical, as distinct from the speculative judgement. Newman's reference to a 'question' rather than an 'assertion' may simply be a manner of speaking. See J. Coulson, *Newman and the Common Tradition*, Oxford 1970, pp. 26ff., 254–5.

[2] 'Domine, si error est a te ipso decepti sumus: nam ista ·n nobis tantis signis et prodigiis confirmata sunt et talibus, quae nonisi per te fieri possunt.' *De Trinitate*, J. P. Migne, *Patrologiae Latina*. Paris 1855, CXCVI, col. 891.

II   Papers of 1857 on Mill's Logic, on Imagination, on Arguments for Christianity

Vol 1. p 54[1] Is it not strange to make States of *Consciousness* synonymous with Feelings? I should have used some such word as *Apprehension*. Consciousness seems to me to imply a reflex act, viz that of being aware that you apprehend. 'Conscius' has 'sibi' understood.

P 57. I will not say that for Logical purposes the notion here set down of 'Perception' may not be passed over — though I am not sure. But, metaphysically, it seems dangerous to lay no stress on the active power of the mind, and to appear to resolve all phenomena into passive sensations. 'Perception' seems to answer to the faculty I describe in my Discourses on University Education Lecture 4. p. 107 etc.[2]

P. 60. Why may not substance be defined, not, 'that which exists by itself' (i.e. without attributes) but 'which may be conceived as existing by itself without attributes', and attribute 'that which can be conceived only as existing in, with, and on condition of another'? So we certainly proceed in speaking of Almighty God. His attributes are Himself, His substance. Certainly then Mill is not opposing *Catholics* here — *whom* is he opposing? who, except Martinus Scriblerus,[3] who could fancy a Lord Mayor without any external indication whatever, considers that in *fact* substance and attribute are separated? Yet still 'good', 'true', 'kind' are separate ideas — and that in which they all subsist is much more so.

P. 68.[4] I can't quite stomach the idea, as expressing a *fact*, that I have no consciousness of *Self*, as such, as distinct from a bundle of sensations. Bishop Butler speaks of consciousness as indivisible and one — this is my idea of man — of no unity have we practically experience, but of self.

---

[1] Newman has put 'N.B. Question' in the margin of his copy beside 'A Feeling and a State of Consciousness are, in the language of philosophy, equivalent expressions: everything is a feeling of which the mind is conscious'. J. S. Mill, *A System of Logic, Ratiocinative and Inductive*, London 1851, I, p. 54. See also *Philosophical Notebook*, I, pp. 224 ff.

[2] J. H. Newman, *The Idea of a University*, London 1905, pp. 74 ff. Newman's reference is to *Discourses on the scope and nature of University Education*, Dublin 1852.

[3] A reference to the *Works* of Alexander Pope, Edinburgh 1764, IV, p. 60. See also, *Letters and Diaries*, XI, p. 182.

[4] p. 68, i.e. Book I, chapter III, § 8. Mill's text reads: 'Thus, then, as body is the unsentient cause to which we are naturally prompted to refer a certain portion of our feelings, so mind may be described as the sentient *subject* (in the German sense of the term) of all feelings; that which has or feels them. But of the nature of either body or mind, further than the feelings which the former excites, and which the latter experiences, we do not, according to the best existing doctrine, know anything; . . .'

P. 70.[1] We may not be able to say *what* are qualities, *what* mere sensations — but, as effects imply causes, so the fact that l'opium endormit implies the existence (not as self subsisting, as one with substance, if you please, but still the fact) d'une vertue soporifique in the object.

P. 71 he has the phrase '*nature* of the object'. Well, call it nature, if you please; no matter whether nature, quality, attribute etc. etc. it is an idea attached to the object as distinct from its relation to others, though it may demand a certain nature *in* those others to produce its effect, or be able to act or operate on them.

P. 166[2] It seems a hard doctrine that geometrical truths depend on postulates, or rather a question of words. They depend on certain *conceptions*. 'Conceive a line fixed at one end to move (at the other. By this condition its extremity neither moves from or to the fixed point. Nor can it ever get further from the fixed point). Therefore it must move round the fixed point. (And since the ⟨its⟩ length is always the same, its other extremity will be always at the same distance from the fixed point). And as a flowing point is a line, its other extremity will trace a line or lines, and when the original line, of which it is one extremity has got round to its first position whence it started, this traced line will run into itself, and will have inclosed a space, that is, will have formed a figure. ⟨vid p. 283[3] "geometrical sense, not logical".⟩ Let the fixed point be called the centre, the moving line the radius, and the line or lines traced by the moving point bounding ⟨and making⟩ the figure, the circumference. And the figure be called a circle. It follows that every point in the circumference of a circle is always at the same distance from the centre, or the radii are all equal'. NB So far nothing is determined whether the circumference is one line or many, straight or curved. But I suppose we may go on to say, 'A straight line always proceeds in the direction in which it started, and if prolonged its extremity gets further from its starting point — therefore in this case its extremity does not move in a ⟨only one⟩ straight line': Now'

---

[1] p. 70, i.e. § 9. Mill is arguing that 'for the doctrine of the existence of a peculiar species of entities called qualities, I can see no foundation except in a tendency of the human mind which is the cause of many delusions.' Mill dismisses the existence of qualities as 'a lingering remnant of the scholastic doctrine of occult causes' ridiculed by Molière's physician who explained the fact that 'l'opium endormit' by the maxim 'parce qu'il a une vertu soporifique'.

[2] p. 166, i.e. Book I, chapter VIII, § 5. Mill argues, in words Newman has pencilled at the bottom of page 165, that 'a definition in Mathematics is an assumed fact to which a name is given.'

[3] p. 283, i.e. Book II, chapter VI, § 2. Mill writes about the foundation of the science of Number:
'The fundamental truths of that science all rest on the evidence of sense; they are proved by showing to our eyes and our fingers that any given number of objects, ten balls for example, may by separation and re-arrangement, exhibit to our senses all the different sets of numbers the sum of which is equal to ten. All the improved methods of teaching arithmetic to children proceed on a knowledge of this fact. All who wish to carry the child's *mind* along with them in learning arithmetic; all who wish to teach numbers, and not mere ciphers – now teach it through the evidence of the senses, in the manner we have described. We may, if we please, call the proposition "Three is two and one", a definition of the number three, and assert that arithmetic, as it has been asserted that geometry, is a science founded on definitions. But they are definitions in the geometrical sense, not the logical; asserting not the meaning of a term only, but along with it an observed matter of fact.'

instead of commencing with 'Conceive', certainly one might say 'Let', and then we start with a Postulate; but it seems simpler to call it an hypothesis, condition, conception, etc., nor does it seem very dangerous to call it a definition, viz as being a conception put into words. The original conception is 'A line moving with one end fixed'; and the words themselves are the Definition — From this original Definition *follows* what has been drawn out above — which is commonly and innocently included *in* the definition.

P. 218.[1] Mill here speaks of *authority*. Does he notice a proposition of this sort, 'In Adam all die'? Here is a universal, not gained by induction. Now in Acts in the Theological Schools the greater part of arguments perhaps depend on premises of this description.

P. 243 Here Mill allows that 'all the inductions involved in all geometry are comprised in those *simple* ones, the formula of which are the axioms, and a few of them so called definitions. The *remainder* of the science is made up of the processes employed for bringing unforseen cases within these inductions — or for proving the minors, the majors being the *definitions and axioms*', etc. Then the deductive science *does* start with definitions and axioms — and *not* with postulates. I do not see what he is making a noise about — whether the major premises be gained from intuition, induction etc. does not matter — but is a quasi metaphysical question, or at least one which may be put aside. The great question is *what* are the sources of the sciences. I suppose he would answer that the major premiss is the τόπος [place] of *syllogistic reasoning*, not the *fact*, the minor not coming from definitions and axioms — is the *minor* from postulates?

P. 251-2 'We cannot *conceive* a line without breadth; we can form no mental picture of such a line'. Does he not here confuse conception with imagination? We cannot imagine such a line — but there are many things which we conceive, or (whatever word we use,) which we hold before our intellect, which we cannot imagine. Abstract words imply conceptions which are not still imaginations. What would he call the operation by which we hold in the mind the idea of whiteness? Why is not length without breadth as good an idea or conception as whiteness? It is an abstraction from facts ⟨phenomena⟩. Take again the notion of *relation*; e.g. paternity or friendship. This is something which *goes between* two objects. It cannot exist without those objects and without a process in fact — but we can conceive it in itself, etc., it is like a line without breadth.

---

[1] p. 218, i.e. Book II, chapter III. § 4, on General Propositions. As Mill held that 'all inference is from particulars to particulars', he held that 'general propositions are merely registers of such inferences already made, and short formulae for making more.' He wrote: 'In both these cases the generalities are the original data, and the particulars are elicited from them by a process which correctly resolves itself into a series of syllogisms. The real nature, however, of the supposed deductive process, is evident enough. The only point to be determined is, whether the authority which declared the general proposition, intended to include this case in it; and whether the legislator intended his command to apply to the present case among others, or not.'

P. 252[1] He speaks of *feigning* the radii of a circle equal — how can you feign unless you have an object which you erect. A hypocrite imitates virtue and produces a counterfeit — that counterfeit is a real existing fact, himself. A poet feigns a character, as Hamlet. It does not exist in nature, but it is *one* — it is made up of things which *are* found in nature, but it is not 10.000 objects which *are* found, a bit of this man, or bit of that history or biography, etc. etc., but one complex idea created by him. And so we should never have feigned a perfect circle without a number of imperfect circles, but we do feign it — and since it is not in fact, it exists in our mind, by the process of abstraction.

P. 265[2] Here is a passage which illustrates what I mean by Imagination as contrasted with Reason. The passage, as continued in p. 266 tells for a body being in two places at once. vid also p. 282-3[3] about 'alteration of place and arrangement'.

P. 280[4] There is certainly a great deal to make it plausible to say, as Mill does, that arithmetic and algebra is the analysis or representative science of all things considered as *number* ⟨quantity⟩ — so that geometry is but one of its subjects or instances. And, if this were so, I should be wrong in what I have said towards the end of my last Oxford University Sermon.[5] Yet I have difficulties in admitting it — for Algebra only represents geometry, quà quantity, a certain way — there are properties of quantity, or kinds of quantity, which it does not measure, analyze, represent. E.g. if a^2 were a sufficient explanation of a geometrical square of AB, as a is a part of a^2, so the line AB

---

[1] p. 252, i.e. chapter V, § 1.
'The correctness of those generalizations, *as* generalizations, is without a flaw: the equality of all the radii of a circle is true of all circles, so far as it is true of any one: but it is not exactly true of any circle; it is only nearly true; so nearly that no error of any importance in practice will be incurred by feigning it to be exactly true.'

[2] p. 265, i.e. chapter V, § 6. Newman has marked the passage he refers to here:
'Now I cannot but wonder that so much stress should be laid on the circumstance of inconceivableness, when there is such ample experience to show, that our capacity or incapacity of conceiving a thing has very little to do with a possibility of the thing in itself; but is in truth very much an affair of accident, and depends on the past history and habits of our minds. There is no more generally acknowledged fact in human nature, than the extreme difficulty at first felt in conceiving anything as possible, which is in contradiction to long established and familiar experience; or even to old familiar habits or thought. And this difficulty is a necessary result of the fundamental laws of the human mind.' In the margin Newman has pencilled: 'All this is against Hume's argument against miracles from experience.'

[3] pp. 282-283, i.e. chapter VI, § 2. 'The expression "two pebbles and one pebble", and the expression "three pebbles", stand indeed for the same aggregation of objects, but they by no means stand for the same physical fact. They are names of the same objects, but of those objects in two different states: though they *de*note the same things, their *con*notation is different. Three pebbles in two separate parcels, and three pebbles in one parcel, do not make the same impression on our senses; and the assertion that the very same pebbles may by an alteration of place and arrangement be made to produce either the one set of sensations or the other, though a very familiar proposition, is not an identical one.'

[4] p. 280: § 2 as above. 'But though numbers must be numbers of something, they may be numbers of anything. Propositions, therefore, concerning numbers, have the remarkable peculiarity that they are propositions concerning all things whatsoever; all objects, all existences of every kind, known to our experience. All things possess quantity; consist of parts which can be numbered; and in that character possess all the properties which are called properties of numbers.'

[5] J. H. Newman, *Fifteen Sermons preached before The University of Oxford*, London 1906, pp. 350-1 [pp. 352-4 of the first edition].

would be part of the square which is raised upon it — that property of quantity then, which is called dimensionality, is not expressed by algebra. Therefore the two sciences, though algebra be the deeper, are after all distinct, and there must be a deeper one unknown which they both, one more, one less represent. On this subject vid p. 284-5 — though the objection is not answered there.

P. 293 *'Invention*, though it can be cultivated, cannot be reduced to rule'. So here is *something* beyond science. Memory is something else. I suspect, the power of reason is another thing else too; though for all those there was [sic] be *rules* to a certain point.

P. 295[1] Explicit and implicit reason — vid note — especially 'To the idea of Science', etc.

P. 305-6[2] Mill says, contrary to Whewell, that the ellipse is no *fact* in addition to the numerical *observations* in detail on which it was founded. But surely the *relations* of facts are facts; and therefore new facts above the facts. Hence (he wishes to answer this p. 302?) the ellipse which expresses the relation of the observations *to each other* is something new. Mill himself observes p. 283 something of the same kind, when speaking of 1 and 2 make 3. 3. Question. What Whewell and Mill call 'conception' p. 304,[3] is the object of it the same as 'formal cause'?

P. 306[4] Right investigation, he says, depends on a *habit of mind* — one man does what another can not. Well, this is just what I say of the investigation which leads to faith. He would answer, *'But, though the investigation* requires personal skill, the *exposition* of the *result* is a mere technical

---

[1] p. 295, i.e. Book III, chapter I § 2, in footnote criticizing Whewell's use of the term 'Induction'. 'To the idea of Science, an express recognition and distinct apprehension of general laws as such, is essential: but nine-tenths of the conclusions drawn from experience in the course of practical life, are drawn without any such recognition: they are direct inferences from known cases, to a case supposed to be similar. I have endeavoured to shew that this is not only as legitimate an operation, but substantially the same operation, as that of ascending from known cases to a general proposition . . . In science, the inference must necessarily pass through the intermediate stage of a general proposition, because the Science wants his conclusions for record, and not for instantaneous use. But the inferences drawn for the guidance of practical affairs, by persons who would often be quite incapable of expressing in unexceptionable terms the corresponding generalizations, may and frequently do exhibit intellectual powers quite equal to any which have ever been displayed in Science: and if these inferences are not inductive, what are they?'

[2] pp. 305-6, i.e. Book III, chapter II, § 4. 'Yet it is a fact surely, that the planet does describe an ellipse; and a fact which we could see, if we had adequate visual organs and a suitable position. Not having these advantages, but possessing the conception of an ellipse, or (to express the meaning in less technical language) knowing what an ellipse was, Kepler tried whether the observed places of the planet were consistent with such a path. He found they were so; and he, consequently, asserted as a fact that the planet moved in an ellipse. But this fact, which Kepler did not add to, but found in, the motions of the planet, namely, that it occupied in succession the various points in the circumference of a given ellipse, was the very fact, the separate parts of which had been separately observed; it was the sum of the different observations.'

[3] p. 304, i.e. Book III, chapter II, § 4. 'No one ever disputed that in order to reason about anything we must have a conception of it; or that when we include a multitude of things under a general expression, there is implied in the expression a conception of something common to those things.'

[4] p. 306, i.e. as above. There is no mention of 'a habit of mind' in Mill's text. On the contrary, he speaks only of 'a skilful guess' in reaching a fruitful hypothesis.

ratiocination which can easily be put into form, and level to the meanest capacity — is in like manner the reasoning which leads to faith?'

P. 307[1] There is this difficulty in his remark 'Now Doctor Whewell has remarked that these successive experiments were all correct' etc. — that, when it was said that the motion of the heavenly body was a circle, or again an epicircle, or an ellipse, it *assumed* the fact that its motion, *when not observed, was* in the circle or epicircle — or ellipse+ not only in the *point* where it *had been* observed. Is this induction or what? If it be induction, how do you *prove* the proposition that what in *certain* places moves in an ellipse will in all places?

P. 313[2] Here he oddly says 'It will *scarcely* be contended that Kepler's operation viz+ (there being) interferences from things ⟨cases⟩ known to things ⟨cases⟩ unknown'. This puzzles me indeed.

P. 322 A condition of induction is that 'if there were in nature any instances to the contrary, we should have known of them'. Does not this mean the same to my own condition, that 'if there are apparent exceptions to rule, we should, had we the due means, be able to account for them'?

P. 324 'We doubt not that even in the region of the fixed stars a straight line is the shortest distance between two points'. So 'two straight lines cannot inclose a space'. p. 260 he will not allow it from intuition, vid also p. 265 where he defends it. All this illustrates the controversy about Transubstantiation. 'A body cannot be in two places at once'.

P. 329. Here Mill says that the first investigators *assumed* that the laws of nature were uniform in their first inductions, or rather that if a thing happened once in a certain association it would again, and *afterwards corrected* their *assumptions*. 'Nor were they wrong in assuming that water drowns etc., subject, however, as they afterwards began to see, to an *ulterior revision of their spontaneous generalization*'. *Spontaneous*, observe, spontaneous, why *spontaneous*; if spontaneous, and *before experience*, it must have been from some principle, tendency, etc. in the mind *itself* which he denies, top of p. 320. However, he refers us to ch. 21.

P. 331[3] 'If an induction conflicts with *stronger* inductions etc. the weaker

---

[1] p. 307: 'Now Doctor Whewell has remarked that these successive general expressions, though apparently so conflicting, were all correct: they all answered the purpose of colligation: they all enabled the mind to represent to itself with facility, and by a simultaneous glance, the whole body of facts at that time ascertained; each in its turn served as a correct description of the phenomena, so far as the senses had up to that time taken cognizance of them.'

[2] p. 313, i.e. as above § 5. Mill's text reads: 'All definitions of induction, by writers of authority, make it consist in drawing inferences from known cases to unknown; affirming of a class, a predicate which has been found true of some cases belonging to the class; concluding, because some things have a certain property, that other things which resemble them have the same property — or because a thing has manifested a property at a certain time, that it has and will have that property at other times.'

It will scarcely be contended that Kepler's operation was an Induction in this sense of the term. The statement, that Mars moves in an elliptical orbit was no generalization from individual cases to a class of cases. Neither was it an extension to all time, or what had been found true at some particular time.'

[3] p. 331, i.e. Book III, chapter IV. 3. 'If an induction conflicts with stronger inductions, or with conclusions capable of being correctly deduced from them, then, unless on re-

must give way'. Here is the point in which I should (in my University Discourses, e.g. the third)[1] differ; i.e. if by stronger and weaker, he merely means 'other and other'. He says that a comet is not a religious messenger, *if* it be a physical phenomena; for there is a stronger induction to show it is physical (i.e. an induction from more and clearer instances) than to show it is religious. On the contrary I would say that there are different spheres of agency, and different laws and agents in them, that they sometimes conflict — and that sometimes one gives way sometimes the other. NB. I doubt whether the uniformity of the Laws of nature *is* intuitive, or agreed on by all, but the *ordinary* uniformity. It is quite as natural and instinctive, the belief in *chance* — by chance being meant, *not an event without a cause, but a phenomenon anomalous to the usual course of things,* e.g. something turning up, etc. etc., fear of ghosts, etc. etc. E.g. *unusual* [three words illegible], strange rites, etc.

The following ideas are portions of one consistent whole. They so hang together and are included in each other, that each follows on the admission of the rest, and none can be denied without distorting and disconnecting the rest. If any one of them was to be proved as a fact the rest would be its proof, would point to it as necessary for their own existence, and thus illuminate and give evidence to that one.

In Geometry science in which separate proofs come from Reason	In Theology science in which separate proofs come from Revelation
1 A figure contained by three straight lines, or a triangle	1 A.B. was baptized
2 has three angles	2 sinned
3 has any of its exterior angles equal to the two opposite interior	3 died in state of grace
4 has any of its exterior with the adjacent interior equal to two right angles	4 died with a temporal debt
5 has its three angles equal to two right angles	5 which is not satisfied
	6 which is in the way to be satisfied
	7 is in purgatory
The assemblage of these makes so perfect a unity, that one cannot be denied and the rest maintained without an absurdity in reason	8 cannot sin
	9 cannot merit
	10 is not in heaven
In Natural History	11 nor in hell
	12 is certain of heaven

consideration it should appear that some of the stronger inductions have been expressed with greater universality than their evidence warrants, the weaker one must give way.'
See also *Idea of a University*, pp. 43 ff.
[1] Now the fourth of *Oxford University Sermons*, 'The Usurpations of Reason'.

phenomena are so connected that
a naturalist by seeing a small
bone can reconstruct the animal.
This example does not answer —
because the connexion of the
separate phenomena is not *certain,*
either from Reason or Revelation.

A contradiction to Reason is called an absurdity and to Revelation an unbelief or incredulity. Reason in the imagination holds views at once per modum unius the complex idea of a Triangle with all its parts. Revelation gives all at once per modum unius the dogma of Grace. Deny any part of the first you overturn the authority of Reason — of the latter, the authority of Revelation.

Yet the only really good instance of *evidentia* is a strict science like Mathematics, because the portions of dogma in Theology do not force the acceptance of other portions. If then the case of Theology, as above, is given, it must be as an illustration, *after* the Geometry, with a sort of apology.

NB. A good instance of the difference between imagination and reason is this — that I feel no fear of reading a book like M. Comte's though said to be atheistical, though I *have* an anxiety about looking into Strauss's Life of Christ.

NB. I should begin a treatise thus:- 'there are various dogmas which all the world holds — I do not go *to the question as to their origin*, whether intuitive and instinctive or from experience — but in fact from a child, from the first use of reason, all men all over the world hold or act as if they held, that 'the course of nature is uniform', 'there is a right and a wrong, etc.', (give more instances) ⟨give *all*⟩). Next what *things come under* these abstract forms, there is far less agreement about, i.e. when minor *premisses* have to be found and settled.

NB. Mill, by making axioms come from experience, seems to lay the foundation of this doctrine 'Experience is the source of absolute certainty'. *But,* if we may be certain about one subject matter from experience, why not about another? Hence the laws of physical nature may become axioms as simply as those of geometry, a miracle may be as impossible as that two lines inclosing a space. On the other hand the *advantage* of his doctrine to a Catholic is that it is not *more* impossible *in idea* to conceive that a body should be in two places at once, *than* that two lines should inclose a space; as then we only say we have no *experience* of the latter, so we have no right to say more than we have no *experience* of the former. Moreover we can overcome the *above difficulty* as to miracles arising from Mill's view, by saying 'You yourself allow that the truths of geometry are only from experience and might be otherwise' — as then you cannot be sure except from experience that two and two make four, so you cannot be sure from experience that the dead cannot rise — and there *is experience* to a resurrection. He will fall back on this:- 'nature is ever uniform':- *therefore* the dead *never* can rise — but query — can analogy prove any thing positive — Experience would prove that the dead do not rise — can it *dis*prove that the dead *have not* risen?

July 23, 1857

(a vivid conception being mistaken for truth, vid. Bonaparte in Allison)[1]

1. Reason is the faculty by which we arrive from things known to things unknown.
2. Imagination is distinct from reason, but mistaken for it. What is *strange*, is to the imagination *false*. It tends to doubt whatever is strange. Experience is the measure of truth to imagination. (Imagination is the basis of Hume's argument against miracles).
3. Since man is a being of limited (powers and) knowledge, the conclusions which reason arrives at are necessarily strange, and therefore to the imagination untrue.
4. Hence the instances are continual of strictly rational processes leading to a conclusion which we are ready to reject as irrational, only because it is strange.
5. Thus reason assures us that something or other must be from eternity — yet an eternity a parte ante is a notion which we would reject, if we possibly could. — So of infinite space. So the theory of the horizontal moon — So etc. etc.
NB The argument from analogy dangerous as indulging the imagination.
6. This being laid down, I say that the Being of God is an idea ⟨truth⟩ of this kind, proved by reason, repugnant to the imagination.
7. For, that a Being should concentrate in Himself all excellencies, that He should be the One Individual Power and goodness, and eternity, and there should be nothing else, and secondly that being thus perfect, the idea of creation should be possible, or that a God can in His nature/notion[?] be a Creator, and further, that He should be able from this idea to communicate His excellencies to His creatures, is far more repugnant to the imagination, than the idea of no God, i.e. of a Universe in which all excellencies were defective and distributed. (Again, go on to the creation as a fact. You can't *account* for, i.e. give the final cause for it, on hypothesis of an intelligent Creator, or of its parts. It seems object less.)
8. Corollary — thus imagination, not reason, is the great enemy to faith, vid what Bacon and Butler say against imagination, vid my sermon about the world in University Sermons.[2]

---

[1] A. Alison, *History of Europe*, X, pp. 286–7. See also *A Grammar of Assent*, p. 334, and below, p. 113.
[2] 'Contest between Faith and Sight', *Oxford University Sermons*, pp. 120–35. See also below, p. 145, from *Stray Essays*, p. 78.

July 24, 1857

I do not see how the argument from Design holds in the case of those who admit existence of Instinct. Bees promote certain ends without meaning it.

They are not physical but self moving agents. Why does not Paley argue that if you found a hive you would say that its framers had a final cause? or again, since Bees are directed by instinct, that the maker of the eye is directed by instinct also?

July, 1857

1. The discoveries of modern astronomy make the Creator more wonderful when his existence is proved, but diminish the astronomical proof of it.
2. As space is but as result of the impressions of our senses, it follows that, as we do not know the *substance* of other things, neither of space.
3. Yet question whether the notion of space is not partly intellectual — I mean a conclusion from reason. Given the idea of a cube, and suppose its annihilation, space is the idea what follows not from sense immediately, but from reason.
4. Is perspective an idea of sense or of reason? brutes have it.
5. Question how far can the divine attributes, how many of them, be proved by the physical world? What is de fide here? What have the sacred Congregations determined?

August 10, 1857

PREFACE

Egotism is modesty in metaphysical discussion — for in so obscure a matter all one can do is to give one's own experience, without daring to say one has found out truths which will approve themselves to all.[1] Therefore this work in the first person and personal.

August, 1857

If the man saw the statue gold on one side, it was only an *imagination* which told him to say it could not be silver on the other.

But it might be of transparent *glass*, and then he could be sure of the other side for he could see through. Take a third illustration in which the material on one side makes it impossible it should be a certain other material on the other.

---

[1] See also *A Grammar of Assent*, pp. 344–5, 353, 384 ff., 409–10; *Philosophical Not ebook* I, pp. 14, 79–80, 133, II, pp. 27 ff., 87.

Imagination — thus Protestants won't admit any thing *but what* is *in* the Bible.

September 2, 1857

It seems a paradox to say that God is the author of the physical universe, yet that so great a work does not contain proof that he is the author.

The whole conversation and politia of the Saints, (brought out in their lives) certainly is to be taken as an argument for Christianity, and may be *the* argument, inattention to which, makes the metaphysical and historical arguments of unbelief overcome the mind.

September 25, 1857

The arguments for the Catholic Religion.

1. On man's ignorance — or the state of the case as *we* profess it — there are arguments against every thing. Therefore whatever was ascertained, atheism, ditheism or monotheism, etc., would have argument against it, which *need not* be solved at the same time that the discovery or revelation is made.

2. On arguments *for* every thing — probabilities etc. cases — rising and falling like waves — approximations to views.

3. Reason proves one thing more than another — on certainty — on moral certainty. How far it goes — at length. There is a truth — fabulae cannot be proved.

4. On objections not availing against an *harmonious* proof (Butler sermon 15 note)[1] or against an idea or form when it is found there cannot be antagonist proofs.

5. If we do all we can, it will be hoped that God will do more.

6. On disposition of mind and antecedent probabilities or likelihoods, on the likelihoods of a correlation — i.e. lungs existing, of air.

7. Likelihood that a revelation would be given — draw this out — argument looks very different according as the onus probandi is on this side or the other.

---

[1] 'Upon the Ignorance of Man': ' . . . our ignorance is the proper answer to many things which are called objections against religion . . . From our ignorance of the constitution of things, and the scheme of providence in the government of the world; from the reference the several parts have to each other, and to the whole, and from our not being able to see the end of the whole, it follows that however perfect things are they must even necessarily appear to us otherwise less perfect than they are.' To this passage Butler appended a note: 'I. Suppose some very complicated piece of work, some system or constitution, formed for some general end, to which each of the parts had a reference. The perfection or justice of this work or constitution would consist in the reference and respect, which the several parts had to the general design. This reference of parts to the general design may be infinitely various, both in degree and kind. Thus one part may only contribute and be subservient to another; this to a third; and so on through a long series, the last part of which alone may contribute immediately and directly to the general design. Or a part may have this distant reference to the general design, and may also contribute immediately to it. . . .' *The Works of Joseph Butler*, Edinburgh 1813, II, pp. 263–4. Edited by W. E. Gladstone, II, *Sermons, Etc.*, Oxford 1897, Sermon XV, p. 226.

8. On a revelation as implying infallibility — the only question is where is the oracle.

8. [Sic] The argument, viz. that the present Church is the continuation of the Primitive.

Discuss Papal Infallibility not being the cardo.

Discuss the Greek Church.

9. On the *Notes* of His one Church.

III   Lecture on Logic

(Of course January or February, 1859)[1]

The great difficulty of lecturing on Philosophy, and of course of the study altogether, is the uncertain distribution of its subject matter. Authority does little for us here, and perhaps could not do much — and in the absence of it writers follow their own judgment. Instances of this will meet us on the very threshold of our inquiries, and need not be given here.

⟨Mill has some chapters on the need of a philosophical language.⟩

⟨The books I mean to take are Bonelli, Dmowski, Gerdil. Balmez, St. Sulpice course, Ubaghs, Mill, Whewell, Brown, Reid, Hamilton.⟩

The shape in which this difficulty first meets us when we propose to open the whole subject is this, viz. that we are in perplexity which branch of it to take first. The University of Paris, no great religious authority, though it has of course an influence beyond its proper sphere, begins with Psychology instead of Logic on the plausible ground that, since Logic professes to guide the powers of the mind in the pursuit of truth, till we know what the powers are, we do not know what is to be guided. Bonelli places Ontology last; 'Ex nostrâ methodo, Ontologia, postremo loco posita, caeterarum Institutionis istius partium, veluti consectarium et apex constituitur.' t 2. p. 148. Dmowski's order is that of Logic, Ontology, Natural Theology, Psychologia, Cosmology, Ethics. The St Sulpice course leaves out Cosmogony, unless it brings it under Ontology and Theology. Ontology p. 16 note. Ubaghs does the same (does he place Psychology first?) places Logic second, and Ontology third; seems to bring Logic under Psychology Logic p. 1; and reduces the proofs of Theology (Theodicea p 8) to Logic, Ontology, psychology and the natural sciences.

If the main divisions are so difficult, still more will be the position and treatment of particular subjects. The question of the real existence of bodies is placed by Bonelli in cosmology, by Dmowski under Logic; by the St. Sulpice writer under Ontology. The subject of Ideas is commonly treated under Logic as by Dmowski; but Bonelli constitutes [it] a distinct science, being with Ontology the two parts of Metaphysics, called Ideology.

Nor is this all. Under one general class are placed subjects altogether different from each other in kind. For instance, Dmowski sets down four informants of the mind in knowing truth, viz the sensus intimus, ratio, sensus externi, and auctoritas. Now of these auctoritas is but a secondary informant — for it depends upon reason, as Dmowski grants, that is on facts and the

---

[1] See *Philosophical Notebook*, I, p. 238.

testimony to facts and of reasoning upon those facts; but testimony ultimately depends on our external senses as do facts also, or on the sensus intimus. Again the word ratio includes powers quite distinct from each other; viz the power of abstraction and the possession of first principles, one of which surely is a process, but the other a habit. ⟨Abstraction is either a faculty or a process — as a process it falls under Logic proper — as a faculty under psychology. Abstraction will come under logic proper and first principles under logic improper.⟩

Another cognate difficulty is the varying use of technical terms. For instance take the word *reason*. It is naturally [sic] to understand it as synonymous to the Greek word λόγος; yet in its derivatives, as the word 'ratio' from which it comes, it would seem rather to be the faculty of reasoning — for we speak of ratiocinium, and reasoning. Hence some writers use intellectus, entendement, understanding, to express the faculty of reasoning — others the word ratio or reason. Ubaghs has varied in the use of the two words, as he confesses, Ratio et intellectus in homine non possunt dici diversa potentia; intelligere est simpliciter veritatem intelligibilem apprehendere; ratiocinari est procedere de uno intellecto ad aliud. Multi auctores, et nos ipsi, alias haec nomina aliter usurpavimus. pp 135–6. notes.

This evil is increased by the real difference of opinion. Some writers have ideas for which they find no suitable terms in their own language, or in Latin; they are obliged then to use those which they find to their hand, and take words in new senses. Kant's use of 'reason' as opposed to 'understanding' is, I suppose, a case in point.

The consequence of all this is that to enter upon the study of Philosophy is to my own feelings like entering into a labyrinth. The very first principle of Science is Order; but here we have often 'confusion worse confounded' by the different attempts at effecting Order. And then, I have spoken of Catholic writers only; but where are we, when we turn ourselves to the multitude of views, of those who are not so! And then it must be considered, (I suppose I am correct in saying so) that for the most part ecclesiastical authority does not help us in starting, because philosophy is the creation of natural reason, and only interferes in the event to condemn the conclusions at which we may suppose to have arrived.

I begin with Logic, both because it is usual to do so, and because it has the best claim to be first considered. But here we have to consider what is understood by the word, in which all writers are not agreed.

Different definitions of Logic. The widest is Tandel's — 'Scientia tractans de veritate cognitionis humanae,' or St Sulpice — 'Scientia intellectum dirigens ad verum' — or Bonelli's 'Disciplina rationem humanam dirigens.' The narrowest is Whately's — 'The art of reasoning.' Nay the widest does not comprehend the narrowest — but the subject matter of each is different — for, whereas the larger definitions all speak of truth, Whately's, strictly speaking, has nothing to do with truth at all.

Then again take Dmowski's, an able writer — 'facultas recte rationandi fontesque veri deprehendendi' — 'recte rationandi' is intelligible, but 'fontesque etc' is something like 'cum quibusdam aliis.'

This is not merely a question of words, for according to the definition, will be the treatise, and the subjects included in it. And, in the next place, every science should have its distinct object — what then is the object of Logic? Dmowski, e.g. proposes two objects — one precise and one very vague. Locke, I think, calls it 'the art of reason;' can a definition be vaguer? or, if not, can a science be vaster?

In such a diversity of opinions, I must choose my own. Now I have a definite meaning which I shall give it myself — viz 'The Science of Proof or Inference.' This definition is wider than Whately's — far narrower than the Port Royal — Bonelli's — Tandel's — Locke's. It agrees pretty well with that of Ubaghs, St. Sulpice, and Mill, and with Aristotle's before them.

Aristotle calls it an instrumental art —[1] that is, it is not concerned with any definitive subject matter, but is an instrument which we use whether we are discussing questions of history, of politics, of commerce, of mathematics, or of mechanics ⟨physics⟩. It follows from this that it is not concerned with the truth or falsehood of the subject matter, but is hypothetical. The only truth it is concerned with is that of the act of inference. And its object is truth of inference, and its occupation is the determination of the laws of true or correct inference.

By 'inference' is meant the process of the mind to what is unknown from, besides, and because of what is known. A is true, therefore B is true. If A is true, B is true, or vice versa, B is true, because A is true, B is true supposing ⟨granting⟩ A is true which is called 'proof.'

How different is this from the view of Logic taken by such able writers as Dmowski! I run through his chapters and find one entitled 'De Corporum Existentia' — what conceivable concern has this with Logic? Is there not something evidently wrong in a division of subject, which allows such a heading to be prefixed to a chapter on Logic?

On the other hand the definition goes beyond that of Whately's, that is, as he explains himself. He considers that the syllogism is the only form or analysis of reasoning — consequently the laws of syllogising are with him nearly the whole of Logic; and he hardly recognises any doctrine about the use of terms or of propositions except with reference to syllogisms. On the other hand I conceive that generalization is a sort of inference — for it implies a conclusion about the similarity of the things generalized. If I threw together Christian Sacraments, benedictions and relics into one class with magical incantations, phylacteries, amulets, philtres, and horse shoes, under the common name of spell or charm, it would be an inference, and a false inference but not a syllogism.[2] And when Linnaeus classifies in an original way, who can

---

[1] *Organon*, the title given to Aristotle's logical works.
[2] See *Philosophical Notebook*, II, p. 9.

deny that he throws great and new light on the subject of living things; the new truth being that this is like that. Again, if I said no Christians are bad men, therefore no bad men are Christians; I should be inferring and correctly inferring, though from a false premiss, but I should not be syllogising and, if I said, All men are animals, therefore all animals are men, here again I infer and falsely, but I am not transgressing any law of the Syllogism. I say that in all these cases there is a new enunciation or judgment true or false, quite as really, as if I said 'Since I am one of a race universal mortal, I shall certainly die.' What great advance do we make in this syllogism, which is not quite equalled by the above instances under the first and second parts of Logic.

But now you will ask me, if I thus define the science called Logic, what am I to do with the heap of subjects, to which I have referred, which are so often brought into it. Ubaghs will help us here.

It is usual to divide Logic into two parts, proper and improper, as I should call them — the former of which is pretty much what I have described Logic to be. Dmowski and Bonelli agree pretty well with Ubaghs here.

Ubaghs says that Logic may be considered in two points of view — first as directing the intellect, secondly as directing the reason. The intellect is the faculty cogitandi, of thinking or reasoning; the reason, the faculty of knowing, cognoscendi. Log. p 2 p 136. Therefore logic is the science first of thinking, secondly of knowing. Of these the former is that instrumental science or art, to which I would confine the name of Logic. Ubaghs calls it Logica stricte sumpta, formalis, subjectiva. (It is also called dialectica). The other kind of logic is that which lays down the laws of knowledge; it is accordingly not an instrumental art, but aims directly at truth, as an end. It is called Logica realis or materialis, or objectiva; and its office, according to Ubaghs, is two-fold; first, the knowledge of truth — 2 our certainty of our knowledge. Bonelli calls these two kinds of logic, dialectica and critica. In other words, Logic is not a science but a generic name, comprehending two sciences, as metaphysics may be, comprehending Ontology, etc.

We now have advanced some way, and with the consent of various authors in clearing up the difficulty which we have complained of — first of removing the vagueness of the province of Logic, and secondly of simplifying the definition. It is the science of Proof or Inference — but then the question comes what is to be done with the second department, which is concerned with truth and certainty.

To answer this question is no part of our present duty — but I will remark as follows. The science which treats of objects external to the soul is called Ontology; the science which treats of the soul itself and its faculties is called Psychology. Now a science is necessary which treats of the connection of these two with each other; of their mutual action, and intercommunion; on the one hand of the channels by which external objects are introduced into the soul, and on the other the criteria by which we are certain that we have possession of them and distinguish them from counterfeits. This is pretty much what the second part of Logic treats of — it is very nearly too what Bonelli contemplates under the name of ideology. I would throw these two departments together; I would do so, because I consider they have one object, and that proper to themselves; I call their one object the intercommunion or concern of the soul to what is external to it, or in other words truth, or rather the ascertainment of truth. The subjects in detail would be such as the origin of ideas, the certainty of the senses, the common sense of nature, the nature and grounds of faith, and all those other matters which relate to the truths of the premisses from which Logic proper argues. Logic proper ascertains the truth of the inferential process — the science in question of the premisses. I do not profess to have clearly made out the limits of each science; for instance, I have some difficulty at the moment to know which of the two should lay down the laws of testimony or evidence or authority as a source of truth. ⟨Yes. I think it [would] be under Ontology. The argument from authority as from testimony I should place under Logic proper, as one of its *applications*. The Sensus intimus or conscientia under the second or Noology⟩ I am inclined to think, as I have expressed it that the justification of the principle of faith would come under the latter science, but the justifications of good testimony or authority under Logic. Lastly for the name. I would then make Logic not a science but a generic name for two sciences, Dialectica and Critica, the Science of Proof ⟨Inference⟩, and the science of knowledge — or the first might be called Logic; the second Noology or Gnoseology ⟨from Aristotle's νοῦς Ethic. lib 6⟩[1]

Logic Proper

Ideas   Names   Classifications   Definitions   Divisions

Judgment   categories   propositions

Ratiocination

Dianoetics

1   Character of Proof

Science — Demonstration

Probability. 1 verisimilitude — 2 reasons of proofs

presumptions

likelihood

[1] pp. 13–16, one folded sheet, seem to have been lost.

2 Instruments of proof — 1 observation — experiment —

2 testimony — experience

3 Method of proof ⟨?⟩ — Deductive Method

Disputation

investigation — Inductive Method

4 Errors and Fallacies

A very difficult question arises whether the subject of ideas comes directly into the province of Logic. Or in other words, whether names or terms stand for ideas or for things. It will be said that ideas and things go together, and therefore the question is unimportant — but there is the case in which there is, or is imagined, an idea without a thing, that is, the case of Universals — Accordingly those then on the side of Things against Ideas, say that there are *not* universal ideas; and a controversy ensues which is nothing else than a portion of the old scholastic controversy, between the Nominalists, Realists, and Conceptionists.

⟨1. No one whatever doubts that what the mind contemplates, at least in corporeal objects, is not the object itself, but a representation of it, which we call an idea.

2. It follows that, at least in all such cases (corporeal) though the word denotes an object, it denotes an idea also.

3. But the question is 'what do I mean when I use a name, e.g. Caesar?' do I take the word to stand for the idea Caesar or the thing ⟨object⟩ Caesar, each or both of which I can make it to stand for — certainly, for the object or thing Caesar.

4. But when I reflect on my meaning, I am contemplating my *idea* for to say 'I mean Caesar when I say Caesar' and 'I have the idea of Caesar' are synonymous.'⟩

It is usual with Catholic writers to take the part of Universals — and in consequence to take the part of Ideas against Things. My own long habit has been the same — and it is difficult for me for that reason to do otherwise, but I confess the onus probandi is with those who maintain Universals, and it is difficult to prove their necessity — and taking that question away, it certainly does seem more simple and natural to say the words stand for the things.[1]

Now let us first clearly see what the question is. ⟨To say words *mean* things is incorrect for *words* can mean nothing. *I* mean.⟩ There is no doubt but objects or things create ideas or images; and that words stand for both

[1] On Newman's attitude to Universals and Nominalism, see *Philosophical Notebook,* I, pp. 108, 167 ff., II, p. 13.

ideas and things — but the question is *what I mean, what you mean*, when you use a name or term.

When you say Augustus was Emperor of Rome, are you really meaning any thing short of Caesar himself?

Is it not so always when the question is of *facts*? Well, and I suppose facts are good part of the subject matter of reasoning. Take, for instance, Scott's Essay in the Atlantis on 'the Birth' etc.[1] it is a series of arguments; facts are throughout the subject matter — does he mean anything short of facts? How do ideas come in at all in his *meaning*? He does not mean the *idea* of Augustus; he does not think of his own mind at all, or whether he *has* a mind — much less whether his mind has ideas — but he is simply looking at something external. And so the greater part of mankind, what do they know of their ideas — they not only do not think of them, but they know them as little as the man in the play knew he was talking prose.

But you may say that some one may doubt whether Augustus was Emperor — for Imperator means a victorious general — not an Emperor — and so, if we say, Napoleon was a great man, we shall have to discuss what we mean by 'great' — True, here is a reflex action. We mean a *thing* — but we *examine* our *meaning*, or in other words *that* is, our idea — Then indeed we do begin to speak and think of ideas — but observe, this is not the enunciation of words and propositions itself, but a reflexion before or enquiry *into* that enunciation, or what we mean.

It is notorious we do not perceive external objects — we see them through a medium, namely in a certain idea, which is created in our minds by our senses and in other ways — as if in a mirror. Now supposing we are looking at a landscape or concourse of people in a glass or camera obscura. We point to the figures in the glass and say 'there goes Tom'; 'Dick is mounting his horse,' 'Jack is getting over a style,' 'Hodge is coming in from ploughing.' We do not mean 'there goes the image of Tom,' 'the image of Dick is on image of horse- back.' etc. But supposing we could not make out some part of the scene, we might say, 'The glass is dusty, or smeared,' and we might take a cloth and clean it. Then we should be examining what we *mean* by our words, or reflecting upon our idea, and we should clean it up by definitions. ⟨There are two kinds of universals — one by abstraction as 'a man', another by ratio pura as a whole is greater than its part ⟨virtue is good⟩. Locke denies the latter? and Mill both? There is a universal which is not abstract, and an abstract which is not universal.⟩

I consider then that words are used by us primarily to denote things — but that when we doubt what the thing is, we are obliged to reflect upon the image which it forms on our minds and which is its representative and then we use it to denote an idea and we define the idea in order that the word may

---

[1] W. H. Scott, 'On the Dates of the Nativity and Crucifixion', *Atlantis*, vol. II (1859), pp. 43 ff. See also, 'A note on the passages omitted from Scott's article in the 'Atlantis', *Irish Ecclesiastical Record*, vol. CVIII (1967), pp. 203 ff.

best convey, not the idea but the thing, as we rub the glass, not for the sake of the glass, but for the sake of the real objects which the glass images. Definition then *has* to do with ideas, but still the *proposition* in which it is still has to do with things. ⟨Again, you may be taking your own idea or fancy *for* a thing, but you *mean* a thing.⟩

If we assume that reasoning is but an instrumental art, and has nothing to do with the objective truth of the premisses or the (factness of their) terms, then I should say that the science of Mathematics is founded upon a hypothetical basis, and that these bases are the Definitions. Here I differ from Mill, for Mill says that a definition is (1) directly an account of the meaning of the word and (2) *involves* the truth ⟨fact⟩ of the object it stands for. He would say then that, whereas definitions are carried out into reality by postulates, postulants [sic] are the foundation of the science; for the postulate is in [a] fact (2) on which and not on the definition (1) the science depends. But I should draw out as follows:-

Let there be such a thing as a point — Let there be such a thing as motion. (I don't assume the fact that there is such a thing), and let a line be the path formed by point moving to point. Let there be two points is space — Let point A approach B in such a way that an eye stationed in B thinks that A is not moving, I call the path of A a straight line.

Let two straight lines A and B of indefinite length cross each other. Let a third straight line C move through ⟨along⟩ the straight lines A and B — I call the path of the straight line C a superficies, and a plain superficies.

Two straight lines in the same plane, which do not cut each other, however far produced are called parallel lines — when they cut each other the inclination of one straight line to another, where they meet, at the point at which they meet, is called an angle. ⟨Lines which cut each other diverge for ever, (prove) never cut each other again.⟩

Proposition:

No two straight lines can bound or inclose a space. Straight lines either may be considered as cutting each other or not. If they do not cut, they do not do so ⟨inclose it⟩, by the hypothesis. If they do, then (as has been shown) they diverge for ever on each side after cutting — and therefore do not inclose a space.

Three straight lines can inclose a space.

Let two straight lines (A and B) cut each other. Take any two points in A and B respectively, and join them and call the joining line C; and A, B, and C inclose a space.

(I call the space, inclosed by the 3 lines, a triangle). Every figure of three sides has three angles — for A and B originally met; and that is *one* angle, and C was drawn from a point in each of A and B and this makes two others. And so on.

That so far forth as definitions consist in *giving* or *explaining names*, I grant what Mill says — I grant also that if 'Let there be such a thing as a point' be a postulate — that he is right too. But this is giving a new sense to the word postulate and there must be many more of them. They ought to be called *hypothetical facts* or *conceptions* expressed in definitions.

It is awkward to have a hypothetical science, though logic may be an instrumental art — therefore the premisses ought to be certain.

Mill p 170 will not allow that we can *conceive* length without breadth, but that we *attend* to length. (Here we must define our word 'conception' — and thus metaphysics are a sort of basis of logic. We conceive the Almighty, though in another sense we as little conceive him as we conceive length without breadth, which we never say. Who *conceives* an abstraction? who *conceives* whiteness? yet Mill will allow of abstract ideas). Well then, find some other word, e.g. we *imagine* it.

Surely the faculty which I speak of is the power of taking views or aspects. Mill will say that it is attending to one part of a fact — but it is more than this — there is an act of mental separation. Let us call it apprehension? understanding? intelligence? contemplation?

A *conception* seems to me to be an act of putting together things, or therefore has something complex in it. Thus we conceive of a *whole*. We conceive a proposition, truth or falsity — we conceive a situation of affairs, as Napoleon had a singular genius for conceptions in battle, i.e. of positions of troops, the consequences etc. etc. The ability to enter into character is a power of conception. It is a sort of *picturing* or *composition*. In *this* sense length without breadth is *not* conceived — much less is it *comprehension*. Yet still surely it is more than what Mill calls *attention*. Length without breadth is at least a phrase. Well — length we can understand — breadth we can understand — without we can understand — all three together then we, not *conceive*, but understand. As we cannot conceive the doctrine of the Holy Trinity, though we understand the meaning of each statement which goes to make up the doctrine. Therefore we have understanding of length without breadth, or intelligence, or contemplate it. Contemplation would be a better word than attention. Some word, which, like abstraction, implies separation, is wanted.

There needs a chapter on acts of the mind ⟨intellect⟩ to start with. It seems to me a great paradox in Mill to say that we have not not [sic] a separate, independent idea of abstract *line*. (But if a line may be an abstract idea, why not 'man'?)

It seems somewhat fussy to make such a to-do about 'Definitions' not being the grounds or principles of mathematics — Why may we not call '*Defined things*' the first principles of mathematics. I do not see why a line should require a postulate more than whiteness — the mind *does* it.

January 11 1859

Questions of greater consequence

1. Whether ad veritatem (aut metaphysicam aut) logicam requiratur aliquod objectum a mente et actu mentis distinctum —. Dmowski p 24 note 1.

Again whether the actus or idea mentis are the same p 5 and whether the idea is attended with an imago sensibilis. ibid.

2. whether perceptio and apperceptio or perceptionis conscientia are different from each other. Bonelli t. 2 p 102 note. Dmowski pp 39, 40.

3. whether subjective certitude may be legitimately produced by probable arguments. vid. Saint Alfonso Homo Apostol. t 1 p 9 *probabilitas* talis, quòd *moralem certitudinem* fundare valet. Dmowski simply denies this, p 27 (text and note) of *proper* moral certainty. ⟨Gerdil seems to grant it t 1 p 219⟩

4. whether induction can issue in certainty. Negat Dmowski Log, p 22, n. 27.

5. Whether words stand for ideas or things, or rather *primarily* and directly, for they *must* stand for ideas any how. I incline to say for things — for 'facts' are *things* not ideas, and we argue from *facts*. When a man talks of his *idea*, he implies it is not certainly a fact. What is assumed as true, *all* will hold and therefore it is no longer a mere *idea*. Thus 'a view' — till it is proved *true*.

One *thing* has many ideas, i.e. *aspects*. Hence the *thing* is 'one and the same' — but the idea is 'consistent.' The word identity applies to the one — consistency to the other — and we use 'ideas' as we may x and y in algebra, as means of working out things.

When Ubaghs p 8 speaks of the Principium identitatis he speaks of the thing: when he says 'logicè, quidquid cum cogitato etc.' —

From this it follows that since reason is hypothetical, we mean to say that we use our *idea as if the thing* — If the thing be ascertained, it is no longer hypothetical — but science.

This would seem to be that words stand for *things* — but, for the purposes of logic ⟨reasoning⟩, only for ideas. How is this?

[Undated but probably 1859][1]

(NB. Mysteries do not address themselves to the judgment, but are simply null incomprehensible).

§ 2

By the doctrine of the Holy Trinity I mean a collection of eight propositions, viz. that from eternity 1. God is One 2. God is a Father, as giving a being to a Son 3. that Son is God 4. the Father and the Son give being to the Spirit 5. that Spirit is God 6. the Father is not the Son 7. nor the Son the Spirit 8. nor the Spirit the Father . . . And so of the Incarnation. 1. He who speaks and acts is God. 2. He who speaks and acts is man. 3. He, by the force of the singular pronoun, is one in as true a sense as that in which each of us is one. 4. That God is not and cannot be man, by the fact of nature, because one thing cannot be another thing.

---

[1] See also, *Letters and Diaries*, XIX, pp. 530 ff., 548 ff. *Philosophical Notebook*, II, pp. 101 ff.

§ 3

Having reviewed what may be considered the ecclesiastical doctrine of the Holy Trinity, which is de fide, I am led to pursue the sacred subject into what is the province of theology rather than of divine? faith, that is, so far as to state what is the point of the Mystery, or in what it distinctly and utterly surpasses the range of human ideas, or where the lines which Christ and His Apostles have laid down, being followed out by the human reason ⟨intellect⟩, end in what to that intellect is profound darkness, and nothing but darkness.

This characteristic of our intellectual powers ⟨reason⟩, viz, that their ⟨its⟩ clearest and most vigorous exercise leads it by most certain steps to a termination from which it simply revolts, baffled and amazed, is not peculiar to the theological doctrine before us.

The most obvious instance of this phenomenon is of such trite application that it can hardly [be] used without apology; but it represents a number of others in its own science, and is selected here as being the most convenient and familiar; the superable difficulty contained in the notion of the asymptotes to the hyperbola. A cone is a real intelligible figure, and, though as really formed, from the peculiarities of material phenomena and our own limited skill, will never exactly come up to its intellectual notion, can be conceived as an idea without any difficulty. It is perfectly intelligible ⟨simple⟩, and has nothing of what is called mystery about it. A perpendicular to a plane of a circle drawn from its centre and of a definite length, is as easy to conceive, (*not* to comprehend — here comes a subject), and so is the revolution of a line of indefinite length, (each way) from the extremity of that perpendicular in the curve of the circle; and so again is the consequence of that revolution, viz the formation of what is called a cone.

[There follow some erased and illegible lines].

Nor is there any difficulty in like manner by successive steps to conceive the formation of a certain curve which runs on to infinitude too of indefinite length, to which the name hyperbola is given, nor to conceive the formation of a certain straight line which lies in the plane of their ⟨the hyperbola⟩, curves and ad infinitum accompany them ⟨it⟩, nor to see so that from the nature of the case, that ⟨they will always be approaching the curves⟩ it never can meet it, ad infinitum, yet again for certain of its conditions that it is ever getting nearer to it; nor lastly is there any doubt at all that when we have got as far as this, we have suddenly plunged into a difficulty or mystery which is simply unintelligible.

There is nothing difficult in conceiving a straight line continually approaching a curve till it reaches it, for this is the case which both tangents and secants, nor again any difficulty in conceiving a straight line, never reaching another though prolonged ever so far, ad infinitum ⟨for this is the⟩ for it may have passed the line already may be diverging or it may be parallel to it. But to conceive ⟨grasp⟩ of both together is simply beyond the powers of our mind or is what is called mysterious.

This mystery then in the doctrine of the Holy Trinity it follows next to investigate; but, before proceeding to do so I next proceed to clear the ground of some objections, for which in part an answer has been provided in the last section and in part an explanation will have to be given.

The following argument is sometimes used by those who consider themselves able to rank themselves among the opponents of orthodoxy . . .

IV Assent and Intuition

1860?

INTRODUCTION

I must explain some of the words which I am to use in the following chapters.

Phenomena. When I speak of phenomena, I mean those impressions upon the mind which it is usual to call sensible. I use the word *impressions*, because the mind seems to itself passive as to their coming or going.

Sensations. By sensations I mean those impressions upon the mind, which are not sensible, yet are passive. Such is the coming and going of pure memory, of sense of conscience, right and wrong, of the sense of beauty, of shame; of the passions, as anger and fear.

Regard? The mind actively contemplates these phenomena of sense (as well as a multitude of subjects besides, which are not to our present purpose). It remembers them when absent; it recognizes them when they come again; it observes when they come in the same order. It forms them into separate wholes; it traces that wholeness to a unity beyond themselves or external to itself, and gives names to these assumed unities. Thus from the sight of colours variously disposed, it traces outlines, which it finds ultimately to run into themselves, and to circumscribe figures, and it gives these figures the names of dog, horse, etc, as objects which do not depend upon itself, though united to itself through the sensible impressions. This section of the mind I call *regard.*

Reflection. In like manner, the mind actively occupies itself on its own sensations, and in that way uniting all its sensations together, and tracing them to a supreme unity beyond themselves, calls that unity by the name of self. Again, it has a sensation of heroism — and goes on to the judgments, right or wrong, that heroic souls are too great for this world, and to the conclusion, right or wrong, that heroic souls are destined for a higher state of being. These acts of judgment or inference upon the sensation as well as the recognition of the sensation itself I call acts of *reflection.* (NB. Then this 'reflection' is abstract, it determines the fortune of 'heroic souls', though such souls never existed.)

Thought. (By *thought* I mean a general embracing regard and reflection together).

Regard and reflection may be expressed by the general word Thought, Imagination, Conception.

Things. By things — I mean those alleged objects, whatever they are, (or whether they are,) or as far as they are, which the mind (professes to have) ascertained by thought exercised on phenomena and sensations.

A thought. (At the same time these objects or things are not really before the mind or in the mind, they are only *thought* of). A Thing thought of is a thought. A thing may exist without there existing ⟨its being thought of by⟩ any thought of it in the mind. On the other hand a thing might be annihilated, yet its image, first in memory, then in abstraction might remain while the mind lasted. Whether, supposing things exist, the presence of them while it lasts, takes the place of the thought of them, I do not think it is necessary to decide.

True and false, is applied to thoughts, and denotes the exact agreement or the disagreement of the thought with the thing to which it belongs.

An assent of the mind. ⟨An affirmation⟩ An assent is thought. To assent is to decide this thought is a thing, or this thought is true. If this is so, really, it is a right assent; if not so, it is a wrong assent.

§

The assent, which I give to my thoughts as true, is either absolute and simple, or conditional and complex.

Absolute or simple assent is my recognition of the truth of a thought on its own account, and independently of everything else, as far as I can determine about myself, and whether it actually admits of proof or no; that is, it is assent to what I see to be ⟨is to me⟩ self evident. Such, for instance, is the assent that I give to 'I feel (there is an unseen world)': 'Truth is praiseworthy'; 'Self-preservation is a duty:'

Conditional or complex assent is that which I give to a thought as true, viewed with and within ⟨in⟩ another thought. Thus, 'God must be omniscient,' that is, *in that* He *is* God. 'He preserves whom He has created;' that is, in that very circumstance, or since, He has created them. 'The Creator has power over His own work,' that is, *because* it *is* His work. 'Error cannot exist in the word of God.' 'Space has no limits;' 'two straight lines cannot inclose a space', as is evidently true, *as soon as* I *picture* ⟨before⟩ to my imagination the meaning of those propositions.

When the assent which I give to a truth, (that is, to a thought which faithfully represents a thing) is simple and absolute, I shall call it an *intuition*, as being an insight into things as they are. When it is complex, I call it a *contuition*, as being a sight of a thing through and by means of the things which lie about it.

Thus any belief in a moral law is an *intuition*; and any belief in its penalties is a *contuition*.

The word *contuition* I must be allowed to invent; as to intuition, it is frequently taken to mean an assent to a truth which does not *admit* of proof, as being a first principle; but not always ⟨necessarily⟩, and not consistently. For instance, Catholics are bound to allow that the being of a God can be proved

64

by reasoning, yet great authorities? among them have held that it is an intuitive truth. ⟨again the religious sentiment, that is, the belief in man's relation, present and future, to an unseen state and unseen agents will commonly be *considered* intuition yet surely it can be justified by argument⟩ Again, there are writers who hold that our knowledge of the uniformity of the operations of nature is intuitive, yet they know well that others consider it is learned by experience.

Though *intuition* and *contuition* are in their respective notions as distinct from each other as a proposition is distinct from a syllogism, yet at times it is difficult in fact to determine whether in a particular case I am assenting to the one or to the other. ⟨Nay I am disposed to question whether such a distinction between necessary truth and induction or ⟨?⟩ empirical truth is possible in fact, though Kant makes it the starting point of his treatise (p 2)⟩. For, on the one hand, I have described intuition to be, not a common assent of all men to what cannot possibly under ⟨on⟩ any circumstances ⟨supposition⟩ or in any way be proved, but as my assent to what is self evident specially to me, though I have not before my mind any actual proof of it: accordingly, it is relative both to me and to my circumstances, and these two may be called its *conditions*. On the other hand, in contuition, that truth which comprises the special object of my assent, may be so wide and so obvious and familiar, or so evidently objective, as merely to constitute the medium, or *condition* of my assent. Thus both intuition and contuition may stand for an assent upon a condition.

For instance, take the truth, 'There is an unseen world;' this I cannot deny, *for the phenomena of sense, of which I am conscious, imply something beyond the object of sense*: The words which I have placed in Italics are a *condition*. This truth then is an intuition to me, as a being of five senses, who assents according to the conditions or circumstances of his state. But it is a contuition, if I directly contemplate the phenomena of sense, and which they imply, when I make the assertion that an unseen world exists, and include it in my assent.

Let us then have recourse to the testimony, and let it ⟨this⟩ be our criterion of an intuition that the testimony is uniform and universal. What is assented to by all men in all ages is a right assent, and the thing assented to as self evident is true. Thus, for instance, if all men everywhere held without reasoning that the soul is immortal, this might be said to be an intuition both of its existence and immortality.

This is plausible, but let us examine it more closely.

§

What the universal human nature assents to, ⟨what the mind naturally assents to⟩, as self evident is true. This, it seems, is to be our criterion of an intuition. It is very difficult to get a good foundation to build upon. I do not wish to cavil at this criterion ⟨proposition⟩, but let us see what it implies. Is it an intuition itself? if not, it takes for granted various previous propositions without proof. For instance.

1. It assumes that *what nature attests or enunciates is true*. Now we ought to be quite sure that this principle is one of universal acceptance. But is it so? So far from it, that, at least in the religious world, there are large masses of men who consider human nature to be depraved, and its thoughts, opinions, and sentiments which are natural to the human mind to be thoroughly and hopelessly false.

2. It assumes as self evident that *all human minds have one nature*. I do not know that this would be indisputable, even though we assumed that all men were of one blood, which we cannot do without the aid of revelation — and what is revealed ⟨needs revelation⟩ is not intuitive. Much less is it clear that all minds are of one nature, when it is not even certain that all bodies are more than generically one. How do we know that any two men have ⟨are⟩ exactly the same nature ⟨similar⟩? and if not, how can we argue from the agreement of their testimony?

If the nature of the mind is different in different men, then different men ought variously to be affected by the same objective facts. The eye is so variously constituted in different men, that what seems red to one is green to another; or at least what to ordinary men looks green, and what looks red, to certain eyes are indistinguishable from each other. It said, that in the war of Independence, an officer or commander of troops was made prisoner with his men by the green Americans whom he had mistaken for the red British. In such cases agreement in testimony is no corroboration of a fact in dispute.

3. The third assumption is that *in this one nature there are many minds*. Supposing a speculative mind takes the contrary view, and such we know there have been, and asserts that there are not a multitude of individual minds under a common genus or species, how are we to answer him? I am conscious of myself, but may not what I call 'other minds' be [no] more than reflexions in some sort of my own mind, as if I saw myself in a multitude of mirrors, each placed, so to say, at a different angle from the rest, and having surfaces sometimes plane, sometimes curved, and curved variously on a multiplicity of laws? This I certainly must allow, that in dreams the interlocutors, whom my mind introduces, sometimes support characters or take courses ⟨do acts⟩, which at the time I do not understand or have no consciousness of creating, but which I wake and reflect upon, I see to have a meaning and to be carried out on some principle or towards some end. Or to take another hypothesis. Revelation shows me that one essence can be several persons at once, or (if it means the same) can have several personalities; now the Divine Nature is sui simile; but still may not I, in some way or other, also have a variety of personalities? And if so, how do I know but that all minds are more than the myriad personalities of one soul, the nature of which being one, its assents in its various minds will be only one individual assent, though they seem many assents?

4. Another assumption, apparently involved in this intuition, has been denied by various philosophers, and the denial of it made the basis of their philosophy. It is, that *there is a nature external to the mind,* either at all, or at least short of the Supreme Being. That the phenomena of sense, as they are called, inflict an intuitive conviction on the mind or an external something, I should have hoped might have been maintainable; except that, when one has got as far as this, it may be urged that the general feeling of mankind is quite as strong for that something short of God, which they call matter, as for there being any thing at all. It seems then a merely private opinion to go half way, and has the odium besides of a half measure. And then again, as to the notion of no being external to the mind, if this has ever been true once in one way, it may happen elsewhere in another. Now the Supreme Being from eternity has existed ⟨been blest⟩ in the fulness of His own ineffable thought, without any external world at all; so that the idea is not in its nature absurd of mind energizing supreme by an internal vigour and without any objective intercourse.

On the other hand, it seems we are to take it as an intuition that what the mind naturally assents to, is true; but how very few assents there are of any kind which do not pre-suppose an external world? ⟨No (the mind as a *thing* is *external* to phenomena and sensations).⟩

5. And another assumption of implication without which this supposed ⟨alleged⟩ intuition cannot be admitted ⟨stand⟩, is, that in fact the mind is able to reach objective realities or things.

These, or such as these, are conditions to the intuition that what the mind naturally assents to is true; but supposing these allowed, there are difficulties of quite a different kind. (I *can't* recollect).

§

If we are to advance to conclusions of any kind and extend the range of our knowledge, we are obliged to recognize certain assents as the primary premisses of our investigations and their results, and as self evident neither requiring nor admitting of proof. They are moreover present to our natural discernment, congenial to our minds, and claiming our homage though they were simply barren and nothing came of them. This is the obvious argument for the existence of Intuition.

And in fact the great bulk of mankind are believers in their existence, and all men at least act as if they directly recognized them as existing.

On the other hand, there is very little agreement in the world or among philosophers what these truths are, whether they are many or few, and what their characteristics. In saying this, I am as far as possible from denying their existence: I maintain it steadfastly ⟨Nay, as will be seen, too strongly for many men to receive⟩: but while I maintain that there are such, I also maintain that there is nothing like a consensus among men what they are.

Writers attempt to set down tests of an intuition or truths, and three are given especially (by Brown) [p. 77]; that the assent given to them is universal, is irresistible, is immediate. Of these the last is undeniable, for it is the very definition of an intuition, as contrasted with a conclusion.

The two former seem to imply each other; for if the truth is irresistible to the human mind, all men, who have the use of reason, must receive it; and if all men receive it, this must arise from the force with which it addresses itself to the human mind, considered in its very nature.

There are some such: consciousness of self, belief in something external to self; assent to the truth that a thing cannot be and not be, (and the consequences of it) these are irresistible in their self-evidence, and universal. But, though there are many others which *ought*, as their supporters consider, to be held by all men, there are few that actually are. To say that, though they are not, they ought to be, is to beg the question. It is confessed ⟨undeniable⟩ that very few intuitive truths are as self evident as the sun in the heavens. There are very few thoughts, however false, but receive the assent of some minds; there are very few thoughts, however true, but from some minds fail to attain it. If for an intuition an assent must be universal and irresistible, the first principles on which our general knowledge rests are scanty indeed.

(If I urge this point by further illustrations, it is, as will be presently seen, in order to increase thereby, not to diminish the number of the intuitions which are possible to our natures.) (Thus) individuals then are sometimes found who are dead to the distinction between virtue and vice. There have been philosophers who have denied absolutely the existence of any being ⟨thing⟩ whatever, external to their own minds. The doctrine of the uniformity of the operations of physical nature, though the cornerstone of certain ⟨recent⟩ philosophies, is utterly foreign to the turn and course of thought of a barbarous or ignorant population.

Races, communities, polities, reject the assents which other races, communities, and polities assume as intuitions. To vast populations ⟨various families and nations⟩, from the beginning of history, the doctrine of a Creator and Moral Governor comes as an elementary self-evident truth; but it seems to be excluded, or even denied, by aboriginal populations and widely spread populations ⟨institutions⟩. Neither the educated Chinese nor the Australian savage has a name to denote the God of Christians, Jews, and Mahometans.

Again, What, according to our own perceptions, proceeds so directly from the very depths of our nature, as the anathema we pronounce upon those brutalities, which the Cynical philosophy sanctioned? Yet not only an eccentric sect, but a whole community seems to have been dead to their odiousness, if we trust the narration of Captain Cook about the South sea islanders. 'Privacy', he tells us, 'is little wanted among people, who have not even the *idea* of indecency, and who gratify every appetite and passion before witnesses, *with no more sense of impropriety*, than we feel when we satisfy our hunger at a social board'. First Voyage ch 17.[1]

Universality of reception then is in no sense necessary to the absolute assent which I give to certain truths. They would stand their ground with me, though I have no evidence for them, whatever evidence could be brought against them. I should be intensely conscious that I existed, I should be certain that virtue differed from vice, though every man I met assured me of the contrary. What others might hold, would not enter into my mind to consider, when I reflected on my certainty about intuitions such as these.

On the other hand there are intuitions about which I am not certain; I assent to my thoughts as truths, and that for their own sake, not on evidence; but I should be glad of stronger light. Thus a Pagan, who by chance found, and read by himself, the gospels, might pronounce deliberately, not on a random feeling, not as a guess, yet not on any intelligible argument which he could unravel, that our Lord was what He declared Himself to be. He would accordingly be assenting absolutely or intuitively, yet not so firmly as not to desire proofs in confirmation.

An assent then may be an intuition, though it is neither universal nor irresistible; and such is our ordinary use of the word. Intuition is allowed popularly to stand for particular truths hid from the many, (partially) ⟨dimly⟩ or occasionally seen by some, and visible only to particular classes, as to a particular stage of life, a particular sex, or particular description of talent. Thus we talk of 'the intuitions of genius,' 'the fine intuition of a woman', 'the intuitions of the child or the peasant ⟨unlearned⟩,' 'of innocence, sanctity, or wisdom'.

This seems to me the more accurate way of viewing the subject. Intuition, though it is the absolute assent which we are naturally capable of giving to the first principles of all knowledge, may be exercised on other truths; it is the gift of the few as well as of the multitude. It is the exercise of a faculty, which is stronger or weaker in this man or that, but of which in every state truth is the object; nor is there any other limit to the number of possible intuitions, than that of the things on which thought can be employed. Those things, which ordinarily are known by means of reasoning, may by some men be ascertained by intuition. We can fancy the whole of Euclid's elements being to a mathematical genius intuitively true; and in fact Newton, as a youth at College, on his first glance at it, called it 'a trifling book' Brewster.[2] A mind may be supposed so extraordinarily gifted, that all the knowledge contained in

---

[1] Newman was quoting from *An Account of the Voyages undertaken by the Order of His Present Majesty for making Discoveries in the Southern Hemisphere*, London 1773, II, p. 196.

[2] About 1661, shortly after entering Trinity College, Cambridge, Isaac Newton came upon a figure in a book of astronomy 'which he could not understand without a previous knowledge of trigonmetry. He therefore purchased an English Euclid, with an index of all the problems at the end of it, and having turned to two or three which he thought likely to remove his difficulties, he found the truths which they enunciated so self-evident, that he expressed his astonishment that any person should have taken the trouble of writing a demonstration of them. He therefore threw aside Euclid "as a trifling book." ' Sir David Brewster, *Memoirs of the Life, Writings, and Discoveries of Sir Isaac Newton*, Edinburgh 1855, I, pp. 21–2.

all the books that ever were written by his fellow men ⟨the product of the human mind⟩, would be to him the object of one all-embracing intuition.

And, while genius has its own intuitions, so, as I have already suggested, particular races or individuals have their own, in this or that particular province of thought. Thus the Greeks had extraordinary intuitive power in the large province of the beautiful; and the Hebrews, (apart from what is supernatural,) in the province of religion. This has much to do with what is called talent; a man is fond of, and successful in, mathematics, or political science, or historical search, when he is able to see immediately as truths without proof, what others only reach by long courses of reasoning or of instruction. Thus the grasp of truth in things speculative, is analogous to power of ⟨dexterity⟩ manipulation in matters of art; the one makes a great thinker, the other an eminent artist or work man.

§

That one community or race, that separate individuals should hold as intuitive, what many others, or the mass of men, do not so hold, is no difficulty; for it may imply nothing else than a deficit in intellectual capacity on the part of those who are blind to it. If intuition be a mental gift or faculty, admitting of degrees, as the faculty of correct deduction admits of degrees, then universality of reception not only need not be, but never can be, a property of intuitive truth, unless it is also to be accounted a property of deductive. Mere insensibility to an intuition is not a denial of it. The case is the same, as regards irresistibility. Not only then is it not startling but it is even reasonable and congrous to maintain, that intuitions are neither irresistible nor universal.

But a difficulty does arise if one professed intuition is contradictory to another or to other truth, known and admitted; or if those persons or people, who have least claim to be considered most advanced in the faculty ⟨gifted in this respect⟩, disown our intuitions and maintain instead others to which we are altogether blind. It is a difficulty moreover, if when two professed intuitions seem to fall under one common principle, part of mankind are alive only to the one, and part of mankind only to the other.

For an instance of the first of these difficulties, I may refer to the case of the Sun's motion, which to the child or uneducated seems as intuitive a truth as the existence of matter, far more so than the uniformity of the operations of nature; yet we know that it is apparent not real. Such too is the doctrine that a body cannot be in two places at once; the Catholic believes the contrary as part of his religion, but the Protestant thinks it an intuition. Again, there are men, especially at this day, who treat it as if an intuitive truth that the Almighty cannot inflict eternal punishment; yet it is a doctrine on the very surface of Scripture.

For an instance of the second difficulty, I refer to a characteristic of that very race, which is reported to have been dead to the first elements of modesty in conduct. Cook says: 'How a meal, which every where else brings families and friends together, came to separate them here, we often inquired, but could never learn. They eat alone, they said, *because it was right*; but, *why* it was right to eat alone, they never attempted to tell us: such, however, was the force of *habit*, that they *expressed the strongest dislike*, and even *disgust*, at our eating in society, especially with our women, and of the same victuals. At first, we thought this strange singularity arose from *some superstitious opinion*; but they constantly *affirmed the contrary* . . . Even two brothers and two sisters have each their separate baskets, with provision and the apparatus of their meal . . . When we sat down to table, they would go out, sit down upon the ground, at two or three yards distance from each other, and, turning their faces different ways, take their repast without interchanging a word.' First Voyage ch. 17.[1] Yet they would eat with the English, on the sly, as it may be called, as persons are accustomed knowingly yet with shame to go against their conscience.

This instance might also stand for the third difficulty, under which fall instances such as the following:- Some nations ⟨races or religions⟩ have a special revolt at the thought of certain kinds of flesh meat, as pork or horse-flesh, which are the food of other races; or at the thought of flesh meat altogether. How does it differ from our own horror at cannibalism, which nonetheless, if we are to believe travellers, is widely spread over the earth, and among intelligent, though barbarous tribes? Yet is a judgment, not a mere taste; as is implied in the story ⟨legend⟩ of Atreus and Thyestes. Again, there are races, as the Turks, who are said to be most tender and merciful towards the brute creation, and yet show the most savage cruelty to ⟨towards⟩ human beings. Again, numbers feel a sort of intuitive reprobation of the idea of a married priest; others, who do not feel this at all, are struck with horror at the mormon principle ⟨doctrine⟩ that a man, (already) in a state of wedlock, may take to himself a second wife.

What are we to say to these contrarieties in first principles between man and man? Truth is one and the same; a thing cannot be and not be; if nature tells me that cannibalism is unnatural, how is it that races of men practice it, without any sense of its being wrong? If I see and touch matter, and it is self evident to me that I do so, does it not turn my head, to use the familiar phrase, to be told by clearsighted and subtle philosophers, that after all it is not at all clear that matter has any existence?

§

On insight of the human mind

In order to solve this difficulty, we must think over the account which has been already given of an Intuition; and determine what assents do and what do not fall under its idea.

I have considered it ⟨an Intuition⟩ to be my assent to a truth on its own

[1] *Account of the Voyages . . .*, II, pp. 203-4.

account, independently of any thing external to it; or the direct insight which I personally possess (so far forth) into things as they are. In other words, it is the vision, analogous to eye-sight, which my intellectual nature has of things as they are, arising from the original, elementary sympathy or harmony between myself and what is external to myself, I and it being portions of one whole, and, in a certain sense, existing for each other.

Hence, there are two points to consider, — the nature of the human mind, and the nature of things; and first what is meant by the former.

Here, it must be recollected that the nature of man differs in this from every other nature, of which we have experience, that it has in it in a special sense a principle of internal progress and perfection. When we speak of the nature of a stone, of fire, of a plant, of a horse, of a dog, we speak of what is (on the whole) uniform in its specimens ⟨all its individuals⟩, and in its whole course; so that, for the purposes of observation and deduction, one specimen is as good as a thousand. But when shall we learn what the nature of man is? What individual, what family, is like another? nay, what class, what race, will stand for the whole kind? nay, what individual is like itself, and will represent itself in all its stages? The ascertainable laws of the human mind are far too large and general to help us in the delicate, abstruse investigation necessary for determining its intuitive knowledge.

But its laws go thus far; viz to show, as I have said, first that there is a process of change and improvement, and next, that this process is a growth, analogous to other growths, that is, an internal development of powers, appropriating and turning to account what is external. Here then at once are two senses of the word 'nature', either of which may be assumed as the right one in the present question; its start, and its termination. What it starts with, it may be argued, is the matter and substance of what it will terminate in; therefore its special unalloyed nature is best seen in its beginnings. What it ends ⟨terminates⟩ in, is nothing else than the true form and perfection of what it began with; therefore its whole complete nature is best seen in its termination. And consequently, since intuition is a natural insight into things as they are, intuition is the gift either of the many or of the few; the original outfit of our rude minds, or the rarest fruit of cultivation and refinement.

Which of these two are we to adopt as containing the right idea of an intuition? Have we this insight into things as they are, specially when we are born or specially when we die? Are the intuitions of our nature the spontaneous assents ⟨utterances⟩ of the savage or child, or on the other hand the mature enunciations of those who have taken most pains with themselves and have had the largest opportunities of improvement, of the old, the experienced, the saintly, or the wise? Either view is plausible; each has its difficulties; each may be said to lead us to real intuitions, or to surrender us to counterfeit; and each has its supporters ⟨advocates⟩ and opponents.

What can be said in support of each, is plain from the brief notice ⟨account⟩

72

of each which has been taken ⟨made⟩ above; and it is equally obvious what can be said to the disparagement of each.

On the one hand, it is undeniable, whether we speak from experience or from revelation, that man is born a weak, blind, not to say wretched animal, in some respects inferior to the beasts of the field, helpless against external nature, and possessed within by a brood of irrational passions, which threaten to be worse foes to his life and well-being, even than the manifold enemies which threaten him from without:- what can the assents of so miserable a being be worth? On the other hand, it is quite as obvious, whether we speak from experience or from Scripture, that at least innocence is the portion of the poor being, who seems so despicable. Scripture especially insists upon the perverse and depraved teaching which is dominant in the mass of mankind, in its nations, states, languages, philosophies, occupations, in what by one word the Sacred writers designate as 'the world'. Man, joined to man in society, interchanges ideas, forms a code and an art of life, perilous both because artificial and corrupt, and because self reliant. He makes self his centre, whereas the very weakness of his first nature threw him upon the Unseen. He becomes the creature of habit; and habit is a second nature, as strong yet less true to the Creator. It certainly has its intuitions, but their right name is prejudices, and they represent and report, not things as they are, but delusions and idols. The child or the savage has at least none of this teaching; and though he may have little to tell us, still a few truths are worth more than many lies.

I conceive that both of these opposite views are true in their own place and measure; and thus we have two sources, and those the same, both of real intuitions and of counterfeit.

As to ⟨for⟩ the testimony producible in favour of the first view of Intuitions, we may refer to the proverb, Vox populi, vox Dei; as if the unstudied, impetuous outburst of the rude multitude were the very oracle of truth, lodged by the Creator Himself in the very heart of our common nature.

The same doctrine is implied in the reverence in which idiots are held in the East, as if in them nature spoke purely and simply, without any of the sophistications and conventionalisms which are the creations of society; or as if God spoke through them, because they were simply His work, and had not been able to become their own making and ⟨or⟩ belong to other masters.

Such too is the doctrine inculcated by writers like Rousseau, who depict? the virtuous savage, or by poets in their account of the just? Hyperboreans, or blameless Ethiopians?, or of the simplicity of Arcadian or Sicilian Shepherds, or of the happiness of the golden age.

It is to be traced too to the popular reverence paid to the voice of children, as in the election, as the account goes, of Saint Ambrose, then a layman, to the Archbishoprick of Milan; and in such superstitions, if they be such, as are delineated by writers like Walter Scott, in whose romance, the little child,

Mary Avenel, sees, when others do not see, 'the bonny leddy signing to them to come yon gate.'[1]

It is also taught us in the noble philosophy of Wordsworth in his grand ode ⟨poem⟩, in which he addresses the little child as

'Thou, whose exterior semblances doth belie
    Thy soul's immensity,
Thou best philosopher, who yet dost keep
Thy heritage, Thou Eye among the blind,
That, deaf and silent, readest the
    eternal deep,
Haunted forever by the Eternal Mind,
    Mighty Prophet, Seer blest,
    On whom those truths do rest,
Which we are toiling all our lives to find.[2]

On the other hand, what does the wisdom of the aged, which has become a proverb, teach us, but to look for the true intuitions of our nature in its perfect, not its inchoate condition? And here we can appeal to as great a poet as Wordsworth, who, instead of looking to children as the organ of divine inspiration, seeks truth by long meditation and the acquired knowledge.

        And may at last my weary age
        Find out the peaceful hermitage,
        The hairy gown and mossy cell,
        Where I may sit and rightly spell
        Of every star that Heaven doth shew,
        And every herb that sips the dew,
        Till old experience do attain
        To something like prophetic strain.[3]

And there are the celebrated words of a philosopher as great as Milton is a poet. 'One should attend,' says Aristotle, 'to the sayings and opinions of the experienced, the old, the wise, *though they be incapable of proof*, not less than to proofs; for they see the principles (or, aright v.i.), in that they have *an eye* in consequence of their experience.' Eth. Nic. vi. 11 fin.

Such writers speak with authority, as being spokesmen of a general sentiment. The language ⟨doctrine⟩ of schools may be also quoted, obviously of inferior weight indeed, but still of importance, for no system of philosophy or religion but must have truth mixed with its errors.

Such then is on the one hand the testimony of the widespread Calvinistic faith; for, in teaching the total ⟨utter⟩ corruption of human nature, it must deny any weight at least to its moral assents, as being simply blind and dead to every truth which has a bearing on the unseen world.

On the other hand, the special philosophy of this day, with its denial of

---

[1] . . . the child suddenly exclaimed — 'Bonny leddy signs to us to come yon gate.' *The Monastery*, I, ch. 3.

[2] *Intimations of Immortality from Recollections of Early Childhood*, 109–17.

[3] *Il Penseroso*, 167–74.

abstract ⟨innate⟩ ideas, its view of the lowly ⟨humble⟩ origin of our race, as originating in the brute world, and its theories ⟨visions⟩ of illimitable progress, seems ⟨may be considered⟩ to move in a parallel direction to Calvinism in preferring the ultimate to the primary assents of human nature.

For myself, I have already intimated that I would unite both views in my own idea of an intuition. There seems to me nothing inconsistent or absurd, in holding that rude nature has one insight into things as they are, and that cultivated nature has another; that these separate conditions ⟨states⟩ of the mind partly oppose, and partly support each other; that each has its own advantages and its own wants; that there are truths which the one sees, and the other does not; that there are others, which are seen by both of them; that there may be illusions in untaught nature as well as educated; and obstinate prejudice in the experienced as well [as] wisdom.

As regards moral intuitions, as being the property of both childhood and old age, there are some beautiful lines of a living poet, who suggests to us that what shone before our infant imagination before the mists of passion and sophistry arose, may return to the soul in greater? ⟨full⟩ splendour in the evening of life, when the ⟨its⟩ sky is clear again. He seems to allude to 'the soul that rises with us, our life's star' of Wordsworth's Ode.[1]

> Star of the East, how sweet art Thou,
>   Seen in Life's early morning sky,
> Ere yet a cloud has dimmed the brow,
>   While yet we gaze with childish eye;
>
> Too soon the glare of earthly day,
>   Buries, to us, thy brightness keen,
> And we are left to find our way,
>   By faith and hope in Thee unseen.
>
> What matter? if in calm old age
>   Our childhood's star again arise,
> Crowning our lonely pilgrimage
>   With all that cheers a wanderer's eyes.
>
> (Will not the long-forgotten glow,
>   of mingled joy and awe return,
> When stars above and flowers below,
>   First made our infant spirits turn?)[2]

§ into the nature of things.

Next, we have to consider Intuition as an insight into things as they are, or most ⟨more⟩ exactly, into the nature of things, for if the faculty is natural, so

[1] *Intimations of Immortality*, 59.
[2] John Keble, *The Christian Year*, 'The Epiphany'.

is its object. For instance, let us say that it is in the nature of things that virtue is not vice, that the Almighty is just, that the beautiful is the true; or that two right lines, after intersection, diverge from each other *ad infinitum*. Granting that I directly assent to these things on their own account and because of nothing else, I have an intuition of them.

But again: — it has been shown above that by the nature of man is to be understood not merely what he has with him on his birth, but what he arrives at with its developed capabilities: this being the case, with this enlarged view of his nature and its intuitions, we must admit a corresponding largeness in our view of the things which are their object. Now in the first place I may be said to have an intuition of good taste, of modesty, and of vulgarity, as being definite objects, differing from each other in the nature of things. But secondly further than this, to the very same action I give various names, and say it is done in good taste, is modest, is vulgar, or is neither this thing or that, according to the place, time, and circumstances under which it is done. The very same speech which evidences good taste in a prince, would be an absurdity in a tradesman or a peasant. The action which is tyrannical or rash in Charles the first would have been becoming in Louis the sixteenth. We sometimes say of a man's manners that they are very strange and affected, or very foreign. A foreigner once said to me of a friend of mine, '*We* should call him proud, judging by his gait; but I believe it is not pride in any personal sense in an Englishman.'

Now pride, vulgarity, the sensible ⟨prudent⟩, the appropriate ⟨dignity⟩, the affected, are real things, and are contemplated by the mind as such, and would have their definite meanings, though the created universe were swept away. But in the above instances a second law comes in, not to the prejudice but in application of the nature of things, viz. the constitution of society, and its variations. And there is a power of intuition, adapted to the contemplation, not only of the pulchrum in the abstract, and in its more obvious manifestations, but in all the details through which it lives and acts in a given nation, country, or polity, — the pulchrum, now, here, in this man, and under these circumstances. My insight into what is beautiful under this double law or nature of things, the natural and the social, is it to be called an intuition? I have already granted that it may, and, to say the least, the use of the word in such cases is far from extraordinary.

For instance, and I will take the first that comes, and that not a very grave one; the author of Adam Bede says, 'Ladies, with that fine *intuition*, which is the distinguishing attribute of their sex, see at once that he is "*nice*".' Book 1, ch. 12.

And so in matters of science or skill; for instance, the military art, as in tactics: 'There have been great captains,' says Macaulay, 'whose precocious and selftaught military skill resembled *intuition*' Essays. Frederic the Great.

And so again, as regards the laws of the universe, which of course are not to be considered as identical with the nature of things; certainly not, for we can suppose the existence of a creation utterly diverse from the actual. There might have been a creation, which was neither matter nor spirit, but some third substance which never has been, for any thing that we know to the contrary. And, supposing matter, it is not an eternal truth that the (so called) mutual attraction in its particles should vary inversely as the squares of their mutual distances. It may have been so from the beginning of matter, but matter has not been from everlasting; it has been, but it need not have been, except to effect that certain system which exists, it is not in the nature of things. Yet we may be said to exercise our power of intuition in physical investigation. Thus Mr Max Muller says, 'No doubt with Philolaus the motion of the earth was only a guess, or, if you like, a happy *intuition*', (Science of Language 1861. pp. 17, 18.); and rightly: still here 'intuition' is used, not simply in a question of abstract science, which may be said to be in the nature of things, but in one of mixed mathematics, in one which belongs to the nature of things as energizing in an existing material order.

After these instances of a legitimate enlargement of the province of intuition, as being not only the nature of things, but as that eternal nature applied and modified by various systems, divine or human, which are not eternal, let us go on to consider the abuse to which this freedom gives occasion, and the counterfeit intuitions which are consequent upon the substitution of some personal subjective law ⟨system⟩ for the nature of things.

[The following paragraph is crossed out].

Mr Max Muller, after referring to the guess or intuition of Philolaus, as quoted above, tells⟨?⟩ us that Sir D. Brewster calls it an *imagination*. Whatever it ⟨that particular exercise of intellect⟩ is to be called, certainly there are not a few so-called intuitions, which plausibly as they may plead for themselves, are in no sense natural assents, or have any concern with things as they are ⟨the nature of things⟩, but are results of imagination and nothing else.

Unreal intuitions, I say, are commonly such as arise from giving to systems which are short of necessary, that authority which belongs only to what is necessary and eternal. For instance, I suppose many persons would call the laws of this physical universe, in which we pass our lives, the nature of things; yet surely without sufficient reason. It is not eternal, but created; there was a time when it began, a time when it was not. It is no eternal truth that the squares of the distances of bodies from each other vary inversely as their mutual attraction; it is not necessary that they should do so. ⟨Dec 7 1869 But some one did conjecture it a priori from the necessity of an influence from a point.⟩ If indeed there was to be this given world, then it was a necessity, always was, always will be: but these hypothetical truths cannot be called eternal without an explanation.

When an hypothetical truth is said to be eternal, what is really meant is that some truth, from which it follows, is eternal. Mathematical truth is such relatively to physics. When we say that there is eternal necessity for a world such as this to have laws such as it has, this necessity rests on the necessity of mathematical truth. The hypothesis is eternal, because the truths of mathematics are eternal.

Again: is Power one of the necessary, eternal attributes of the Divine Being? Yes. But it could not be, before creation; till then it was but hypothetical, viz. it would have been eternal, could creatures have been eternal. Still it is rightly called necessary and eternal, for it is contained in that which is eternal, the existence of the Eternal Essence of God; it is one with and in His Nature.

Again: in algebra we say that there is no square root of a minus quantity. Is this a necessary truth or not? X.Y.Z. stand for quantities; are quantities eternal? no; then it is not a necessary truth. What shall we say to this? There are two answers; either we may say that the fact ⟨negative impossibility⟩ in question is a mere defect in the particular calculus (just as it is a defect in the geometrical, that you cannot express a^4, a^5.. a^n ⟨space does not admit of more than three dimensions⟩) or we may say that the expression depends upon or represents something beside itself in the nature of things, which *is* impossible. Of these I adopt the former, considering the whole doctrine of quantities a particular expression in our created universe, of truths which are really eternal.

Take another instance: a body cannot be in two places at once. Is this in the nature of things? Let us examine. Why cannot it be in two places at once? because, if it be here and there, it must be at a distance from itself; which is absurd, if there be such a thing as distance, as extension, as space, — if they be things as well as words. But that space, not only is, but is in the nature of things is an intuition. Is it so really? then it is eternal; but nothing is eternal but the Divine Nature and what It contains. Is space in any sense divine? can the Almighty annihilate space? He cannot annihilate goodness or sanctity or beauty or truth or the archetypes of mathematical science or of musical harmony; for that would be to annihilate Himself; but is space co-eternal with and in Him? Over the nature of things the Almighty has no power, except in the sense that He has power over Himself; is space an attribute of God? — In saying then a body cannot be in two places at once, because the existence of space is an intuitive truth, we use an argument, good or bad, which at least is grounded in an unreal intuition.

To take an instance from a more superficial system, that of plane astronomy. The enunciations of this science surely are not in the nature of things. The sun is at first in the direction of the East, it rises to the meridian; then it declines. A child or a savage might in consequence tell you that it was an intuitive truth [th]at the sun moved through the sky. And so Doctor Johnson, when some one spoke of those philosophers who denied the existence of matter, kicked out and answered, 'Sir, I disprove it thus'. Are the phenomena, which present themselves to our senses, in the nature of things?

Habit, in like manner, weaves around the intellect an artificial system, which is practically mistaken for the nature of things. People seem mad to us, who advocate a doctrine which we never heard of. What is familiar to us is thought intuitive. Take the instance of Scripture interpretation. Men see their own sense in it, and no other; they cannot even imagine any other; they think the matter of interpretation as clear as day. A bishop, according to Saint Paul, must be 'husband of one wife;' what can be more obvious and natural? it was written when polygamy was allowable. But to say it means, what it means historically, 'once married, and not twice,' seems far-fetched, strained, and impossible.

Nay sometimes, an error in the received ⟨authorized⟩ Version has become so familiar to the mind, and found to give such good sense, that devout readers have been impatient and indignant at its correction, as if the work of officious pedantry or arrogance; as in the text 'who strain *at* a gnat, and swallow a camel.' To such good persons, under other circumstances, 'mumpsimus' would be an intuition.

It would be easy in like manner to enlarge upon the so-called intuitions of prejudice, narrow-mindness, and bigotry.

I will set down one example more. To be a man of the world, and to know the world, is to have thorough experience of the motives and conduct of the mass of mankind. In consequence, we have a code of maxims, such as 'Every man has his price.' A mind, saturated with faith in this principle, would sympathise and agree with Simon Magus, who, on contemplating Saint Peter's miracles, had an intuition that he was nothing more than a cleverer knave than himself. In like manner, I have heard of an excellent gentleman, who was so liberal to the tenants, that the report spread that he was bound to be so by ⟨as⟩ the tenure of his property. Was it not intuitive, that a person, unless he had some political or social purpose, or some legal compulsion, never would voluntarily relinquish the fair returns of his rentroll. When the Oxford Movement was in progress some twenty years and more ago, an old Tory Professor stated his suspicion that the Archbishop of Canterbury must be at the bottom of it, over [or] its leaders never would have been so bold. Others, under the same general feeling, ascribed it to some Catholic conspiracy. Such suspicions might easily grow into a sort of intuition. Enthusiasm, fanaticism, romantic generosity, chivalrous sense of honor, heroism, self-denying charity, are absolutely out of the range of vision of such men. There is a letter of the Duke of Wellington's (then Sir A. Wellesley) in the Grenville correspondence, in which he says he signed the Convention of Cintra in obedience⟨?⟩ to his superiors and commanders, as he thought a soldier ought to do; but that he had not said so publicly, because he felt no one would believe him.[1] In like manner in 1835⟨?⟩ he offered to take up the King's government and carry out the King's measures, though they were not his, rather than that the King should want a minister; and he said that he should

---

[1] See the Duke of Buckingham and Chandos, *Memoirs of the Court and Cabinets of George the third, from original Family Documents*, London 1855, pp. 254 and 264.

feel himself fit for nothing but⟨?⟩ the gutter, if he did not do so.[1] Civilians must not then judge of military men, by their own intuitions. In like manner Protestants know nothing of the Catholic Church, *and* the character or feelings of its members: accordingly, they make the most extreme mistakes about them, and thinking such mistakes intuitions.

---

[1] This was in Nov. 1834 after the King had dismissed Lord Melbourne's government. The Duke of Buckingham and Chandos *Memoirs of the Courts and Cabinets of William the fourth and Victoria, from original Family Documents*, London 1861, pp. 143–5.

V Papers of 1860 on the Evidence
for Revelation

January 5, 1860.

ON THE POPULAR, PRACTICAL, PERSONAL EVIDENCE FOR THE TRUTH OF REVELATION.

I am not here to dispute that the alleged fact of the supernatural origin of Christianity ought to be subjected to the same rigid ⟨rigorous⟩ cross-examination and ought to satisfy the same logical criteria of truth, which are applied in the case of secular sciences, such as chemistry, zoology, or political economy.

Nor am I disputing the assertion of theologians, that such an ordeal is actually met, undergone, and satisfied by Christianity; but I am proposing to engage in an investigation, from which, except as a point ruled by their authority, this consideration is necessarily excluded.

I am addressing myself to a question, on which Father Perrone much insists, as demanding a decision in the affirmative, viz that the motivum credibilitatis is personal to each individual as well as formal, public, and what may be called objective, after the manner of a science. My undertaking is founded on the assumption of such individual proof, and is directed to the drawing it out.

Such individual conviction cannot rise from grounds altogether separate from the logical and formal body of evidence; it must be concurrent with and included in that moral and scientific proof. However, it is sui generis and varying with the individual.

By the scientific proof I mean the arguments from miracles, from prophecy etc etc. which have been so often and so carefully drawn out. If I speak of this, it will be but incidentally; for I am aiming at meeting an objection, which is at once most obvious, and most frequently urged and most plausible, and which has great weight with people just now, and it is of the following kind:-

'The great mass of Catholics know nothing of argument; how then is their faith rational? The peasant believes "what he is told," and if his priest told him the Holy Ghost was incarnate, he would have faith in that heresy. Catholics are forbidden to reconsider the truth of their faith. They may have received it by inheritance, they may have embraced it as boys, they have been slowly brought into it by some groove or other which a contracted course of study has formed for them, and then they are told they must take care to be certain it is true, and to force themselves into a sustained pitch of certainty by the action of their will, if they begin to lag, and to repress as poison any doubt or any desire fairly to consider such various aspects of the subject, such new fields of argument, as are at a later time proffered to their consideration. Now is not this a clear token that Catholicism is not proved in the sense that other facts, other sciences are proved? If they are so certain, as they say, what harm can listening to objections do them? Who shuts his ears to an alleged proof that England is not an island? Who is not ready to give his best attention, if called upon, to such proof? If he is afraid thus candidly to consider objections against revealed religion, it is a proof that he is after all not certain — and has but worked his mind into a persuasion which [he] does not like to have disturbed. And that this really is the case is plain from the undeniable fact that few persons have submitted to the Catholic Church upon a demonstration of her divinity, but merely on those chance arguments and mere probabilities which came in his way. How then can his belief be called rational? How can his treatment of his intellect be called honest or dutiful to its great maker and giver?'

This is the objection which has given rise to the following Essay.

I propose to draw out the nature of the evidence, or motivum credibilitatis, on which individuals believe, and to inquire what is meant by the prohibition to re-examine the trustworthiness of the motivum.

My first chapter shall be an exact drawing out of what is meant in *idea* by the body of evidences, — *all* arguments brought together into an *order*, system and focus — how it stands related to the revealed system itself — how it stands analogously to the proof, e.g. of the Newtonian system[1] — whom it affects — who are its guardians — how it stands relatively to the body of Catholics — and what is its right viewed as an *authoritative doctrine* of the learned, i.e. of the Schola, as separate from its intrinsic logical force.

My second chapter shall be an exposition of what is meant by personal proof, giving instances, e.g. (1) Mrs L. comes and says, I want to be a Catholic. Her catechist is frightened, for he can find no motivum, except that I am one and she knew me etc. (2) A factory girl comes, and can only say 'So and so brought me etc'. (3) A boy comes and says he wishes to get his sins forgiven. (4)

January 12, 1860.

THE EVIDENCES OF RELIGION

There are few religious questions of more importance practically in a day like this, than that of the grounds on which the mass of men believe in Christianity, or in other words, the relation of faith, viewed in the concrete as a habit and act of the mind, towards reason. When we speak of faith objectively, we mean the Creed, which, viewed in all its explanations and developments, in its history and the controversies and comments to which it has given rise, is a vast doctrinal system or philosophy. And so again the arguments

---

[1] See *A Grammar of Assent*, pp. 320 ff.

grounds in reason on which this Creed reposes form a vast objective system, known commonly among us by the name of the Evidences. Such Evidences are considered etc.

And now in the first place as to what we call in English the Evidences for Revealed Religion. These are considered by theologians to hold a very high scientific place, and to amount to a logical demonstration. These Father Perrone calls 'Notae divinae ac supernaturalis revelationis;' and he enumerates six, speaking of them at the same time in the following terms. 'Patet . . . dari *certissimas notas,* quibus divina ac supernaturalis, haec revelatio probè secernatur a quâcumque hominum fraude, cujusmodi esse ostendimus, tum ex se, tum ex omnium gentium consensu, extrinsecus (1) *miracula* et (2) *vaticinia* comprobata, intrinsecus (3) *sanctitatem doctrinae,* quae tamquam revelata perhibetur . . . Subsidiariis denique argumentis, petitis (4) tum ex admirabili religionis christianae *propagatione,* (5) tum ex ejusdem non minus prodigiosa *conservatione,* (6) tum ex *martyrum testimonio,* quae, omnibus adjunctis perpensis, non competunt neque competere poterunt unquam nisi uni divinae ac supernaturali revelationi, seu uni religioni christianae, talem certitudinis gradum adjecimus, ut *nihil certius* a prudenti et cordato quolibet desiderari possit.' t. I pp. 214–216.

Scaramelli enumerates seven; viz Prophecy, the Sanctity of the precepts, the authority⟨?⟩ of the Doctors of the Church, the propagation of the religion, the miracles, the martyrs, the conservation of the faith. i.e. to Perrone's six, he adds the authority⟨?⟩ of the Doctors. Direttor. Ascet. p. 2 p. 148–9.[1]

Pascal seems to lay down ⟨lays down⟩ as many as [thirteen] (put it in French) 'Marks of the True Religion. 1. Its concurrence with the articulate requirements of reason. 2. Knowledge of human nature. 3. coincidence with the external facts of the world. 4. its success in inflexibility ⟨fidelity to its traditions⟩. 5. miracles. 6. prophecies fulfilled. 7. conformity to our internal constitution (does not this *include* and supersedes numbers 1 and 2?). 8. history of its establishment. 9. (instances of Christian character sanctity and idea of this realized.) 10. character of Jesus Christ. 11. history and success of the Apostles. 12. State of the Jewish people. 13. perpetuity of Christianity from the beginning of the world.

Nicolas divides ⟨arranges⟩ the Proofs under three heads, adding to the extrinsic and intrinsic of Perrone, the preliminary or philosophical of Pascal:- Thus we have

Philosophical, — Theological, and historical; under each of which

| | | |
| Bossuet | Gerdil | Grotius |

(NB. 1. Conscience implies *fear*; nullâ *pallescens* culpâ — Thus conscience doth make cowards of us all — [2]But fear is of the future.

Conscience implies shame — nullum ⟨summum⟩ crede nefas animam

---

[1] This appears to be a mistaken reference.
[2] Horace, *Epistles,* I. i. 61; *Hamlet,* III. i. 83.

proferre *pudori*.[1] But shame is *towards persons*. Adam hid himself from God, and from Eve by the skins.)

Here again we have a second deep and large philosophy, human from first to last, as the doctrinal system is human in its deductions, but divinely revealed in its basis ⟨*The Assurances of Religion*⟩; but I am speaking of neither the Creed nor its Evidences, when I speak of the importance in this day of investigating the grounds on which individuals believe. As their faith need not be directed towards all parts of revelation, but only its elementary teaching, and such other parts of it as they know, but in other respects is implicit, so the grounds on which they hold their faith are not commensurate with the Evidences of Revealed Religion, but though concurring and found in them, are but a portion, and an accidental, and varying portion of them. The Creed is for public teaching in Church; the Evidences are for public disputations and lectures in the Schools; but the faith and reason, of which I speak, are subjective, private, personal, and unscientific; the mental acts of every Christian whatever, except when they are merely hereditary and mechanical, and therefore unworthy of the name; yet not exactly the same perhaps in any two. The analysis of them is not easy, and, though theologians do not overlook them, it is not perhaps rash to say that they have not satisfactorily explained them.

It is as long ago as the year 1832, that I began Sermons on the subject in the Oxford University Pulpit, which I continued down to the year 1843, when I published them. I shall proceed on the basis of those Sermons, in what I have to say, but I shall attempt to speak with a distinctness which for two reasons they had not; first because I was feeling my way and had not found it; next because, conscious of this, I had not the requisite confidence in my own train of thought. I have at least more confidence now; confidence, not that I am right, but that I have a right to speak, and have something to say; and that though I may be mistaken more or less, yet that on the whole I may say something of one kind or another which the reader may be glad to pursue.

The reason why I think it ⟨the subject⟩ of great importance just now is this:- because just now a scepticism is on foot, which throws on the individual believer the *onus* probandi, in a way never *contemplated*, or at least recognised before. Hitherto a man was allowed to believe till it was logically brought home to him that he ought not to believe: but now it seems tacitly to be considered that a man ⟨he⟩ has no liberty to believe, till it has been brought home to him in a rational form that ⟨till he can state ⟨show cause⟩ distinctly, or at least till others can do it for him, why⟩ he has a right to do so:

Reason for ⟨Occasion of⟩ considering and investigating the Assurances

The question then ⟨to be considered⟩ takes the shape of an objection, and that objection is of the following form:- Faith, which is not based upon rational grounds, is a superstition, or a prejudice, or a fanaticism, or some kind or other of unreality. What are the grounds on which the great mass of religious persons believe? Few of them have any sort of opportunity or means

---

[1] Juvenal, *Satires*, VIII. 83.

of forming any good reason whatever; take away the uneducated classes, young people, men in the business of life, women, and you nearly exhaust the community. Few indeed are there who have any leisure at all for reflection, or the resources of mind, if they have leisure, to turn it to account. All except a very few are merely hereditary Christians; they believe because they have been so taught. Their sole and main argument is the argument from authority — which will serve for the Jew, Mahometan, or Pagan, as well as for the Christian. There is a residue indeed which may be considered exceptions, as having exerted their minds sufficiently to choose or to change their religion; yet is it not plain how many of these are led by accidents, by the authority of some person they meet with, by fancy, by the stress of circumstances to the form of religion which they adopt? And do they not take up such very different forms of opinion, as to refute each other?

If indeed individuals had the same proof about Christianity which a scientific man has of the Newtonian system one might fairly laugh at the notion of re-examining, and say 'Oh yes, if you please, examine by all means; but I have already such arguments to be quite certain that it would be fudge and nonsense in me to say that I was keeping my mind open and dispassionate, I really will try to do justice to your objections' — but such scientific conviction is not the fact as regards the many. They have not really examined the question at all.

You will say that these difficulties are in the nature of things, that I have proved too much; that if no one is to adopt a faith, till he has sufficient grounds for it, religion must, from the impossibility of people doing so, die out from the world — that it is lucky for mankind that my principles are not felt and acted on and carried out — that the Creator of mankind has made man what he is and placed him where he is — and unless we suppose that He can acquiesce in His being neglected and forgotten, He must sanction that irrational faith, as I consider it, which is all the overwhelming mass of men can attain to. I do not deny the force of this answer — but I have two questions to ask — first, how can you even expect to convert ⟨with what force or with what hope can you set out converting⟩ them, while you have the bad conscience that you are persuading them on insufficient arguments, which may be used against you in Turkey or Persia, as they tell for you in Italy or Spain; and next, why do you so peremptorily forbid them to re-examine ⟨at least Catholics do, and all denominations in a measure, in spite of their profession⟩, or rather to examine for themselves, boys when they grow up, men of the lower classes in proportion as they have means of reading and thinking, while you acknowledge that reason has so little to do with their faith? Does it not simply let out your secret, secret perhaps from yourself, that, Christianity cannot stand the full light of reason, or, as it has sometimes been expressed, that ignorance is the mother of devotion?

This then is the thesis which I shall make the occasion of an Essay upon the nature of the personal evidence on which the mass of Christians individually believe. If I give the reader warning that I shall say much which has been said before me, I am only granting what must be the case if what I shall say is true or irrefragable; what I aim at doing is to put into distinct words and to bring into a connected shape what most men have felt and many men have partially expressed. If my reading was greater, perhaps I should find that it has been sufficiently done already; but even if so, every generation has a tone and character of its own, and if I write with existing difficulties before my mind, I have a sufficient justification for writing, which is not to be found in the treatises of former authors, though good in themselves, and on the whole, superior to my own attempt.

Statement of the case

I know the kind of answer then which I ought to make to the suggestion, and I shall try to make it. I grant then that, as soon as a person can use his reason, and so far forth as he exercises it, he ought to exercise it on religion, and should place his faith upon it as an antecedent condition in the order of nature. I say as an antecedent condition in the order of nature, because that faith itself teaches us of itself that it is a divine gift and comes from supernatural grace, according to the text, 'By grace are ye saved', etc ⟨Ephesians 2⟩; but theological doctrine does not come into this discussion. Though the real source and cause of religious faith is beyond nature and natural reason, still reason is its antecedent, and cause *sine quâ non*, and it is in this aspect of it that it falls to me to consider it. And, this being the case, I hope no reader will misunderstand me, and think that I am forgetting its divine origin because I am investigating its human history.[1]

I grant then that mere hereditary faith, in those who can have an intelligent faith, is, to say the least, dangerous and inconsistent; nay, in the case of a religious person, rather I would even say ⟨affirm⟩ that it is impossible. I would maintain that faith must rest on reason, nay even in the case of children and of the most ignorant and dull peasant, wherever faith is living and loving; and of course in a great many other cases besides.

I start then with a deep conviction that that is the case on which the objection I am to answer bases itself; viz that faith, not only ought to rest upon reason as its human basis, but does rest and cannot but so rest, if it deserves the name of faith. And my task is to elicit and show to the satisfaction of others what those grounds of reason are.

⟨*Reasons for thinking it granted* [i.e. that faith must rest upon reason]. N.B. In the same way that we argue antecedently from the nature of the case, that if a Revelation be given as a Revelation, it will have a Prophet or Oracle, and a distinct one, so again, we may argue antecedently that if religion is consequent upon *reason* and at the same time for *all* men, there must be reasons producible sufficient for the rational conviction of every individual.⟩

---

[1] See also J. Seynaeve, *Cardinal Newman's Doctrine on Holy Scripture*, Louvain 1953, p. 31*; *Tract 73* reprinted in *Essays Critical and Historical*, London 1919, I, pp. 30 ff., and Newman's review of Dean Milman, II, pp. 186 ff.

Antecedent idea of the nature of the Assurances

1. Next I observe, since the grounds are to be such as apply to all classes of men, they must lie deep in the constitution of our nature.
2. And further they must be obvious and not abstract: of a natural persuasiveness, of a nature to be intelligible to and to arrest the attention of all, and to touch them and come home to them, and work upon them.
3. And moreover since they apply to all men, ignorant as well as learned, they must not require books or education, or an array of facts, and the like, but they must be portable, like the *philosophia* of the Latin Orator, which *peregrinatur nobiscum*[1] etc etc
4. And the same thing follows from the necessity that they should be lasting, carrying the mind through all temptations to unbelief, and of force in all ages, in age as well as in youth.

In some of these respects they resemble the Notes of the Church, the character of which may be taken to illustrate them, and which indeed will take their place among them. These Notes are described by theologians as having the following qualifications:- 'Deprehendi debet vera Christi ecclesia,' says Father Perrone, 'per signa, quae in *omnium oculis facile incurrunt* . . . Hae notae *non* debent *ad arbitrium confingi*; . . . debent ex *intimâ ac essentiali* ipsius ecclesiae instituti *constitutione* suâ sponte enasci.' t 2. p. 90. (Bellarmine gives the rules better) vide Walenburch de notis ecclesiae. ⟨p 92⟩. 'Sunt extrinsicae, atque essentiae ac proprietatum manifestationes.

(On *practical* truths — which seem unphilosophical which analysed deeper — e.g. *miracles* are 1. natural to the first instinct. 2. unlikely to the reason. 3. true in fact in revelation. Thus first thoughts best.)

(How can a person know that a resurrection is a miracle? for does he know that men cannot under circumstances, i.e. by a higher law of nature, sometimes rise? I answer, how does that person know that *he* shall die? Which he does not. He will find it as difficult to draw out the proof on which he so holds as the proof on which he holds that no dead man ever arose).

(On whether you can be said to understand and receive a proof till you have heard and answered to the objections to its conclusion. Yes — for objections are not sufficient to touch certainty.)

On the fear which children have of being *in the darkness* and similar feelings, what can be argued from it?

N.B. January 26, 1860. The key of the whole system is that God, since a God there is, *desires* and imposes it as a duty on men that they should seek Him and find how to please Him, and that being the case He will bless imperfect proofs, which there is *no* reason to show that He will go [do] in matters of *science*.

---

[1] Cicero, *Pro Archia*, 7. 16.

And the obvious point to be considered is, *can* a science be of a private personal character, and must it not be intelligible to all the world? Since reason in religion, is a reasoning of a *religious* mind, it is plain that its fundamental axioms will not be intelligible except to religious men — ⟨I have been led to think that the greatest modesty in a metaphysical treatise is Egotism —⟩ to the rest it will be like words without meaning. Can this be called a *science*? Aristotle says an ἐπιστήμη [Scientific knowledge][1] is a necessary deduction from principles; and these principles are natural truths and their habit a natural habit. Yet, in like manner, νοῦς may be *supernatural* — and then this science is not level to the comprehension of any who has not the *supernatural* habit.

Antecedent questions

1. a proof *open to all* antecedently likely
2. on science, not necessarily being open *to all mankind*, e.g. if they have not *eyes.*
3. on moral probabilities when cumulative issuing in certainty.
4. Apperception not necessary.

And I shall give the grounds of belief which I am to investigate the name of Assurances, as in opposition to those which in English are called the Evidences of Religion.

There are two or three Preliminaries, which have to be dwelt upon.

Reflex Perception or Apperception⟨?⟩ not necessary in Assurances, as it really is in Evidences.

(Introduce the apparently contrary opinions of some Catholic Philosophers).

Whoever doeth the will, shall know of the doctrine, etc.[2]

1. India is.
2. England an island.
3. all die.
4. practical judgment, cuique in suâ arte credendum.
5. calculating boys.

N.B. There is a vast difference between an argument in abstract and concrete. The same set of considerations, which viewed abstractedly, may seem quite insufficient for certainty, may be conclusive when actually embodied or before the individual mind. I have said this in my first Essay on Miracles, when I spoke of seeing the miracle of the calming the waters.[3] This should be worked into one whole section.

N.B. Enlarge on the *position* actually and in the concrete of a mind *believing* that the eternal God has become man, has died etc., how *can* such a one but

---

[1] *Nicomachean Ethics*, VI. 3. See below, p. 153 from *Stray Essays*, Privately printed 1890, p. 97.
[2] *John*, 7:17.
[3] *Two Essays on Biblical and Ecclesiastical Miracles*, p. 9.

shrink in disgust at the notion of doubt? Can he say 'I will keep my mind open to evidence, etc etc?' how unreal! This will form a section.

March 12, 1860

On the question whether a person need to know or have certainty of, a thing, know what can be said against it, Mill speaks in his work on Liberty, and is answered by Arnold in The Rambler, number for March, 1860 p. 377.[1] The argument of the latter is that a false opinion requires argument to detect — but a true only requires meditation to confirm, — there is a good deal in this — I should observe crosswise by making a distinction between a conclusion ⟨conviction⟩ and certainty wrought out by a cumulation of probabilities, and one relying on a direct simple strong ground of proof. The latter, it might be admitted, does not require to hear what an opponent says, the former does.

March 13, 1860.

As to the belief in India being certainty, I suppose it might be said that it is not — i.e. we are not lawfully without *fear*, because it is derived from the fact that 'every one says it,' but that this is not enough for logical certainty is proved by the parallel case of belief in Catholicity, which in the middle ages would be implicit and absolute because *all men* had it, but which individuals find insufficiently proved, for the very reason that the *fact* of 'all men' has now ceased. Hence I cannot retort on a person who asks 'How can an ignorant person be certain about Catholicity?' by saying 'How can he be certain about India?' for he is *not* certain, i.e. logically. N.B. How can it be said that a man is certain *without fear* who has doubts like muscae volitantes? Is the *acting* without fear the measure of *speculative* certainty?

Personal grounds. March 14, 1860. As to the ground for answers to prayer, it might be replied that the heathen had just the same answers and failures of answer — believed in its inefficacy [sic], yet acknowledged constant failures.

March 27, 1860. Thus:- The Almighty has in all *practical* matters provided for His creatures short cuts to certainty. Thus we are certain that there is a country called India, that England is an island, and that we must all die. The only question is, is this to be called *speculative* certainty. Now you may say we *ought* not to feel speculative certainty in such cases, but *we do*. Not only do we think it safe to act as if there was a country called India, but *we do* think and

---

[1] T. Arnold, 'Mill on Liberty', *Rambler*, N.S. vol. II (1860) pp. 376 ff. See also, *The Correspondence of Lord Acton and Richard Simpson*, Cambridge 1973, II, pp. 19, 27–9, 35, 39.

hold it without doubt *or fear* that there *is* such country. And further, when questions about *persons* come in, we consider it a crime *not* to be certain. If a friend had much brought against him which we could not explain, we should say, 'Well, I will *not* believe, till it is demonstrated' — showing how certainty (or faith) is a matter of the will. If it be said that this proves too much, for many men are confessedly certain when they are mistaken, as e.g. about a friend, this only shows that it requires a 'judicium *prudentis*', and that there is an excess of belief possible, and rules and criteria necessary.

3. Chapter. Contrast between the corpus and the individual motivum. [The one] conscious, objective etc. the other latent, implicit, etc, the one logical, the other rhetorical, moral etc. Individuals need not to be able to analyze, understand, and explain their own grounds. On reasoning as a simple progression or movement of the mind, (Give some *instances* of *good* whether *moral* or *rhetorical* arguments) of which logic is only the nearest account, instead of being an analysis. On calculating boys, not *really* reasoning by *methods*, but by instinct. This will not easily be granted me. I was reading some one the other day, who said *of course* the boys *did* go by method, though they could not bring it out — but I do not think it matters for my purpose, whether we say that the logic is implicit, or that there is no *real* logic except as symbolical — so that *conscious* analysis is not required as possessed by the unlearned etc.

4. Chapter. Next I give the obvious reasons *why* the personal proof *must* be of an obvious character and suited to all and easily understood — else, the great bulk of mankind never could believe on reason. This leads to the discussion of the *Notes* of the Church which *are* popular — vid. the three rules laid down by theologians about them.[1] On the Notes, on rhetorical and moral arguments at length.

On prima facie arguments which at first are sound, next unsound, and lastly sound again. ⟨*Somewhere* should come in the question of 'implicit faith' in the Church, true, but the question is the *grounds* in reason for that faith.⟩

⟨Implicit faith has reference to *doctrine*⟩.

Conclude by ennumerating the *requisites* of the popular proof 1. It must be *portabile*, we must carry it with us for all circumstances of life.

NB. An accurate knowledge of the Catechism is a *motivum credibilitatis*.

---

[1] Perrone gives these, *Praelectiones Theologicae*, II, Rome 1841, *De Locis Theologicis*, I p. 91, in note: 'Bellarminus lib. iv. *De ecclesia militante* cap. ii, tres conditiones assignat, quae concurrere debent ad veras notas constituendas, ac i. quod debeant esse *propriae* et non communes; 2. debeant esse *notiores* ea re cujus sunt notae; 3. debeant esse *inseparabiles* a vera ecclesia cujus notae sunt.'

BOOK ii

The personal proof actually drawn out in

Chapter 1. There are two kinds of arguments for a fact ἐικονα and σήμεια.[1] On their respective provinces. Verisimilitude or likelihood and probable rising to moral certainty.

Of these two the personal argument is mainly founded on the former, though of course the latter ever must be the direct ground of conviction, but the former so heightens even a low probability as to make it enough. Bring out all this fully.

Chapter 2. Now to instance it in detail.

I begin by assuming the Being and Attributes of God — i.e. I suppose any subject ⟨soggetto⟩ or instance to *believe* in God — how he came to do so, being a most necessary point to prove, when people are disposed to doubt it — but I shall here assume that it will not be questioned, and that I may assume it. Then proceed thus:-

Chapter 3. popular motiva credibilitatis.

Chapter 4. On the mode in which the mass of persons thus brought to faith, should bear themselves towards objections to revelation. Should they allow themselves fairly to examine? I say, yes, if it *comes* in their way and they have a duty to do so. They will feel as a person having to examine the Newtonian hypothesis: confident.

Chapter 5. On revelation being directed to a person and devotional and how this affects the question. You may examine with your *will* determinatedly fixed. As when a friend is accused, you do not let yourself doubt him *at all*, till he is found guilty. But if God is not *such* a friend, of course it is dangerous. You have not fortified yourself by religious habits, and you are not worthy to examine.

---

[1] See H. L. Mansel's note on εἰκός, σημεῖον, and τεκμήριον in his edition of Aldrich's *Artis Logicae Rudimenta*, Oxford 1856, pp. 207–16, and the distinction between τεκμήρια — sure signs, and σημεῖα — probable signs in T. S. Baynes (trans.), *Logic or The Art of Thinking : being the Port Royal Logic*, Edinburgh 1850, pp. 42–4.

VI On Certainty, Intuition and the Conceivable 1861–1863

Ventnor. October 12, 1861.

Schema totius Operis.

BOOK I.

First on Intuitions and Semi-intuitions.

⟨Excellence in the Faculty of semi-intuition is Sagacity.⟩

The latter at great length, taking instances and illustrations from books in every line of thought and action, separately.

Secondly on *certainty*, as the mind's reflective ratification of this.

Thirdly, but now this defect — 1. want of criteria that the certainty is justifiable. 2. want of a medium by which we can communicate our intuitions and semi-intuitions, and the reflective certainty, to others.

Till this is done, our only test is the *event* or experience. Hence the proverbs 'The proof of the pudding' etc etc. And our only medium is *faith* in individuals, according to the proverb 'Cuique in arte suâ etc', every one has his Pope.

On the *state of things*, of society, and under the condition of knowledge — ⟨one sided sagacity — how are [we] to know *how far* a man's sagacity extends. On *the mistakes* hence occurring, e.g. Duke of Wellington, Newton. This is sometimes put as if every one had his *weak point*. No. It is rather that every one has his strong point. Most people may have *one* strong point. When they go beyond it they fail. But commonly they do not go beyond it often. Hence people think that such people are generally strong, and only in one point weak.⟩ viz. from history, i.e. before the rise of *science* which is the next subject.

BOOK 2

On science as a criterion of knowledge and a medium of communicating it.

Hence logic, an instrumental art, equalising all men and all discoveries. ⟨N.B. as an instance F. W. N. [Francis Newman] says that theology and philosophy have now been reduced to science.⟩

1. A faculty was [to] be specifically different in different subject matters — yet its nature the same, e.g. memory — that a memory is good in figures does not betoken its being good in poetry. Something like this Dmowski says in his proposition 'Omnes veritates necessario *reducuntur* ad principium (contradictionis) non tamen omnes possunt aut debent per illud *demonstrari*.' t.i.p. 72.

2. A faculty may be specifically different, but the *process* the same on analysis, i.e. proof after all.

On the deficiencies of science.

1. On the necessary assumption of first principles. This is evaded, as is thought, by *induction*; which goes by *facts* but observe (1) the first principles involved in induction, e.g. 'nature if uniform in her operations,'! vid Mill. (2) the *facts* — how do we know the facts? e.g. that England is an island, that all men must die etc etc.

2. On the things to be *taken for granted* ⟨assumptions⟩ — *how* many? and when? e.g. do we take for granted the existence of matter? i.e. any thing over and above phenomena —

or do we take for granted that others see as we see etc etc. or the existence of a Framer as well as matter ⟨substance⟩? if the latter, why not the former? or do we make the two one under the idea of Cause?

On the state of society etc. under the effect of science.

BOOK 3

On the adjustment of the two methods — their separate utilities etc.

A priori proof theological — a sort of meditation (should this be in Book 2?) e.g.

      1. deductive proof. theological.

      2. inductive. physical, etc.

October 29, 1861.

Brown p. 77 etc. speaks of Intuitions as universal, irresistible, immediate. By 'irresistible' he seems to imply their subjective certainty.

And he gives as *instances* of Intuitions, the belief in our Identity, and of the stability of the laws of nature.

It is to me wonderful that he should put these two beliefs on the same level. The latter is hardly universal — on the contrary, the religious sense, so far as it goes, is counter to such a belief — for the mass of mankind consider that Almighty God, and good and bad spirits, continue [to] interfere with its actual stability. If it be said, that there is a universal belief that the order of nature is stable, if *let alone*, I answer that I have great doubts whether an hypothetical proposition of this kind can be called one of universal belief — and whether the bulk of mankind enter into any such abstract speculations.

Further, supposing it to be universal, I do not think it immediate. It seems to me, as far as it obtains, to arise from the imagination. If we are accustomed to things one way, we do not expect them to be in any other. We think that what is, will go on. 'Well then', it may be objected, '*this* is a proposition of which there is universal belief.' No — I do not call it a belief, that is, an act of the intellect. I have no experience of things except in one way, there is nothing to *shift* my imagination for another. It is *change* that has to be proved by the fact, but the imagination becomes a habit. If I had gazed on Lisbon for hours, and then suddenly it had sunk into the earth, I should have distrusted my eyes — but not from any notion that what was would be, but because it was a shock to my *imagination* and an interruption of my *habit*. But any how, the belief would not be immediate, but would depend in these two causes.

But in matter of fact, I think belief in the stability of nature is not at all general, not merely as an explicit proposition, but as virtual and assumed.

Then as to our belief in our identity, I cannot call it *immediate*, for at least it is *through* our mental acts, if not because of the reflection of our mind upon the fact of their existence. Cogito ergo sum — seems to me true. At all events, previous *reflection*, and some previous mental act, e.g. sight, or memory, or hope, or fear, etc. are *necessary conditions* to the intuition. And it is very difficult, if not impossible, in *such* a case, to draw the line between a *virtual* premiss and a sine qua non condition. We see our identity or personality *in* our seeing, or remembering etc. So that it is what I have called a contuition, rather than an intuition.

Further as to *irresistible* — if so, certainty is necessary to an intuition. Whereas I conceive you may have an intuition without knowing it. And if so, they perhaps are *not* few, whereas Brown makes intuitions few, p. 80 apparently contra Reid.

February 13, 1863

LOGICAL METHODS

1. Logic of Presumptions
2. Logic of analysis (a priori) The schola
3. Logic of Synthesis (induction)
4. Logic of facts — e.g. (1) Lay baptism must be valid *else* such a large part of Christians are unbaptized.

   (2) For saying office it is not necessary to understand, for the nuns often *do not* understand it. *Our* bishop can ordain validly; *else* the hierarchy can hardly have the succession. This τόπος is nearly the same as ex absurdo.
5. Logic of Imagination.
6. Logic of Intuition.

September, 1863

Chapter ii

§*1*

I am aware that what I have said at the end of the foregoing Chapter will not be considered by every one sufficient to answer the difficulty to which I drew attention. It will be objected by those who urge it, as a principle to be laid down generally, that things which are above the reason, are incapable, as such, of being the objects of faith. We express these unknown things by means of figures, we argue about them under figurative terms, we have no knowledge at all of the real objects which we are so confidently discussing, we cannot pronounce a judgment this way or that on propositions of which we do not know the terms. We cannot believe in them, we can but use mere words about them. Yet we speak of these verbal propositions, which mean nothing, at least by which we mean nothing, as if they conveyed ⟨were⟩ important truths, which, as received or rejected, brought life or death to the soul. We say that the Holy Ghost proceeds from the Father and the Son; what definite idea has any one, educated or uneducated, of the figurative terms Father, Son, Spirit, or procession, when used of the Eternal God? Yet we discuss and argue from this proposition, as if we had mastered it. Suppose we were to express mysteries in the Divine Nature by numbers, and made them the subject of arithmetical conclusions, should we not understand what was meant by our numbers, those given and those deduced, quite as much as we now understand the doctrine of the Holy Trinity as taught by the Catholic Church?

This objection is not only levelled against the revealed doctrine in question, but against any ⟨all⟩ dogmatic teaching upon the subject of the Being of a God. I wish to consider it carefully in this and the following sections; it opens three questions upon us, our knowledge of God, the language in which that knowledge is expressed and communicated, and the limits of that knowledge. I will enter upon them at once, and must ask leave to be both elementary and discursive in my treatment of them.

I begin by observing that it is the characteristic of the human mind that it can arrive, by continuous and irrefragable processes of thought at conclusions which baffle all thought, and even seem to contradict the first principles on which it carries on its thoughts at all. Our power of logic outstrips our power of conception. We are irresistibly forced forward upon avowals, from which, while we make them, we as irresistibly recoil, as though 'scared? at the sound ourselves have made.'

The simplest instances of this phenomenon are found in our elementary treatment of the ideas (of Time and) Space. Space either has a limit or it has not; we cannot conceive it running out in every direction interminably, yet we cannot conceive the possibility of a limit. (And so of Time, we cannot conceive either that it had a beginning or that it had not; yet) this dilemma is strictly logical. Thoughts like these make us giddy, and dismay us with a sense of the feebleness of our intellectual powers. No ideas are more wild than those which are relentlessly reasoned out by the hard heart and the sober judgment.

This combination of strength and weakness in our intellect is, as might be expected, especially brought to view, when it begins to inquire about the Divine Being. How we originally gain our knowledge of Him, is as obscure, as the fact is clear that we do gain it; but, having the idea, and the conviction, that He is, by whatever means, when we attempt to employ our logical powers upon the great truth, to develop it, to bring it into a consistent shape, steadily to contemplate it as a whole, and to give it an objective reality, we are confronted by a host of conclusions as overwhelming as they are inevitable. Our imagination cannot keep pace with our analysis, and our words partake more and more of the nature of signs and symbols from the increasing difficulty of interpreting them.

For instance, the most just account which can be given of the Supreme Being is that which He had deigned Himself to deliver to His creatures, when He said to Moses, 'Ego sum, qui Sum'. He is emphatically 'Qui Est', The Being, all other beings vanishing from our view in comparison of Him. But, it is plain, that, while to call Him 'I am' gives the amplest matter for exercising our reasoning powers, it at once baffles and discredits our powers of conception. When we so call Him, we attach a vague and, as far as it goes, a true meaning to our words; but, when we reflect ⟨dwell⟩ upon them, we find ourselves hurried on, by a few steps, each of which we master, to conclusions which we cannot master. For, if He is the Being, He must have a title to the name in a sense in which no one else can rightly claim it; what is that sense? We answer by negatives, that He has no parts, no relations, no mode, form, or quality of existence, no stages of life, no history; we answer affirmatively that He is self-dependent, that He is ever one and the same, that He is a stationary Now, that He is pure existence, that His being and His nature are identical:- propositions, all or nearly all of which are at once intelligible, as far as the terms are concerned, but simply beyond us, when we consider the truth which those terms are intended to convey. As, in matters of this world, did I make the assertion, for instance, Caesar was a great man, the general sense of the proposition would be intelligible even to a child, yet only a scholar, well-versed in Roman history, would be able to understand the truth to which I intended, in so speaking, to give utterance, [Newman worked a great deal on this sentence in pencil. To begin with he substituted *Napoleon* for *Caesar* and continued:] ⟨Yet only an educated man who was conversant with ⟨had a sufficient knowledge of⟩ great facts of human nature and of history, who understood character and the influence of man upon man, ⟨who knew what was meant by personal influence of man upon man⟩, and the bearing of the individual and his circumstances upon each other, would be able, I do not say to judge of the truth, for that would require a knowledge of the special history of Napoleon besides, but to understand what it was meant to say.⟩ so, in a parallel way, we may have a hold upon the sense of theological words sufficient to argue about and from them, yet have the dimmest of conceptions of the object which they represent and intend.[1]

The negative proposition that the Divine Being has no parts, is in reality ⟨declares what is intensely⟩ positive, if our minds could embrace what in its fulness is meant by it; but to us in this life it is but a logical statement, separating Him off from this world of which we have experience, and presenting no object for the imagination to fix upon. And so of other negatives, what is their effect, taken by themselves, but to turn our eyes away from Him? To say that He is invisible, immaterial, immutable, incomprehensible, incommun-

---

[1] Newman inserted here in pencil, with reference either to what precedes or what follows: 'Not on the subject vid infra (and so say generally).'

icable, infinite, and then to stop, to say what God is not is practically much the same as to say that He is not. The more we remove Him from us, so much the more do we remove ourselves from Him. Such was the course of thought pursued by the philosophers of old. It is illustrated in the story of one of them, who, having asked for two days before he determined what God was, at the end of them asked for four, and so then went on doubling his time for thought whenever he came to the end of it. This was truly to adjourn the decision *sine die*.

The same is true of the affirmations which we make about the Divine Essence, though in another way. For, if our negative propositions practically present no object for our conception, our affirmative present an object which at first sight [is] ⟨unmeaning, or⟩ self-opposing or even impossible. Thus, to say that God has neither beginning nor ending is negative; shall we take the affirmative that He is everlasting? What will be our course of thought? We begin ⟨commence⟩ with the idea of time; then we imagine time continuing without limit, and speak of 'omnia saecula saeculorum'. Next we correct ourselves and say that in these perpetual 'ages upon ages', and this 'for ever and ever' there is no succession. But these words imply ⟨have⟩ succession in their very form, *nor* can we rid ourselves of the idea; so that, when we would imagine to ourselves the eternity of God, we describe it as time evolving itself without evolution ⟨[time] succeeding time without succession or duration with uniformity of state (vid. de Lugo)⟩;[1] and though we know this is not the true account of it, and suggests no determinate view to the mind, we know not how else to speak of eternity.

In like manner, when we say He is self-dependent, we know what 'self' means, and what 'dependent' means, and thereby what the two words put side by side mean; but, when we have gone as far as this, we see also that they stand respectively for ideas which ⟨in their literal fulness⟩ are not compatible. 'Dependence', literally taken, implies an external correlation, and 'self' cannot stand ⟨be⟩ for such a ⟨that⟩ correlation; yet we cannot state the divine fact which we aim at stating in any clearer way. We aim to grasp in our intellect what we cannot grasp, for nothing, of which we have experience, is independent of every thing else. If we say that He is of or from only Himself, the same difficulty will be found to recur. Two ideas, which we can barely reconcile together, are combined by us as our nearest approximations towards the possession of an incomplex truth, which is shown to be beyond our conception for the very reason that it is beyond our expression.

And so again, from the experience of causes which we have in the world, we rise to the idea of a First Cause, from whom they all proceed. But such a cause must be His own Cause; therefore he is a Cause *sui generis*; therefore in the sense in which He is a cause, He is the Only Cause; and therefore other so-called causes are not really such. Thus we have run to a conclusion which undoes, or at least confuses our premises; a conception of the human truth

[1] *Theologia Scholastica, De Deo Uno*, XXX. ii. 2, p. 327.

with which we started fails to secure us a conception of the divine truth with which we end.

And so of all terms, affirmative and negative, by which we attempt to speak of ⟨describe⟩ the Supreme Essence, they are logical statements, true in their wording, positive in their drift, and the best ⟨adapted⟩ ⟨useful⟩ that can be found for their purpose:- but they do not profess to suggest or to express the real thing in concrete of ⟨on⟩ which they give piecemeal and abstract information. We have no means of conceiving One who is and never came to be, who has no other essence than ⟨essence beyond/besides⟩ His Existence, no qualities beyond ⟨besides⟩ His essence, who endures ⟨has duration⟩ without succession, who has life without evolution, who is ever active yet ever quiescent, who is infinite, yet most definite, who is abstract yet at the same time concrete, who can make without materials, who can foresee without *media*, who is His own all-sufficient object of thought, observes and stores up for Himself the innumerable details that exist and that are done in the material and spiritual worlds. We believe each proposition ⟨can understand and command our belief to [each proposition]⟩, as it passes before us in succession; we cannot combine, we cannot realise the whole.

I have been speaking of the Almighty, as He is suggested to our minds in contrast and antagonism to the universe, viewed as a whole. The very fact of that universe carries us on to the idea of One who has caused it, and who, while so far related to it ⟨with whom it has relations⟩, is also independent of it. Then we ask ourselves, if such a one that be, what is He like? Who is He? Scripture in answer tells us that He is 'The Being', and thus at once places Him at an infinite distance from everything else. This leads us to analyse the meaning of that title, and to enumerate the list of supereminent characteristics which it involves, His eternity, all-sufficiency, infinitude, creative power, omnipresence, incomprehensibility. Attributes such as these are suggested to us from the very fact that He is, and are scarcely more than various aspects under which we contemplate the fact. But there is another and more numerous series of appellations, which arise from our actual experience of the world in all its details as it lies before us, and which, while they involve a second argument for His existence, at the same time clothe and enrich the great idea and intimately connect it with ourselves and with the universe. That He is the omnipotent 'I Am', and all that that Title implies, is a truth mainly irrespective of this world; but that He is the Good God, in a like fulness of meaning, is a conviction which we attain by regarding Him as the limit and archetype of all possible ⟨conceivable⟩ perfection, and this is a consideration suggested to us from the experience which we have of His creation. We contemplate Him, not in contrast, but in union with other things, as within not without them. There is an instinctive feeling in our hearts ⟨minds⟩ that all that is good and beautiful in this visible scene in which we live, does but intimate something, tend to something, come ⟨proceed⟩ from something more perfect than itself. Whenever we see excellence, of whatever kind, here below, we find it, from one reason or other, stunted in its growth or thwarted in its efforts after manifestation. It has its artificial boundaries, appears in accidental and varying measures, has a field and a scope which it does not satisfy, and raises expectations only to disappoint them. The fairer, the more delicate, the more exquisite is its promise, the more frail is its life, and the more inglorious its end. The flowers of the field, which are cast into the oven, are the truest image of the condition of this world. Hence it is so rightly called vanity, for by the word is meant, not simply impotence or worthlessness, but the profession of excellence which mocks us by its failure. But we cannot bring ourselves to believe that what we so unhesitatingly pronounce as good and worship as such, that what we pronounce to have a substance and a power in it which nothing else can claim, should come and go yet from no source, and should only exist in such gleams and scintillations as it here exhibits. What we experience of it is an augury to us of what we do not experience. We yield to the presentiment that there is behind the veil of phenomena a transcendent excellence, and a perfection which is the supereminent source and original of all perfections; and we understand that it must be found in Him, whom by other proofs we already know to exist.

This, it is plain, is a far richer and more copious subject of thought than that which I considered in the first place; for, whereas that was the analysis of but one idea, viz. of (God as) the All-sufficient Existence of the I Am (I Am), this on the contrary ⟨is⟩ has important accessions to it in the fresh and fresh discoveries which we make, through the senses, of the excellencies, endless in diversity and nature, of the creation, His handiwork. In the words of the Poet,

These are Thy glorious works, Parent of good,
Almighty! Thine this universal frame,
Thus wondrous fair: Thyself how wondrous then,
Unspeakable![1]

Whatever there is of good here below is nothing more, as it were, than the footprints, the shadow, or at most the image, of what is in fulness and perfection above. All there is of order, harmony, and majesty in the universe, all that is powerful and vast, all that is beautiful, all that is wonderful, all that is wise and just, tender and faithful, beneficent, noble, and great, find its true home in Him.

In That One Great Spirit meet
All things mighty, grave, and sweet.

We have His tokens on all sides of us; but, while they remind us of Him, they remind us also how dissimilar ⟨unlike⟩, as well as like must that Perfection be to the earthly phenomena which suggest it to us; and we are reminded, still more forcibly than in the case of those attributes which first employed my attention, that the words, in which we speak of Him, are improper to their subject, as being all drawn from the creation, and that, before they can stand for His incommensurable sanctity, benevolence, and truth, they must be

[1] Milton, *Paradise Lost*, V. 153–6.

understood in a sense which is higher than their own and are the symbols of realities which are beyond our conception.

The word 'perfection' itself is an instance in point; by an analysis of grammatical formation we shall see at once that it is but improperly applied to the Divine Being. Quite as much as 'self-dependence', or 'self-causation' or 'everlasting', an attempt is made by a combination of ideas drawn from experience to approximate to an idea beyond experience. The word properly denotes the completion of a process ⟨an elaboration, a process, and its completion⟩, as being taken from the view of things which have an origin, progress, and maturity. All things here below grow to their perfection; and perfection in its etymology? implies first a making and then a carrying out. But Divine Excellence begins with what its created ⟨human⟩ adumbrations do but end. It is perfection without elaboration. Our Lord says, 'Be ye perfect as your Father'; but the word literally belongs to us and is transferred in a secondary sense to Him, that in its new sense it may belong primarily to Him as Archetype, and to us but improperly and partially formed after His image.

But here is a second mystery. As everything of which we have experience is composed of parts and powers, there is no perfection here but what is as complex in its ultimate state, as it is elaborate in its attainment of it. Much more is this the case with the world, taken as a whole, made up, as it is, of so many perfections conspiring into one. But its Maker and Archetype, owns, as I have said, and absorbs into Himself all these various perfections, as truly His and His alone, in a transcendent and supereminent mode indeed, but still possesses them all at once in one. He is an infinitely more wonderful world than that into which we are born, and this He has been from eternity. He is the divine immense universe, the true increate rerum natura, which has ever been in being, and by reason of which, not only was there not emptiness and nothingness in the everlasting period gone by, but a vastness in it and a fulness, in comparison of which this whole creation dwindles and fades away. He is that Living All, a million times more varied, (more multiform), more profound, more mighty, than this world of matter and spirit, the real pattern of an optimism which we seek in vain in our experience, and a standard of good and truth, by which no other being can, except figuratively, be measured. But then, let it be observed that this Seat of infinitely numerous perfections is also in His being infinitely one and simple; as transcendently above every idea we possess of numerical oneness, as drawn from our experience, as He is transcendently innumerable in the aspects of greatness and glory under which we contemplate Him. And here again is an antagonism, not less perplexing to our reason, more startling to the imagination, than that which is contained in the idea of duration without succession, or being without relation, suggesting to us that the words which we use of Him do not express the divine truth, but merely created semblances, which serve to instruct us up to a certain point, but betray their imperfection by their mutual incompatibility. Did we really know and could we express adequately the divine at once manifoldness and simplicity, those two words would not stand in that contradiction, the one to the other, of which we cannot rid them.

Once more:- perfection, as we are led from our earthly experience to ascribe it to the Divine Being, not only is a combination of many various excellencies, but of excellencies, which require to be combined in various proportions, relatively to each other, if they are to form a symmetrical whole ⟨to coalesce symmetrically⟩. The perfection, for instance, of a Christian does not consist in the unlimited cultivation of a particular virtue, apart from all others, but in the cultivation of all virtues together in their due measures respectively. Each, as united to the rest, has a *maximum*, and becomes actually a fault, if allowed to extend itself beyond a certain limit, and without reference to the whole circle of virtues. The case is the same with the arts, the useful and the fine. Subordination is of the essence of combinations which are to be beautiful. The designer who is determined to lavish on his architectural structure all possible beauty of form and colour, of light and shade, of curve, angle, and dimension, will end, as is evident, in utterly defeating the purpose for which he is so profuse. But it is otherwise with the Supreme Being. In His infinitude all excellencies may freely expatiate, yet without interference with each other; for the range which is to bound them, and the centre in which they are to meet, is large enough, and is distant enough, for the exercise of a myriad of infinities. But the words used are the same both for the infinite attributes of God and the finite endowments of man; and hence the judgment we pass upon human excellence we shall with difficulty be found to withold from that which is divine. ⟨June 6, 1868. Question. Are His attributes as well as His Essence infinite? Because His attributes are only *our mode of viewing* His Essence, and our mode of viewing *must* be finite?⟩ Attributes or their exercise will seem to us incompatible because they are incompatible in us, and our imagination will be unable to accept two attributes as reconcilable in the same object, which seem to us to be at variance because we cannot understand that they are ⟨[because we cannot] comprehend them as⟩ infinite. As certain attributes, taken by themselves, have, as I have shown, an intrinsic incoherence, from the infirmity? of our intellect, ⟨from their being beyond our experience⟩, as the simplicity and the multiform perfection of the Divine Nature are in their very conception, that is, as men conceive, irreconcilable, so also the divine attributes generally, viewed as an assemblage, seem to us, as if of necessity to oppose, to impede, to exclude one another. Thus, we cannot, for instance, reconcile the perfection of sanctity with the admission of moral evil; sovereignty of will with toleration of the rebellious; the omnipotence of the Creator with His diligent subtlety of contrivance; His profusion of resources with His economy of power; justice with mercy; majesty with condescension; His supreme quietude yet His everwakeful governance of all things. These antagonisms, I say, lie in our ideas of God, as we gain them through human resemblances ⟨earthly phenomena⟩ and express them in human language; they do not exist in the truths themselves, which are far above those phenomena and that language. But as we do not know those truths as they are in their own nature, and are unable to interpret language which we use of them in that analogical sense in which alone it is true, the apparent antagonisms ⟨incongruities⟩ remain; and much more will they perplex us in the case of such characteristics of the Divine Mind, as are conveyed to us by purely metaphorical expressions, such as God's anger, grief, repentance, jealousy and hope, human infirmities, which are but mere symbols of unknown truths and have no resemblance whatever to any characteristics of the Immutable God.

Such is the true answer, as it seems to me, which is to be made to those who object that the doctrine of the Holy Trinity deals with figures, and with proofs and inferences from figures. I reply that, from the nature of the case, all our language about Almighty God, so far as it is affirmative, is analogical and figurative. We can only speak of Him, whom we reason about but have not seen, in the terms of our experience. When we reflect on Him and put into words our thoughts about Him, we are forced to transfer to a new meaning ready made words, which primarily belong to objects of time and place. We are aware, while we do so, that they are inadequate, but we have the alternative of doing so, or doing nothing at all. We can only remedy their insufficiency by confessing it. We can do no more than put ourselves on the guard as to our own proceeding, and protest against it, while we do ⟨frame⟩ ⟨adhere to⟩ it. We can only set right one error of expression by another. By this method of antagonism we steady our minds, not so as to reach their object, but to point them in the right direction; as in an algebraical process we might add and substract in series, approximating little by little, by saying and unsaying, to a positive result. We lay down that the Supreme Being is omnipresent ⟨everywhere⟩, and yet nowhere; that He is everlasting, yet not for ages upon ages ⟨age after age⟩ ⟨does not live for ever⟩; He is ineffably one yet He is exuberantly manifold. We draw lines, which seem to us parallel, because the point at which they meet is so distant; and we do not ever see that they do meet in it, we only know by calculation that they must.

Such is the character of our knowledge in this world about the Supreme Being altogether; our knowledge of the Holy Trinity, given us by revelation, is the same in kind as this; (1) as determinate and as obscure; (2) as logical, and as inconceivable; (3) as dogmatic and as mysterious; — but all this will become clearer, as I proceed with the argument which I have begun.

December 1, 1863

November 26, 1863

Chapter 2 § 3

Every assertion, true or false, affirmative or negative, received ⟨assented to⟩ or rejected, may be viewed under two aspects, as logical and as formal. By a logical assertion, I mean one in which the wording is intelligible; by a formal one in which there is an intelligible sense. In the first we understand the subject, predicate and their relation to each other; in the second we perceive an image or a sort of object which is the result of the whole proposition. Thus algebraical statements are logical not formal, but those of (arithmetic and) geometry are formal as well as logical, they are the direct representation of an object. 'Bacon was Newton', though unmeaning, is a logical assertion, and so is 'Bacon was a Greek', though it is false, for the wording is clear. 'Islamism is more manly than Christianity' is a formal assertion, for, it suggests an image which may be intensely realized by the mind, though it be a detestable falsehood. 'Sin does not pay' is only logical to the young; though they perfectly understand the proposition; it presents a definite image to the mind, or becomes formal, in proportion as a man advances in years, and has had experience of life.

Next comes the question what is the discriminating mark between assertions which are only logical and those which are also formal. The answer is that the sine qua non of formal assents the terms should be seen not to be incompatible.

Applying this distinction to theological science, first I would lay down that all propositions made of ⟨concerning⟩ God and the Holy Trinity by Catholic divines, are true or probable. Next that they are all logical; but thirdly that not all of them are formal. They are not formal, not from any fault in themselves, but because our minds cannot take in what they are calculated to convey, e.g. the negative proposition 'God is infinite', first is logical, secondly it testifies to a positive truth, but thirdly, since from its negative form it does not image any positive truth to us, therefore it is not what I have called formal.

And in like manner the affirmative proposition God is eternal, if explained to be 'an Abiding Now' or 'duration without succession,' in each case is made up of two propositions each of them logical, but, according to our present faculties, incompatible; hence the complex proposition resulting, viz. 'God is eternal', though it is real and positive in its design, is not what I have called a formal assertion.

On the other hand, though [']unchangeable,['] is grammatically a negative, we have experience of it and it suggests to us a positive image. We affirm then that God has that attribute of being continuing one and the same, of which we have in an inferior sense instances in this world. The proposition then is formal as well as logical.

And so all such propositions as are used of the Supreme Being from the analogy of what we see on earth, convey a distinct image to our minds and whether affirmative or negative are formal assertions.

December 2, 1863.

Propositions may be accepted in four ways.
1. implicitly by faith in another

2. logically as conclusions
3. as conceptions from seeing the *consistency* of the subject with the predicate. (These admit of *conception*).
4. as assents, viz with the assent of the judgment.

Question: What are the poetical or imaginative, as centaurs, chimaeras, and whatever else is poetical? Do they come under the *third* head, as appearing conceivable. τινί?

On this point I should say as follows:-

[All that follows is crossed out]

1. By what is conceivable we mean that what is likely or verisimilar or at least not unlikely.
2. By verisimilar we mean what is conformable to our experience of ——
A man of genius 1 arrives at quasi logical conclusions 2 and CONCEIVES THEM when others do not.
3. By what we have experience of, we mean, (what has been conveyed to us, in some way or other through our senses or), which is parallel to the information conveyed to us through our senses.
4. Therefore what is conceivable to one man is not to another, for it varies with his experience. To a Poet or an unscientific person a mermaid may be conceivable but not to a naturalist or comparative anatomist. To a person of great imagination who knew science is opposed to poetry, not

There is a large field between what is according to all experience and is against all experience. This is the field for men of great imagination, sanguine speculations, and for real philosophers in distinction to mere men of science.

In this way science is opposed to poetry, nay even to philosophy.

Natural truths are inconceivable — as the speed of light.

No one can conceive what is directly contrary to all his experience.

These truths of religion are either, according to experience (analogical) or *not against it* under [word illegible], yet anyhow, for we have not experience of a first couple.

December 3, 1863.

§1 Conception [First version]

The knowledge which is most intimately our own and directly personal to us lies in our experience; and by experience I mean the results of our self consciousness and of our use of our senses. By our self consciousness we know about ourselves; by the use of our senses we are informed of phenomena external to us. Those novel acts through which the matter of our experience is created, are, logically speaking, either acts of complex apprehension or of judgment vid Dmowski p. 10[1] according as we view them.

Such acts of ⟨direct⟩ apprehension, however, would do little towards

---

[1] J. A. Dmowski, S. J., distinguishes the judgement from a simple apprehension of its terms on p. 10 of *Institutiones Philosophicae*, Rome 1843.

enabling the mind to avail itself of its powers or actively⟨?⟩ to think, were it not for the possession of that instinct, which is commonly called the association of ideas:- I mean that spontaneous proceeding, by which it views henceforth as united ⟨related to each other⟩, such objects as it has found united (by) ⟨in⟩ its experience ⟨its practice of observing the union or apparent union of the phenomena present to its senses; so that these phenomena are not viewed one by one, but in connection, succession and order; and further when it has found two united⟩ If one of these recurs, it suggests ⟨we feel it natural to anticipate⟩ the recurrence of the other. And in like manner, if one thing has happened by itself, we look for its happening again; for it has happened in the succession of days or weeks ⟨years⟩, and that succession goes on as those days and weeks as they still repeat themselves, so it seems to us may that which has already occurred in them. If spring has come three months after winter, we should involuntarily look out for its parallel return; and, if the cuckoo sang in the first spring, we should listen for it at the second. And if it does not happen or does not happen in the way which we were led to anticipate we are proportionally disappointed.

And this applies also to complex facts and occurrences, as indeed all facts and occurrences really are. I carry off an idea of a person on seeing him for the first time, and a superficial one. When I see him again, I expect a similar impression; and find myself baffled and astray, ⟨on⟩ at the new view which I gain of his person and character. Or, if I have not seen another for a lapse of years, my reason indeed tells me to expect a change and in his appearance, but in spite of this, a spontaneous impulse, independent of reason, carries me on to feel surprise at the particular change in him, whatever it is.

And as we expect such repetitions of the past, before they happen, so when they actually take place, or are reported to do so, we give them or the news of them a warm welcome, more or less cordial according to the impression they have already made on us, because we have already expected them. And still more so, when they have happened again and again; till at length their presence becomes too familiar to us to excite our interest, but it is taken for granted. And this applies not only to *fac-similes*, so to call them, of our past experience, but to what in any way resembles it. When two things have happened in connection, though we cannot look for ⟨expect⟩, yet we are not surprised at, events similar to one or both of them, or similar to one on the recurrence of the other, or parallel to one or both, or analogous, and this whether they are witnessed by us or reported to us. Our past experience has given them a place in our minds, which altogether new ⟨novel⟩ occurrences have not. Thus for instance the association of ideas already in our minds created by the familiar knowledge of horses and cattle, would greatly modify that intense surprise which the first sight of elephants and ⟨or⟩ camels would cause in a people who had never seen or heard of quadrupeds of any kind. And so again the existence of living things on the earth suggests the idea, and would support and recommend the reported fact, of there being inhabitants in the moon; and this of course, quite independent of any logical proofs.

This association of ideas has been sometimes developed into an intellectual principle, and made to imply the axiom ⟨intuition⟩ that 'the laws of nature are uniform'; but this seems to me an assumption. We have no sort of proof of the existence of such an intuition, as this view ⟨hypothesis⟩ would advocate, in the mere fact of the characteristic in question; and we have a proof to the contrary in the fact that brutes are actuated by it as well as ourselves. The dog that has been whipped, runs away at the sound of the crack with which he associates the stroke; but he knows nothing at all of the uniformity of nature. There is no (thing to show) ⟨evidence⟩ ⟨token⟩ that he is ever exercising an act of reasoning; or that he exercises any volition in the association ⟨his action⟩. And what does not prove the presence of intellect or will in the inferior animals, cannot by itself prove it in the case of man.

It ought not, indeed, to be called an instinct, if an instinct must be unerring, for this on the contrary need not be always true ⟨tell truly⟩ but requires safeguards as I shall presently notice. However, it plays a most important ⟨foremost⟩ part in the formation of the circle of our elementary notions and affords the means, the matter for knowledge, where it is not the special instrument of it. Since I know from self-consciousness my own existence and my mental faculties, my own personality and identity, and the connexion of them with those phenomena of sense which I know to be personal to me, I spontaneously expect ⟨attribute⟩ a parallel existence ⟨being⟩, individuality, and self action in those phenomena which do not belong to me, and are like those which do; and I view the latter in a very different way from that in which I should view them, did I not find a pattern in myself which would serve for an interpretation of them. I recognise fellow men, and fellow-units, in the phenomena which surround me; I group them and class them, and invest them with the relation of cause and effect.

This is but the beginning of a large ⟨vast⟩ assemblage of informations which by means of the association of ideas we gather from the recognition of self and the world of phenomena. A large body of thought ⟨facts and truth⟩ is thereby obtained for us, common to us all, as to which on the whole we have no differences of opinion, and which is thus attested to be true and trustworthy ⟨facts and truths⟩ by that universal consent. All this, though it is not simple experience, as I have defined it, may be brought under the notion of experience; so that we may say ⟨pronounce⟩ that we have experience of nature, of society, of persons. Other acts of the mind, besides the exercise of association, necessarily contribute to this large knowledge; as, for instance, minute logical processes, which it is not necessary to analyze [This sentence has been crossed out and corrected illegibly]. We may even go on to include in our experience qualities of character and conduct, the instances of virtue and vice, wisdom and ignorance ⟨barbarism⟩, beauty and deformity, because the intellectual sentiments and the moral dictates, which are our natural standards

⟨which we find in us for⟩ of judging the phenomena which we have already learned to call the actions of individuals, cannot be kept from criticising, viewing, forming, and colouring them in accordance to their proper modes ⟨with their own principles⟩ of criticism. Then we may speak of our experience of good and bad deeds, and of brave or refined men. The testimony of others, moreover, is to a certain point considered as a sort of personal experience. On all this I have no need to enlarge here; it is as difficult, of course as it is imperative ⟨scarcely possible⟩, to draw the line round experience, and to determine what is properly to be included in it and what not; but I have no call to do it here. Much of it is common to the whole race, much belongs to particular states of society, much of it is apparent. On the whole it is ever growing both in the individual in society I only have to describe generally what is meant by experience, this alone being necessary for the inquiry in which I am engaged ⟨but it is not to my purpose to even if it were possible⟩. [Further corrections added here, largely illegible].

In this creation of what may be called our *formal* experiences, to use the language of the schools, association of ideas, as I have said, has a very considerable share; but this is only the beginning of its influence in the formation and growth of our knowledge. It is ever making itself felt; it makes use of the memory, or rather it has its origin in the faculty of memory. The sun rose in the Eastern quarter of the heavens this morning; if it is to rise again, in the East we shall look for it. The sun and the East are objects, first united in our experience, then in our memory. They remain united as a complex idea or conception on the memory, as a man's face is imaged to us in our memory, or the connexion of a blow and a wound, or of a horse and his speed, so is it with all things which we have experienced. The past facts live as conceptions or associations of the memory; and, being conceptions, they have a sort of argumentative force, though such is not intrinsically their nature. They seem to urge upon us, 'Things which have been united are unitable'; and this at least is more than can be said for things which have not. In such cases the associations of physical fact with physical fact, moral fact with moral, moral with physical, are conceptions impressed on our memory by past experience. That I saw an accident on a railway, that a railway servant conducted himself bravely, and that the passengers were allowed to reward him on the spot, are facts of experience, which remain, when they are over, as conceptions on the memory, of a railway and an accident, a railway servant and good conduct, and good conduct and its reward. These complex ideas become easy to my mind in a sense in which other complex ideas, which I have never thus learned, are not easy. The trouble of learning them is over; I am familiar with the association. Thus the association may be called the conception in action, and, though I may lose the direct memory of the facts, it ⟨the association⟩ may remain. I have learned that two things are compatible, because they have already been patient of each other's presence; I have learned that they are consistent, because they have already stood together in union. I may forget the experience, but I have still remaining with me a sense, which is called ⟨elicited⟩ out on the fitting occasion that the objects, which the conception of my memory once embraced, are congenial nay correlative to each other; and when I see or hear of the one, I spontaneously look for the other.

These conceptions then, as viewed separately from the memory of our experience, become abstract and general; and are called by various names, correct and incorrect; as, for instance, intuitions, first principles, axioms, dictates of common sense, presumptions, presentiments, prepossessions, or prejudices. I say correct or incorrect; because it would be going out of my way to state more than the fact that they are among the things called by these various names. I have learned from my own self consciousness the fact ⟨existence⟩ of a cause; and I look for a like fact elsewhere, or at least embrace the idea without difficulty, and easily conceive it, when I hear instances of it. (Whether Caesar was a great man) I have a turn and I have had opportunities for studying character; I read history, and find myself able at once to form a conception of the Emperor Charles the 5th, or Henry the 4th, or Sully, or James the 1st or Lord Bacon, though that conception may be peculiar to myself. A suspected murderer has blood upon his clothes; my power of conception outruns the serious calmness of my logic, and I go on [to] pronounce him guilty. A friend makes a remark to me; I take it up at once, and say that it had never struck me before, but that it is incontrovertible. It comes to me as proved already assimilated to my mind, and as if it belonged to me of rights. This is one of the causes of those sudden sympathies which one man has for another, for the intimacies formed at first sight, and of the powerful effect of sermons on individual hearers. Once more Doctor Franklin's bargain of his whistle was a lesson which at once becomes a first principle of his life ever afterwards.[1] A man comes with a tale of sorrow of sin; I have already in my person been a witness or a sufferer or a principal in a like history; I cannot help believing it at once, it so comes home to me, for I say it is so natural and I am sure that it is true.

---

[1] 'When I was a child, at seven years old, my friends, on a holiday, filled my pockets with coppers. I went directly to a shop where they sold toys for children; and, being charmed with the sound of a whistle, that I met by the way in the hands of another boy, I voluntarily offered him all my money for one. I then came home, and went whistling all over the house, much pleased with my whistle, but disturbing all the family. My brothers, and sisters, and cousins, understanding the bargain I had made, told me I had given four times as much for it as it was worth. This put me in mind what good things I might have bought with the rest of the money; and they laughed at me so much for my folly, that I cried with vexation; and the reflection gave me more chagrin than the whistle gave me pleasure.
This, however, was afterwards of use to me, the impression continuing in my mind; so that often, when I was tempted to buy some unnecessary thing, I said to myself, "Don't give too much for the whistle"; and so I saved my money. As I grew up, came into the world, and observed the actions of men, I thought I met with many, very many, who gave "too much for the whistle". When I saw anyone too ambitious of court favours, sacrificing his time in attendance on levees, his repose, his liberty, his virtue, and perhaps his friends, to attain it, I have said to myself, "This man pays too much for his whistle" . . .'
In short, I conceived that the great part of the miseries of mankind were brought upon them by the false estimates they had made of the value of things, and by their giving too much for their whistles.' 'The Whistle, a true story. Written to his Nephew', *The Works of Dr. Benjamin Franklin*, London 1835, pp. 143–4.

[Revision of the previous page]

. . . already stood together in union. I may forget the experience, but have still remaining with me a sense, of the objects of it, once in my memory, being congenial, nay correlative, to each other, and, when I see one of them, I am led to think of the other also.

These conceptions then, as viewed separately from the memory of our experience, become abstract and general; and are called by various names, correct and incorrect; as, for instance, intuitions, first principles, axioms, dictates of common sense, presumptions, presentiments, prepossessions, or prejudices. I say, correct or incorrect, because it would be going out of my way to state more than the fact that they are among the things called by these various names. Whatever be their character, they are the formal life, intellectual and moral, into which our experience has developed. They rule us in a way in which mere logic cannot rule us, and from their great diversity they answer to our need, whatever be the subject matter of our inquiries. Thus from the experience of the power of our own volition over our body, we gain the conception of cause and effect. On the other hand, in his story of his Whistle, which he purchased as a boy, Doctor Franklin has shown us how an hour's⟨?⟩ experience in his boyhood gave him the conception of a practical first principle which he turned to account all through his life.

I add, lest I should be mistaken, that such a view of our principles of thought and action, in no sense (disparages or ⟨is derogatory⟩ ⟨passes a slight on to⟩ ⟨undervalues⟩) slights religious knowledge, natural or revealed; for (revealed religion) ⟨revelation⟩ is specially a portion of our formal experience, and natural religion is the joint result ⟨teaching⟩ of phenomena and our self consciousness.

December 12. 1863

§ 1   [On Conception. Revised Version]

The knowledge, which is most intimately our own, and directly personal to us, lies in our experience; and by experience I mean in the first instance, the results of our self consciousness and of our use of our senses. By our self consciousness we know about ourselves; by the use of our senses we are informed of things independent of us.

Such sense, however, of things within us and without us, would do little towards enabling the mind to think and to know, were it not for our possession of a certain instinct, which may be called in a large sense of the words, 'the association of ideas'; I mean, our spontaneous recognition of a union in the phenomena presented to our senses, and a method of connecting them together; so that these phenomena are never viewed by us one by one, but in groups, and with an order and in a succession; not as objects of simple incomplex apprehension, to use the language of logic, but either of complex, or of judgment. Nor is this all; by this method of association, we not only view phenomena as connected, if we have once united them in a certain way in one experience, we consider them ever afterwards in the light of that union. The fact of the recurrence of one of these correlatives suggests the prospect of the recurrence of the other. And in like manner, if a phenomenon has happened once, we look for its happening again; for its appearance was in the succession of days or years, and that succession continues; as then days and years still repeat themselves, so, as it seems to us, may that which has already occurred in them. If spring has come three months after winter, we shall involuntarily look out for its parallel ⟨like⟩ return; and, if the cuckoo sang in the first spring, we shall listen for it in the second. And, if the thing which we have experienced, does not happen again, or does not happen in the way which we were led to anticipate, we are proportionally disappointed.

And this applies to complex facts and occurrences, as the example which I have taken shows; indeed there are really no other facts or occurrences, but complex ones, as I have also implied. I carry off an idea of a person whom I see for the first time, and a superficial one. When I see him again, I expect a similar impression, and find myself baffled and astray, upon the new view which I gain of his person and character. Or, if I have not seen another for a lapse of years, my reason indeed tells me to expect changes in his appearance, but, in spite of this, a spontaneous impulse, independent of reason, carries me on to feel surprise at the particular change which time has wrought in him, whatever it is.

And, as we expect such repetitions of the past before the event, so upon the event, or the report of it, we give them a welcome, more or less cordial, according to the impression which their first occurrence has made upon us. And still more so, when they have taken place again and again; till at length their presence becomes too familiar to us, to excite our interest, but is taken for granted. And this applies, not only to *fac-similes*, as they may be called, of our past experience, but to what in any way resembles it. When two things have happened in connection, we are not surprised at the occurrence of things similar to one or both of them, or of what is similar to one on the recurrence of the other, or of things parallel to one or both of them, or analogous, viz as either presented or reported to us. Our past experience has given them a place in our minds, which altogether novel occurrences have not. Thus, for instance, the associations already created in our minds by the sight of horses and cattle, would greatly modify the wonder which would be caused by the first sight of elephants or camels, in the minds of a people who had never seen or heard of quadrupeds of any kind. And so again the existence of living things on this earth, suggests the idea, and would recommend the reported fact, that the moon was inhabited, and this, of course, quite independent of any logical process.

It is sometimes indeed said that the ⟨an⟩ act of intellect and to reasoning is at the bottom ⟨the animating principle⟩ of this association of idea, viz the axiom and its application, that 'the laws of nature are uniform'; but this seems to be an assumption.[1] I do not see what proof we have of the existence of an intuition of this kind in this association; on the other hand, we find this argument against it, viz that brutes are actuated by the association of ideas as well as men. The dog which has been whipped today, runs away tomorrow at the sound of the crack with which he associates the strike ⟨stroke⟩; but he knows nothing of the uniformity of nature. He gives us no evidence of there being any reasoning, or any volition in his act; and what does not prove the presence of intellect or will in the inferior creation, cannot by itself prove it in the case of man.

I have called it therefore an instinct, though the name is not well chosen, supposing it is of the essence of an instinct to be unerring; for this the association of ideas evidently is not. It need not tell truly, and it requires safeguards, to keep us from being misled by it. However, though not infallible, it plays a foremost part in the formation of our elementary notions, and supplies the matter and the occasions of knowledge, though it be not the special instrument of it. For instance, since I (know from selfconsciousness) ⟨have experience of⟩ my own existence and my mental faculties, of my own personality and identity, and of their connexion with those phenomena of sense which I know to be personal to me, I am led without effort to attribute a parallel existence, individuality, and self-action to those groups of phenomena who do not belong to me, and are like those which do; and I view the latter in a very different light from that in which I should view them, did I not find a pattern in myself which serves as an interpretation of them. I recognize fellow-men and fellow-units in the phenomena which surround me; and I invest them, so far forth as they resemble me, with parallel attributes respectively.

This instance is but one of the first of a vast assemblage of informations, which, by means of the association of ideas, we gather from our experience of self and what is external to self. A (large) body of facts, and particular and general, is thereby obtained for us, which is common to us all, about which on the whole we have no differences of opinion, and which is thereby attested to be true and trustworthy as by universal consent. All this, though it is not simple experience, as I have defined it, (for it includes the results of the mutual bearing of one kind of experience on another and of such acts of the mind as make it available), nevertheless may be brought under the notion of experience; so that we may fairly profess that our experience embraces nature, society, and persons in its range. We may even go on to assign to it the knowledge or apparent knowledge which we have of character and conduct, of qualities of mind and also matter, of deeds virtuous and vicious, wise and reckless, of things beautiful and hideous, great and contemptible; because the intellectual sentiments and the moral dictates, which are the standards which we find within us for judging the phenomena which we have already learned to call the actions of individuals or the properties of body cannot be kept from criticising, disposing, and colouring them in accordance with their

[1] See also *A Grammar Assent*, pp. 68 ff.

own principles. Thus we may speak of our experience of good and evil, of brave men and eloquent speakers. Moreover, testimony is to a certain point considered as an instrument of personal experience. On all this I have no need to enlarge here: it is neither practicable indeed nor necessary to draw the line or to determine what is properly to be called experience and what not, though such a line there must be. Much of it is common to the whole race; much belongs to particular states of society; much of it is apparent or conventional. On the whole it is ever growing, in the individual, in society, and, I may add, in the world. It is impossible then to assign its limits in fact, and unprofitable to define it in its idea.

But what is very much to my purpose to observe, is, the share had in its formation by what I have called the association of ideas. Such association is the first element of order. Even the brutes show a sense ⟨have perception⟩ of it, for they discriminate between individual and individual in that mass of phenomena which strikes their senses as they strike ours. They recognise their own selves in some sense; for a dog, for instance, never would mistake my hand for his own paw, and he tolerates the sight of his own limbs as he does not tolerate the reflexion of himself in a mirror. But with us this association of ideas is a principle of advance. It is ever leading us to the tokens, or ⟨to conjectures⟩ suggestions, or to the materials of truths which we do not yet know; and it suggests to the mind ⟨us⟩, which is ⟨who are⟩ at first merely passive under its operation, the active employment of it at our own will and the use of it for our own purposes. Thus the mind ⟨we⟩ comes to form associations for itself; ⟨This leads the mind which at first submits to it unconsciously to form associations for itself.⟩ it connects things together, or their portions in its own way ⟨and of its own will arbitrarily⟩, and it enlarges its imaginative powers, and goes beyond ⟨reach out beyond⟩ experience for the ultimate benefit of experience itself.

⟨These acts of association whether they relate to facts or are simply arbitrary, I shall call conceptions.⟩

[*Newman's Conclusions*]

§2 The Conceivable

We have⟨?⟩ now passed from conceptions ⟨already been speaking not only of conceptions⟩ to the conceivable and inconceivable: for that which falls under our existing conceptions is the conceivable, and the inconceivable that which runs directly counter to them.

⟨The conceivable evidently much wider than the conceptions.⟩

What I have already said, leads me to the following conclusions: There are things conceivable by all; there are things inconceivable by any. The (conceivable and) inconceivable are ⟨is⟩ not the same as the self-contradictory in terms, nor the self-contradictory in idea; not the same as the logically inconsequent?, nor as the untrue. The conceivable and inconceivable are things compatible ⟨coherent⟩ and ⟨or⟩ incompatible ⟨incoherent⟩; they admit of more or less; they vary with our experience; they vary in various minds; they vary with ages of the world and states of society. Nothing was conceivable, when there was no experience; nothing will be left to conceive, and nothing therefore will be inconceivable, when experiment has reached its utmost limit.

[Undated]

§2 The Conceivable

Now let us take these propositions one by one, and test their correctness by such illustrations as easily come to hand.

1. The Inconceivable is not the same as the self-contradictory in terms; for no one would speak of its being 'past conception, that black should be ⟨is⟩ white'. Nor is it what is self contradictory in idea; for neither would any one say that it was inconceivable that the sublime should be the beautiful. Rather, we should call such positions unmeaning and absurd.

2. Nor is inconceivable equivalent to illogical, and the conceivable is logical. It is logically certain, for instance, that Being cannot have had a beginning; yet who can conceive eternity *à parte ante*? It is demonstrable that the asymptotes of an hyperbola are ever approaching the curve ad infinitum, without ever reaching it; yet who can adjust in his mind these two opposite facts? On the other hand it is quite illogical to say that education will make the lower classes discontented with their station and unfit for its duties; but it is not difficult to conceive such a result, because we may have had experience of individual instances of such a result.

3. Nor are conceivable and inconceivable the same as the possible and impossible, though the words are often used for each other. It is conceivable that there is no Creator, but it is not possible. It is possible that my friend should deceive me, but it is not conceivable.

4. Nor are they the same as true and false, that is, as fact and not fact. The conceivable is not the true, but like truth; like truth, because it is, as I have said, the experienced. What has happened once, may happen again; what has happened often, is still more likely to happen; what is in one shape, may be in another; what we know in this sense, is conceivable analogically, but after all, the supposed case is only like truth or verisimilar. Likely or like truth is a subjective word; it admits of degrees; but a fact cannot be more or less of a fact; it either is a fact or is not. Therefore the conceivable is not the same as the true.

We may often conceive what is not true. Historians tell us that one of the great gifts of the first Napoleon was his power of conception; that he saw the state of things at a glance.[1] On the other hand that this very talent was the cause of his mistakes; for he was taken captive by the vividness of his combinations, and mistook the perception of the picture which he created for an

[1] See also *A Grammar of Assent*, p. 334.

objective truth. It is not of course here denied that such a power of conception may not sometimes become an anticipation, or, as it were, prophecy of facts afterwards to be brought to light. It is one of the inspirations of genius to put things together in a way of its own, and to elicit conjectures which lead the way to logical conclusions, and discoveries of fact. Columbus was led on by a great conception. But still for one happy conjecture and correct conception, there are a hundred false ones, as we learn from the history of speculations in every kind.

The most imposing form of the conceivable is consistency. An object is consistent or coherent, when its many parts are such, when viewed together, as to harmonise happily with all one's experiences, having in itself multiplied instances of this conceivable. Now we know nothing is more common, or more dangerous, than to take the consistent for the true, whether in philosophy, religion, or in intercourse with others. The truth is consistent, and hence they say that liars must have long memories, in order not to betray themselves, and this too is the principle which so often shows itself in judicial cross examinations: but the consistent need not be truth. It is the very art of a writer of genius, as Defoe, to put things together so naturally that his readers are led to stake their character for discernment in behalf of his relating scenes which he saw, whereas it is all fiction. It is the business too of impostors, as those who come with tales of distress, to lead us to mistake the consistency of their statements as a satisfactory criterion of their truth. And in matters of observation and experiment ⟨sciences⟩, one hypothesis often succeeds another, yet each in its day has had its success on the ground, and so far not unfair that its consistency was a primâ facie evidence of its truth; still even if it were in all respects consistent, that quality of an hypothesis, even in matters of scientific research, and when the whole field of fact was thrown open to our knowledge, could hardly suffice, without further reasons, as a demonstration of its being objectively true; as more keys than one may open the same lock, so one consistency may be more perfect than another, and the most perfect of all may be as yet unimagined. To such imitations of fact we give the names 'specious', and 'plausible'; in matters of controversy, especially religious, we use a harsher word, and call them 'sophistical'.

And as the conceivable is not necessarily true, so the inconceivable is not necessarily false. Light passes at the rate of nearly 200,000 miles in a second, or 12,000,000 miles in a minute, whereas the fastest railway, which is the measure ⟨limit⟩ of our experience, goes scarcely more than one mile a minute. We may say this, we may understand what our words mean, we may prove it, we may have no doubt about the fact; but, as to conceiving it, no one can expect that of us; no one, I was going to say, will imagine that the time will ever come when we, mortal men, are able to conceive it. It is true, but inconceivable; it inconceivable because it is simply dissociated from all experience; inconceivable, I mean, as *motion*, for as such I am considering it. If I heard, for instance, of a conveyance such, that, as soon as you entered it, you found yourself at your journey's end, I should not call that inconceivable; for it is as easy to me to conceive one house next door to me than [as] another. The houses and land in London and Dublin are not so unlike each other, that I should feel any thing contrary to my experience that they should be in juxta position; nor is the change from one to another more startling than the sudden change of a dissolving view; but the idea which we cannot embrace is that [of] a motion of such a velocity. If we said that it was a velocity such that every object passed appeared only as drawn out horizontal lines, if we said that it came and went like a flash of lightning, if we said that it took away our breath and left us senseless at our destination, we should have something to measure it by; but we say that the motion is one of twelve million miles in a minute, it cannot be said to present any sort of image before us, and to be more than an assertion of which we understand the terms. And yet we receive it without any difficulty as true, its conceivableness as we feel not having any bearing whatever on its truth, one way or the other, but being quite in a different medium of thought.

Nor does the logical force of past experience, of which I have lately spoken, avail to touch the certainty of the fact, if it be proved by its proper instruments of observation and calculation. For, as I have said, our past experience does but make a certain fact which is in question, likely or unlikely, and this does not touch the question of fact. If the fact is proved in a strictly logical way, all that our past experience will have shown is this, that a proved fact was most unlikely to have turned out such, before it was demonstrated ⟨did so turn out⟩.

Applying what I have said to the question of revealed religion, I would observe, what I suppose is very plain, that a strong antecedent argument against it is its strangeness, or inconceivableness. This is the really influential force of those arguments, so commonly brought forward by unbelievers, which turn upon its likelihood. When Hume, for instance, speaks[1] of its being against experience and therefore not verisimilar, he uses a fair objection, which has to be met; but its real force is upon the imagination, not upon the reason, viz that the revealed truths are not simply unlikely, but that they are inconceivable. It is easy to reply that the Supreme Being and His providences are so far above us, that we cannot determine ourselves what is likely and what unlikely as regards His dealings towards us. This is unanswerable to the objection as such, and covers the whole ground; but it does not touch the distress occasioned to the imagination by the particular doctrines revealed. The persons in question find their minds recoil from them as so strange, so alien to the whole current of their experience, and structure of their thought, so inconceivable, when confronted point by point in detail.

Apparently to meet this difficulty, Butler wrote his great work on the

[1] See also: J. H. Newman, *Two Essays on Biblical and Ecclesiastical Miracles*, pp. 10, 14–16, 20, 26, 47, 54, 155–7, 175–7, 353–4; *A Grammar Assent*, pp. 306–7; *University Sermons.* pp. 195, 231.

Analogy of Religion;[1] the word Analogy being in fact a denial that the doctrines of Revelation were inconceivable, for what is analogous is not inconceivable, and he has succeeded in a still [more] remarkable way in quieting the imagination than in convincing the reason, though of course I am not denying the argumentative power of his Treatise. He had too clear a mind himself, not to confine his argument within its due limits; but, since his time, there has been a tendency, on the part of some of his admirers, to make natural religion, not only a defence of what revelation is, but a pattern and measure of what it should be. Butler defends revelation, so far forth as it is of an historical and empirical ⟨probable⟩ character, by the analogy of the natural world, but that argument does not hinder its being dogmatic in another aspect, only it does not subserve it in that aspect; but there are writers of the day who understand the argument from Analogy, not merely to be negative, but to prove something positively and a priori about the character of Revelation.[2] But nothing we know by nature can avail to determine for us what our Maker will say, should He speak to us directly from Himself, and this indeed is the very⟨?⟩ subject of one of Butler's chapters.[3]

The case would really seem to stand thus:- so far as revealed doctrine is after the analogy of our natural experience, so far it is conceivable; so far as it is beyond that analogy, it is inconceivable; it is partly the one, and partly the other; but, whether the one or the other, its truth is independent of either. It is according to the analogy of nature, or conceivable, in what it teaches: the fact of a revelation, the world's ruined state, redemption through vicarious suffering, probation, reward and punishment; and it is beyond the analogy of nature or inconceivable, in the great dogmas of faith in their definite form, those of the Holy Trinity, of the Incarnation, of the Holy Eucharist, the Resurrection, and the like. And so much on the conceivable and inconceivable as true or false.

5. The conceivable and inconceivable are the coherent and incoherent, or the compatible and the incompatible; and the conceivable admits of degrees.

There can be no degrees, of course, in the inconceivable, strictly speaking, but the conceivable if its essence is coherency, is of various intensities. Not any experience at all of a given complex fact is *necessary*, provided we have no actual experience of its intrinsic incoherence. The formal conception may be simply the work of the imagination, though its material will be from experience. On the other hand if a complex fact has come for the mind again and again, and in various shapes, and in fulfilment of various tests, we shall be able to conceive it with the force of an intuition ⟨as if it were intuition⟩. Thus

---

[1] Not, at least, as it was formulated by Hume. Butler published *The Analogy of Religion* in 1736 and Hume only published his *Inquiry Concerning Human Understanding* in 1748.

[2] See *A Grammar of Assent*, Note II, pp. 495 ff.

[3] 'Of our Incapacity of judging, what were to be expected in a Revelation; and the Credibility, from Analogy, that it must contain things appearing liable to objections.' *Analogy*, Part II, Chapter III.

the specimens of the conceivable range from what may be called ⟨we believe to be⟩ an intuition to what we know to be an imagination.

This may be illustrated in various ways. One man can make his experience go much further than another. He can combine separate facts or truths into a consistent whole. He can abstract from facts variously, and throw his thoughts into various concrete shapes. Then they are called creations. Such is the talent ⟨gift⟩ of the poet, bringing into form, position, and life, what has no existence out of his own mind, yet in its matter may all be traced to his experience. Hence the dramatic conception of character, seen in such men as Shakespeare and Walter Scott, so original, yet so necessarily drawn from the stores of their experience. And so again whether we turn to Homer or to Milton, however grand their conceptions may be, it is plain they paint their Olympus and the Empyrean⟨?⟩, gods or angels, after the patterns of this lower world, and could not do otherwise.

Still they are real conceptions; they are complex wholes, struck off or wrought out by poetic genius, and consistent in their constituent parts. Such too are many of the conceptions of novelists, especially of one living author, who, whatever be his other merits, is remarkable for the study which he gives to the formation of his characters.[1] And in like manner we speak, and rightly, of the conceptions which actors have of a character which they have to represent and the conception which musical performers form of the composition which they have to play. The business of these artists, to use the word of the day, is to reproduce in their own persons the conceptions of the great masters, dramatists or musicians; and they have no pretence to do their work, if they [do] not study their parts, and trust to voice and countenance and figure, or to mere powers of execution, and so merely go by rote.

And in the case of painters and sculptors, in like manner, without conception no greatness of execution, skill in drawing, colouring or expression is of much account.

Intellectual ⟨supremely creative⟩ as such conceptions are, ⟨Yet the very perfection of such conceptions⟩ still any perfection lies in their not losing sight of the origin ⟨source⟩ from which they proceed. Experience, which is their source, is also their rule and limit. Not even the most eminent poet can safely venture on imaginations which directly offend against the teachings of experience. Such imaginations are not conceptions, not conceivable even to him. His miracula must be speciosa, that is, plausible, because in some way like the truth. I never will believe that Virgil had a conception in his mind of a ship turned into a sea nymph, or Milton of a rebel angel discharging a cannon, ⟨acting the part of an artillery man.⟩[2] Their ideas outran their conceptions, just as a man's talk may outrun his meaning. These are only the blemishes of poets really great, one of whose characteristics ever is that sobriety of thought and good taste, of which what I have been saying about the

---

[1] This presumably refers to Thackeray who did not die until the end of 1863.
[2] *Aeneid*, IX. 120–2; *Paradise Lost*, II. 64–60.

source of the conceivable is, I consider, the analysis. And on the other hand the luxuriance of fancy, the prettinesses, and glitter of secondary poets, which are so wearisome, mainly lie in their not forming conceptions of what they are saying while they say it. This may be called the conscientiousness and truth-fulness of a poet; the observance, not of truth, (for truth is not his province), but of verisimilitude, taking that word in a high and large sense. Thus Homer's comparison of the Graecian forces to birds upon the Cayster is a true conception; but the Oriental poet's comparison of Timour's army on march to the bursting forth of vegetation of Spring is hardly more than a clever and brilliant fancy. Copleston's Praelect. p. 453.

Next, the ⟨a great⟩ philosopher's conceptions are almost as bold and excursive as the poet's. He has especial need of a large mind. He demands and exercises perfect liberty of thought within the bounds of experience. He has the power of a boundless speculation, which he carries on by his originality in abstracting, generalizing, and applying. He far more than the poet ventures, and ought to venture, on the extreme limits of the conceivable. His concep-tions need not be defined as the poet's are, but that two things may possibly be combined is enough to for him to theorize and imagine the combination. We have a special instance of this in Lord Bacon's works, whose speculations about physical fact and law are of all sorts, thrown out with great profusion and variety, as seeds scattered over the field of inquiry, and left for the event to determine which will prosper and which will not.

Next among those whose conceptions lie further from experience, may be reckoned the ignorant. To a man who has never excited his mind upon his experiences, one thing is as likely and conceivable as another, and he has nothing to guide him. This is what is meant when it is sometimes said that he has no view on any subject if he has stored nothing ⟨as little as possible⟩ in his memory, and has as few conceptions as possible. Ignorance has nothing to guide itself by, and conceives too much, and too little. The King of Siam could not conceive the existence of ice; on the other hand in this way it is that ignorant persons are credulous; for if any story comes to them of any sort, they have nothing to compare it with, — cannot say which is the more, and which the less probable.

And as these classes of persons give the widest range to the conceivable, men of science give the least. In consequence they are in continual opposition to them. A common person on hearing a report about a mermaid, is sensible of nothing inconceivable in the idea. The component parts of the supposed animal present no incongruities to his experience, and he has no difficulty to believe it, in the same sense in which he believes any other report. But a man of science cannot even tolerate the notion. His cultivated and practical experience teaches him, as a naturalist or comparative anatomist, that such a head and shoulders cannot possibly be joined to such a termination, and he pronounces it an idle tale or an imposture. Each conceives according to his experience. In such a case the man of science is right, but in others he is quite as likely to be wrong. Science is jealous of science, in as much as each has its own experience, and throws its experience into its own narrow moulds; hence a proficiency in one of them it is slow to conceive the information conveyed by others of a different kind; the physicist comes into collision with the metaphysician, the linguist with the ethnologist, and all with the true philosopher, whose range is wider than each and all of theirs. The same antagonism shows itself between the students of the human sciences and divine. This is why a profound physical adept will find it nearly impossible to admit the existence of miracles.

Define on starting the limits of the conceivable better ⟨a *law* and *how* can it be?⟩ — any *thing* conceivable about which we do not feel a positive revulsion from its being against experience — sometimes barely not inconceivable — *one* instance only. Sermon *striking*. 'But never *struck* me before'. blood on clothes. King James's fear of swords and a blind boy. Denial of plurality of worlds not *in*conceivable, yet resented!

VII   Papers in Preparation for *A Grammar of Assent*, 1865–1869

1865[1]

Now in applying what I have been saying about the moral sense to the subject of certitude, I must not be supposed to assume that there is a true analogy between them — but I think the consideration of the moral sense, as it comes before us, a real principle in our nature, exposed to perversion of every kind in the case of individuals, and protected in each individual by the name of science on the one hand, and his own personal skill ⟨activity⟩ ⟨energy⟩ on the other, will serve first to illustrate the view of certitude which I am about to take, and next in some sort at least to remove any thing which may seem at first sight paradoxical in it. I use the parallel then to introduce ⟨recommend⟩ a doctrine on the subject, which, though far from new, may at first sight be to many men strange: for by strange we mean what is difficult first to enter into and secondly to receive.

I observe then, certitude being an assent to a thing as true, as the moral sense is an assent to a thing as right.

1. The moral sense is so intimately one with our minds that it may justly be considered a natural principle. The same remark applies to the assent of certitude; it is an act which is natural to us.

2. There are so many perversions of the moral sense i.e. false consciences, as to obscure the just claim of the moral sense to be reckoned among the faculties given us by nature; and in like manner there are so many false certitudes as to obscure the evidence of its being natural.

3. ⟨In this difficulty⟩ there are two methods of enlightening and strengthening the mind in the exercise of its moral sense, the scientific and the personal; and there are ⟨in like manner⟩ two methods of making the mind equal to the exercise of its acts of certitude, and they are the same, the scientific and abstract, or the personal and concrete, the way of reason and the way of practice.

4. The scientific method as regards the moral sense is the most perfect and satisfactory, as it maps the whole territory of the moral sense, enunciates the right and wrong on every thing, accounts for every thing, proves every thing and teaches every thing. And this holds good of the same method in regard to certitude. It makes every truth, so far as it goes, public property: and acts of

---

[1] This extract is in part a conflation of two distinct drafts and is taken from a longer discussion on the force and origin of the moral sense. See also *Difficulties of Anglicans*, I, pp. xii, 270–1; *Apologia Pro Vita Sua*, ed. M. J. Svaglic, Oxford 1967, pp. 498 ff.; and below, p. 153 from *Stray Essays*, p. 97.

certitude, not only depend for their value upon individuals, but use the unanimous acts of multitudes ⟨bodies of men⟩.

5. As there is a personal conscience, which judges by a sort of instinct derived from moral practice, and reasons without scientific generalizations, so there is a personal certitude, which proceeds not by logical proof ⟨demonstration⟩, but by practical and personal tact and skill.

I consider then that certitude is a faculty or disposition of mind natural to us, and that never to exercise it would be most unnatural; rather I should say, simply impossible, constituted as we are. That we are not able to live even if we would without some exercise of certitude, just as the worst of men cannot be with[out] some sort of conscience, however strange or debased may be their standard of right and wrong. That though we cannot live without the exercise of certitude on the whole, yet every particular exercise of it is in our own power, as we cannot live without breathing, and yet each inspiration we make is in our power to suspend. That certitude is not the compulsory effect of any process of argument as its proper cause, or any thing else that we have in common with others, but a free act (to speak generally), just as the acts of conscience are free and depend upon our will. That, while certitude has truth for its object, what we thus take to be truth, may be falsehood, as what our moral sense tells us is right may in fact be wrong. That in such cases it is not really certitude that we exercise, but persuasion or delusion, but still, since no direct available test exists by which we can at once discriminate between truth and falsehood, it may for convenience be called by the general ⟨generic⟩ name of certitude. That not to have certitude, i.e. to make assents to a proposition or its contrary as true, when there is a call of duty on us to have it (to the best of our ability), because we may have before now assented to falsehood instead of truth, is a parallel fault to that of not listening to one's moral sense because we have before now mistaken vice for virtue. That in many cases indeed it is not necessary to be certain, that is to assent to a proposition (or its contrary) as true, e.g. whether there are inhabitants in the moon; but in other cases it is imperative, or it is a duty, ⟨there is a call of common sense or of duty⟩ to be certain, that is to assent to a certain proposition as true; e.g. that we are not made of glass, and that there is a life after death. That (when it is a duty to be certain, one ⟨we⟩ must do one's ⟨our⟩ best to fulfil the duty, and) that our best ⟨the way of fulfilling the duty⟩ lies in the use of our best judgment. That this judgment or good sense is not of a scientific character, any more than is the practical judgment by which we determine points of conscience; that is, it is not capable of being exhibited, and thereby superseded, by a series of principles, arguments, conclusions and rules, but is a habit of mind which acts *pro re natâ*. ⟨That it is gained by practice and experience as other habits of mind.⟩ That, at least in concrete matters, science never leads the mind to certitude.

That acts of certitude, i.e. assents to things as true, made under a sense of duty and the guidance of the judgment, generally succeed in having ⟨attaining⟩

a true object, that is, in being acts of real certitude, and not mere persuasions or delusions; or, if they are not such acts, perhaps they are made to objects in substance true, however they may be coloured, or distorted, or maimed, or even (if so be) leavened with falsehood, or, if after all mere persuasions, they are inefficacious, and have no root in the mind. That even mere persuasions and delusions, if the result of our best judgment under a sense of duty, are more consistent with our nature and our position in the world than a simple suspense of assent. That a man who has made acts of certitude on his best judgment is in a state of mind more favourable to the possession ⟨attainment⟩ of true certitude and more consistent with his nature, than he who in such a case has, if it be possible, abstained from any act of certitude, real or false, altogether.

July 20, 1865.

Certitude is an assent, deliberate, unconditional, and conscious, to a proposition as true. It is a state of mind, which in its acts is familiar to us all, as we all experience it as regards a great multitude of things. When we say that we are sure that Queen Victoria is alive, or that Prince Albert is dead, we mean that we do not at all admit the contrary idea; nay, that we cannot admit it without an effort of mind; that the very supposition of it is an absurdity; that nothing could make us say it; that it is mere unworthy trifling and mockery to bid us listen to reasons in favour of it; that Prince Albert is dead beyond any chance whatever of his turning out to be alive.

Thus it is that we feel and speak when we are sure about a thing. We repel and reject the insinuation that there is the faintest chance of our being mistaken, and of that being false which we fully acquiesce in as true. As soon as ever we go so far as merely to entertain, that is, seriously entertain, the supposition that we are mistaken, even though we go no further, we have *ipso facto* lost our certitude.

We have ceased to be certain the very moment that we entertain the supposition that perhaps after all we are wrong. In saying this, I do not mean that we lose our certitude, if we allow that in the abstract it is possible that we are wrong, or that there is a mathematical chance of it. Nor do I mean that we are no longer certain of a thing, if we admit its contradictory into our minds as a mere conception, as I may read or write poetry or fairy tales, and dwell upon the beautiful or extravagant marvels which take place in them; or, as I may throw my mind into the hypothesis of some pagan philosopher, and follow it out as such; but we lose certitude, if we admit the contradictory of what we have hitherto held as a fact, and that, deliberately. Nor is it inconsistent again with certitude to listen to arguments which tend to the denial of its object. Arguments against the grounds of our certitude about any object have no direct power to destroy our certitude, even though we confess we cannot answer them, as daily experience shows; — they are but directed against the grounds. An experienced judge, (if he allowed his mind to escape from its habitual caution and self restraint,) might own to the certainty that a prisoner at the bar was guilty, though he felt at the same time that there is enough plausibility or cogency in his counsel's defence of him to think it right that he should be acquitted. A philosopher may be a careful and candid listener to a speculation, while he is simply incredulous as to its soundness or reasonableness; and his incredulity will not be the less for his patient attention to what can be offered in its behalf. Did any one promise to show me that a trilateral figure could have four internal angles, my very confidence that it was impossible would keep my mind awake to ⟨the proof of it offered to me, in order that I might come down⟩ light at once upon the weak point in it, as soon as it turned up. Of course a prejudiced hearer is more difficult to be convinced; but prepossession need not be prejudice. Not till I listen to arguments in opposition [to] my present belief in the spirit and temper of an inquirer, should I have lost my certitude in it. Unbelievers may be quite fair to this or that proof in behalf of the (occurrence or the) fact of miraculous occurrences, and yet remain all along steady ⟨in⟩ to their unbelief. And so I might listen to some fanatic, who professed to prove to me that justice or purity or veracity or benevolence was a sin, and might do justice to his arguments; or to a man who would persuade me there was no Supreme moral Governor of the world; or that Our Lord was an impostor; or that there was no day of final retribution.

Even insoluble[1] difficulties would not necessarily touch my certitude in ⟨as to⟩ the proposition against which they lay; but whether they were great difficulties or small, if they went so far as to affect it at all, they would destroy it altogether. For certitude, being an unconditional assent, and a rejection of all doubt, does not admit of degrees. As soon as I entertain the objections adduced in a particular case as really telling, not upon the proof, but on the fact itself which is the object of my certitude, then, I am no longer certain at all. This delicate sensitiveness of assent is the very *differentia* of certitude; and it must be recognised as such and respected accordingly, if there is to be any room or liberty left to the human mind to be certain about any thing. To forbid us in any case whatever to reject doubt peremptorily, is to forbid us ever to be certain.[2]

A first and essential characteristic, then, of certitude is, that it cannot co-exist with hesitation or doubt, or with the admission into the mind of the very supposition in any shape that it is misplaced as to its object. On this follows close a second. Such a state of mind, it is plain, cannot be immediately dependent on the reasons which are its antecedents, and cannot rightly be referred back to them as its producing cause. If it were the direct result of sight, or testimony, or argument, then, as it has been gradually created by

---

[1] Note not 'unanswerable', see *Philosophical Notebook*, II, pp. 101 ff. See also W. Ward, *Life of John Henry Newman*, II, pp. 248 ff.

[2] The paragraphs up to this point have been lightly erased in pencil, and occasional pencil corrections inserted. The two last paragraphs of this paper have been similarly erased, perhaps, in both cases, as a sign that they had been sufficiently provided for in *A Grammar of Assent*.

them, so might it be gradually destroyed, and each objection would weaken it according to its own force. But, as I have been saying, certitude does not admit of more or less — but is a state of mind, definite and complete, admitting only of being and not being. To fancy that it may be strengthened, is to imply that it never has been attained. Conclusions indeed may be strengthened, by the adduction of fresh arguments, and strengthened without limit; but certitude, being already a full assent, and nothing short of it, for that very reason cannot be any thing beyond it. This being the case, it is plain that it does not then rest on sense, reason, authority, or an other informant of the mind, as its proper and intrinsic cause.

Thus, if there were twelve witnesses to an occurrence, a thirteenth makes the fact that it took place more evident to the reasoning faculty ⟨⟨i.e. the evidentia greater)⟩; but, on the other hand, if twelve have been in matter of fact sufficient to lead me to be certain, the thirteenth is simply superfluous, because inoperative, in that respect. I am speaking of the matter of fact, not of any abstract or scientific considerations; not of how I ought to feel mathematically, but how I do feel in my proper person. Nor do I deny that the more witnesses I had, so much the more encouragement I should feel in maintaining my point, as I might be encouraged by the presence of a friend; but this is a moral, not an intellectual consideration ⟨result⟩; I am not here speaking of the boldness and energy with which I might cherish my inward conviction, nor of that inward conviction itself. If twelve witnesses did not make me certain, then (*caeteris paribus*) thirteen would not make me so. Certitude then is not to be measured by the logical force of premises; the very arguments which create certitude in one mind, fail to do so in another; as if there were no rule external to the individual mind itself, of sufficient subtlety to decide the question when it ought to be certain and when not.

Indeed if certitude could not exist without logical completeness of proof, both as a *sine quâ non* condition and a creating cause, then, at least in concrete matters, certitude could not be at all (; and that) from the very nature of the case, and without examining particular cases ⟨instances⟩ when it was professed on their several merits. The very fact that separate persons are certain about contradictories is in itself an objection against all certitude whatever, and ipso facto precludes the possibility ⟨idea⟩ of an unexceptionable proof. And much more so, when we consider that not only are certitudes so contradictory to each other in the world at large, but that one and the same individual, at different times of his life, may have been certain, as he may recollect well, of opposite propositions. Yet assuredly I am certain in my own innermost mind of certain things, against which this objection ought to tell ⟨be fatal⟩, which certitude was the direct result of logical proof. I am certain I have never been in Iceland; though a man were to swear that he had seen me there twice, he would not tend to remove my confidence in my own memory. He might be a man of honour, quite sincere in what he said; he might be my friend; but I should not set his certitude against mine. I should think him mad; or leave thinking of his act as simply unaccountable. And so again, we will say I once believed in the divinity of Christianity, and was certain of it, as far as I know myself; and now I am certain, as far as I know myself, quite certain that it is not properly divine; yet I am, to my own consciousness, as certain now as I was then, in spite of my experience now of my own fallibility. It may be said that I ought not to be certain; that is, ought not, if argumentative cogency was its sole and sufficient basis; well, that is the very thing that I am saying. The state of mind does exist; that is a matter of fact; and very widely too; it is familiar to us all; and it is created and maintained, not indeed without the exercise of the reasoning faculty, but undeniably ⟨still⟩ not by it alone.

This is plain of certitude in concrete matters; but what is to be said of it in abstract? Is it not at least then the inevitable effect of the demonstration which precedes it? for, while a logical conclusion from undeniable premisses has an irresistible claim on our unconditional acceptance, so again for that very reason neither others nor our former selves can, by the fact of having disputed it, become an argument against that acceptance. Yet even here I answer the question in the negative. For after all, in any intricate or new calculation, especially if it leads to an unexpected conclusion, no mathematician would be satisfied with his own uncorroborated investigation, however carefully he had conducted it. He would suspend his act of certitude, till his process of proof had been verified by another; in other words, his demonstration is not accepted as sufficient for an unconditional assent; it is not the sole preliminary or the immediate instrument of certitude; it is not his demonstration, but he himself, who makes himself certain. But first he consults, perhaps, a second and third person; he finds they all agree with him; how many ought he to consult? ought he not by publication to challenge the criticisms of the world upon him, before he allows himself to be certain? Whether he ought or ought not, any how the decision is left to himself. It is left to his sound judgment, good sense, long and wide experience, practical wisdom, to something or other personal, and independent of logical or other rules.

But ⟨Again⟩, it may be, the conclusion to which the demonstration comes, is not of a character to interest him; there are many conclusions such. In consequence he takes no notice of it, perhaps he forgets it. That is, he has never fixed it in his mind, never catalogued it; in a word he has never taken those steps by which a demonstrated conclusion passes into a certainty. And even though he has not lost it, yet his knowledge of it is implicit, rather than explicit, and has never been ⟨involved⟩ an assent. And again the conclusion may be of a character so strange to him or paradoxical that nothing can persuade him to accept it, as the motion of the earth (in mixed mathematics) to those who firmly believed, in consequence of the letter of Scripture, that the earth was immovable. In such a case, though he cannot refute the demonstration, he will suspect a fallacy somewhere or other, though he cannot find it out; and will elude the necessity of certitude. This is the meaning of the well known lines, 'A man convinced against his will, is of the same opinion still.' He refuses to be certain of a demonstrated truth.

Acts of certitude being then of a personal character, not the necessary effect ⟨consequence⟩ ⟨impression on the mind⟩ of antecedents of the ⟨a⟩ scientific character, but in the power of the individual exercising them, and exerted or not according to his particular mental constitution, the question occurs ⟨follows⟩ whether they are arbitrary acts or in any way directed by reason.

If acts of certitude are of this personal nature ⟨character⟩, not elicited of necessity by the intrinsic force of argument, but originating in himself and dependent on his particular mental constitution ⟨complexion⟩, it may be ⟨then it would seem to follow⟩ that they have no connexion with truth and are simply unmeaning and fruitless.

In the foregoing chapter, I have spoken chiefly of argument as the preliminary to certitude; but so in its own place is testimony, so is authority, so is sensation, and so is intuition. It is possible to hold implicitly in our thoughts and to be actuated in our conduct [by] information conveyed through intuition, prepossession, teaching, reasoning, testimony, tradition, or revelation, without having a definite apprehension of them, or recognising them as truths. And when it recognises them, and becomes certain of them, this it does not do arbitrarily, but by means, as I have said above, of its own judgments, good sense, experience, and the like, which both completes the evidence and determines what it is worth.

Certitude then is not the passive admission of a conclusion as necessary, but the recognition of it as true. It is not the mere acceptance of a conclusion as a conclusion, or of a testimony as a testimony, or of a sensation as a sensation, or of an intuition as an intuition. What is brought home to the mind in whatever way as having an objective existence, this it elevates (whatever it is), into a higher order of thought. It gives it, as it were, an *imprimatur*, or accords it a registration on the catalogue of things which are to be taken for granted. Or, to keep close to the word itself, the act of certitude is a *certifying* it or giving a *certificate* which henceforth will be its passport and protection.

Certitude then does not come under the reasoning faculty; but under the imagination. When I make an act of certitude in the death of Prince Albert, I am contemplating a fact in itself, as presented to me by my imagination, and apart from the means by which I gained it. Sense, logic, authority, testimony, belong to the process; the result is beyond them and independent of them, and stands by itself, as long as I choose, created and dependent on myself as an individual and free agent.

September 25, 1865

I do not wish to attempt definitions of ⟨in⟩ the things ⟨subject⟩ ⟨matters⟩ about which I am to write, further than is practically useful ⟨necessary⟩

towards attaining a clear and consistent idea of them. With this explanation I observe that by certitude of mind I mean the state of being certain; and that, like other states or habits of mind, it is a disposition or adaptation of the mind towards certain acts, which acts are the evidence of its existence ⟨existing⟩. And, as others habits, it is created, in the first instance, by means of those acts; and therefore, viewed as a habit, admits of growth and of being stronger and weaker. The word may also be used to express the abstract types and generalizations of the acts in which the habit manifests itself; in which sense of course it does not admit of degrees, as it does when viewed in the concrete. So much in general.

Next, what is an act of certitude? it is an unconditional assent to a proposition as true; by an assent to a proposition as true, I mean the assertion of my intellect, that what it is contemplating subjectively, has an existence outside of me.

Further, the propositions to which I give the assent of certitude, are, as falling under the particular category of 'true', are necessarily of a complex character, being of the form, not of 'a is b', but of 'that a is b is true.'

Moreover, the act of the mind in certitude is reflex; for, as being the assertion of a correspondence between what is without and what is within me, it involves a recognition of myself. Thus it differs from knowledge, which is the simple contemplation of truth as objective. Hence we speak of having knowledge and feeling certain.

Lastly, it is an unconditional assent; that is, it is more than a belief, an opinion, or a judgment, but such, that we reject from our minds, as out of the question, the very notion of our being mistaken. And thus viewed in its acts, it is as exclusive of degrees as it is in its abstract idea. Though it admits of more or less when viewed as a habit, for a habit may be but partially formed enabling us to act, only now and then, or in some cases not in others.

Thus, to take an instance: we may acquiesce in the thought almost unconsciously, or again we may have the clear perception, that Napoleon the First was deficient in heroism. Next, if our opinion is asked about it, we may give expression to it. These are assents, conscious or unconscious, to a simple proposition and if the proposition is true, more or less answer to what we mean by knowledge. Next — an argument ensues; we have to defend ourselves for expressing it. In consequence we look out for the grounds of our judgment; we are led to contemplate it; and it may happen that we find perhaps that we cannot speak confidently on the subject, and have to modify our language, though I have definite and strong opinion to the same effect still. That is, we assent to the proposition that Napoleon was wanting in heroism, conditionally. However, at our leisure we reconsider the whole matter; and at length find that the point is too clear to admit of any dispute; we see there is no room, no corner, for a doubt, we have no fear at all that we can be mistaken in maintaining it, whether I can convince another of it or no:- that is, we give it ⟨to the proposition⟩ an assent, unconditional, deliberate, and conscious, or the assent of certitude.

This is what it is to be certain; and that there really is such a state of mind, manifesting itself in acts congenial to it, it would be a great paradox to deny. If there be those who do deny the existence of certitude, it is that they define certitude ⟨it⟩ otherwise ⟨differently⟩, or because they consider we never really have grounds which are sufficient for being certain of the truth of a thing, and that therefore, though we may think and call ourselves certain, we really are not. Taking the word then in my own sense as I have described it, I shall show that certitude is a phenomenon of mind and such as not to admit of being ignored or put aside; that it is a state of mind, ordinary, natural and familiar to us, necessary, and obligatory upon us.[1]

I think that on the whole I shall [be] considered to have given a concrete account of what we mean by certitude and certainty. So a thing is certain when it does not admit of a question, or is unquestionable; and the mind is certain when it refuses to admit a question about the truth of a thing.

Whether and when it is legitimate to be in this state of mind ⟨exercise certainty⟩, I do not inquire in this chapter, in which I intend ⟨merely propose⟩ to show that there is such a state of mind as certitude; that it is a natural, an ordinary, familiar, universally experienced state of mind; that it is a necessary state; and that it is a state obligatory upon us.

1. In matter of fact, we do feel certain, in the sense in which I have used the word, of a great number of things. For instance, we make no question at all that we exist.[2]

It is in this latter sense in which I am using the word in this Chapter, viz. as relating to truth and falsehood, or, what Catholics call 'a speculative certainty;' or, as I shall call it, a 'theoretic' taking the word from Aristotle Ethic. vi. and it is simply against certainty in this sense, that the objection, which I have stated, is directed. It does not lie against practical certainty, for we may know enough, at a given moment, call that knowledge, conviction or persuasion to decide our actions, and we must act for the best according to the moment, and may do so without hesitation or anxiety, by our knowledge real or apparent and our conscience true or false; but it is another thing to speak of certainty as a conviction that a thing is actually true. Thus a man may be certain, as a practical point, that he ought to accept Scripture as the Word of God, though he be not certain, as a speculative matter, that it is such; and again he may [be] certain of its being his duty to perform acts of religion, whatever becomes of his doubts about the existence of a God. But speculative certainty, to be really such, must have a truth for its subject, and it must be a conviction of that truth; and on both these accounts is pronounced to be impossible ⟨unattainable⟩; — on the one hand it cannot claim to be a conviction till it is proved not to be a persuasion, and this proof, I have said, is

---

[1] This paragraph has been erased.
[2] These last three words have been erased.

beyond us; and on the other hand it cannot claim to have a truth for its subject, for in concrete matters no proof that [we] can ⟨may⟩ frame can pass beyond probability, greater or less, according to the measure of the arguments which are adduced for it. Therefore, speculative, that is, real certainty, or a state of conviction, or the conscious possession,[1] real mental attainment, and conscious attainment of what is true, is impossible in our present state of being.

I have no direct and sufficient answer to give to this objection, but, whatever be its proper force and whatever the proper solution of it, I consider it is overset by the common sense and universal practice of men, that is, by the laws of the human mind. Solvitur ambulando. In spite of the absence of a decisive test between conviction and persuasion, in spite of the merely probable character of the evidence on which our concrete conclusions rest, nevertheless mankind at large cannot help entertaining a certainty of the truth of things, which they are unable to demonstrate, a certainty not merely practical but really speculative, so absolute that they even think it would be absurd in them not to entertain it. Thus, for instance, I am only doing what all the world does, when I allow myself to be certain of the existence of the English possessions in the East; yet what do I know about India personally? What is the proof that has come to me as a definite individual, into my eyes, nay to my ears from eye witnesses, — that such a country even exists? Yet I am certain about it as a fact, not merely as a probable fact, safe to believe for practical purposes, for mercantile or monetary considerations, but an absolute, undeniable, truth. Again I have no doubt at all that this earth is a globe; I am as sure of it as that I once shook hands with the Duke of Wellington; and I am as sure, as my own feelings and consciousness are concerned, that I did shake hands with the Duke, as that two and two make four. You may say I ought not to be equally sure of all these three, but I am sure, as far as I can witness about myself, and I do not know why I am not a better witness here than any one else. But moreover, as to other people also; are not others too as firmly convinced in their own minds that the earth is a globe, as that two and two make four. Yet what warrant have I, what warrant have most of them, for this certainty? I am no circumnavigator; I am no mathematician or physicist; yet I, not only think to [sic] safe to act as if the earth were a globe, but in my own heart of hearts I believe it actually to be a globe in the same sense than an orange is.

Again, I am sure that the Great Britain is an island; I have no reserve of doubt in the matter; others are as sure as I am, and, instead of speaking under correction, they would think me a paradoxical fool, if I did not believe it as absolutely and frankly as themselves; yet what is my and their real, substantial proof that it is an island? There may perhaps be cogent arguments at bottom; it may be said, for instance, that all our knowledge of the earth, of men, of history, of present politics, would come to pieces and be nought, if it was not

---

[1] These three words have been erased.

an island; and that this vague, implicit, latent argument is felt indirectly, though it is not consciously before us; I am not denying this, but, if so, there may be the like circuitous, impalpable demonstration leading to certainty, of many other things too, and there may not be any such demonstration in other things which seem parallel to them; and then comes the question, what is the *test* between those vague impressions leading to a sense of certainty, which are really logical, and those which are not so? It will be great gain to be put into possession of such a criterion between what is conviction and what is persuasion, for that in fact it will be. Meanwhile, if I were asked to assign reasons, why I am certain that Great Britain is an island, I should certainly feel the task beyond me, and should prefer to leave it as a question for the candidates at some competitive examination rather than attempt it myself. I never have gone round Great Britain by land or sea — I never met with any one who had, or any number of persons who had done so between them. I have never met with any one who had sailed from Norway to the Scheld; or coasted from the Scheld to Brest. I only know that every one says that we are in an island; and that every one relies on every one else; and that, when I attempt to trace down this universal belief to its tangible originals, I simply fail and have to give over:- but yet I believe it as firmly, I am as convinced of it, I have as unconditional a certainty of it, beyond all hesitation or misgiving,

August 4, 1866.[1]

The voluntary does not enter into assents, for our assents often, as sensation, precede any act of will, thus 'a is a' we are obliged to assent to — an assent is an inward assertion.

But to reflect on this and say that a is a is true, cannot ⟨is not⟩ be done without ⟨against⟩ the will.

1. A is C, B is A therefore B is C — the proposition therefore B is C is not the expression of an act of assent, but of inference. It is a conditional assent, if it is an assent at all; or rather, an assertion.

2. B is C is an assent. It is in its nature unconditional. It need not be voluntary. It is in its nature a *direct*, unconscious, objective, and indeliberate act.

3. That B is C is true, is in its nature an assent. But there are various kinds of this

   (1) involuntary — e.g. when a thing is borne in upon the mind. This may be, or rather is? a mere persuasion.

   (2) conditional. Under this head comes the formula 'It is true if he says so'. Which is maybe an individual act of certainty — or implicit faith.

   (3) unconditional certainty. That A is B is true. When it is conscious, voluntary, deliberate, unconditional. Of course there may be *previous* acts which previousness is often ⟨always ?⟩ a condition of certainty,

[1] Newman has drawn a line through much in these papers of 4 and 17 August 1866.

but they do not *enter into the act* of certainty. A condition *does* enter into the act of implicit faith.

And Faith itself is a *complex* act of assent for it is to assent in a subject on account of an object. What is necessary for salvation is to assent to a revelatum ut revelatum, virtute medii that there is a God Deus remunerator ac Pater et ille revelans.

What is necessary for Baptism is Est Deus et ille qua revelans.

Being thus dependent on our . . . . will it is a personal act. . . . Sense in which questions or mere inferences cannot be so called. It is an inward assertion or act of acceptance, of a proposition of which we know at least the meaning of the predicate; it is direct, absolute, unconditional, unargumentative, dependent on the will alone, unless in cases when the very laws of our nature make it a compulsory act, more or less unconscious and personal.

August 17, 1866

It was noticed above, that, though the three affirmations, of question, conclusion and assertion are simply incompatible with each other ⟨distinct in kind⟩, yet the proposition which is the subject of one of them may at one and the same time [be] the subject of all; there being no inconsistency in at once asserting a thing and yet to ⟨in⟩ proposing it as a subject for additional or for different proof. And in like manner, assent to a proposition, yet in such sense question it as to go on to wish and attempt ⟨attempt and secure⟩ a proof of it. Assent indeed to a professed truth and doubt of it are incompatible; but not assent to it, and doubt of its admitting of proof, or of its having been proved.

This remark may be extended to the case of those acts of mind corresponding to those affirmations. We may still question a proposition though we have inferred it; because no proof exhausts all possibility of proving. And we may assent to a proposition at the same time that we give reasons for it, though our assent is independent of our inference. And lastly, though doubting or questioning about it is incompatible with assent, yet we may assent to it at the same time that we seek for proof of it and doubt whether proof is forthcoming. And thus a fresh assent is led to.

Thus a youth may have assented to the being of God from his childhood, yet, as his reason opens, may wish to ascertain on what grounds the doctrine rests, and may become perplexed and anxious because ⟨if⟩ he cannot obtain so neat and clear a proof as he wishes. It is not that he for a moment doubts it, and still he does inquire and reason as truly and simply as if he did. Then let us suppose that at length he ascertains and comprehends what mode and character of proof he has a right to look for and attains to such a proof, then he comes to a decision or act of judgment makes a second or reflex assent to the doctrine and this reflex assent, while it has the characteristic properties of assent as is plain, must always be conscious and deliberate. ⟨comes to a decision which is an assent to the proposition 'That there is a God ought to be affirmed' on which he proceeds to assent to the proposition.⟩

Again, let him be brought up as a Christian; he may never have realized its internal power, and, as he grows up, he may unconsciously arrive at the conclusion that Christianity is a mere human work; this is an act of inference, still, he may continue his inward assent to its truth; then after a time it may burst upon him, and he can no longer disguise from himself that his reason is against its divine origin, and then I make ⟨he makes a⟩ new act of assent, reflex, contrary to his original assent.

Lastly it may happen that on revising the grounds of the act of inference which precedes his assent, he cannot bring sufficient [reasons] for any conclusions ⟨act of judgment⟩. There are reasons one way, reasons [another]. In that case he will not proceed to make any act of assent at all, whether affirmative or negative. These second assents, as I have said, conscious and deliberate, are what is commonly called rational. At the same time all assents even those which are primary and unconscious, are really such; for reason is ultimately the only motive on which the intellect assents to any proposition. If I assent to the facts brought home to me by the senses, it is from an unconscious sentiment that it is . . .

July 7, 1867

Divine Faith, whether habit or act, involves two conditions; first that the material object is true, secondly that the formal object in its subject (that is, the mind of the individual) is the authority Dei revelantis.

A peasant, taught by his parochus that God the Holy Ghost was incarnate, believes it on the authority of God revealing, but he believes an untruth. Therefore he does not believe it by the grace of God operating Fides divina in his mind.

A philosopher, taught by his accurate reasonings that there is but one God, believes a truth, but he does not believe on the authority of God revealing. Therefore neither does he believe it by the grace of God operating Fides Divina in his mind.

A sufficiently instructed Catholic, in accepting with an internal assent the definitions of the Church, is secure of both conditions, — he believes what is true on the authority Dei revelantis per Vocem Ecclesiae infallibilem.

The question follows is there any other security for possessing these two conditions, that is, for Divina Fides, besides the guarantee Ecclesiae definientis?

A private revelation may possess that security, though in what that security consists is understood only by the mind which is the subject of it.

A particular ⟨An adequate⟩ knowledge of Christian history may involve that security at least to certain ⟨quasdam⟩ Catholic doctrines ⟨veritates⟩, for it may bring home to the mind possessing that knowledge that they were taught by Christ and His Apostles, i.e. à Deo revelante.

A penetrating insight into the sense of Scripture may involve that security, as regards particular given doctrines, for the same reason.

Here are three *private* channels of revealed truth, (Visio, Scriptura, Traditio divina), distinct from the definitions of the Church, by which that truth may come to the mind, and be received by it on the authority Dei revelantis, i.e. by divine faith.

But they differ from the channel of Definitio Ecclesiae *in that* they are private, they have no public guarantee; and though obligatory on the mind possessing them, cannot be imposed upon others. Accordingly they are not received by Fides Divina *Catholica* (though by Fides Divina), and those who do not receive them are not called heretics whether material or formal, or can they be spoken of as invincibly ignorant, a term which is correlative with Fides Divina Catholica.

A fourth private channel of revelation may be mentioned, viz the necessary conclusion (though undefined) from a defined premiss; but this again, being a revelation only to the mind apprehending it, is not received by Fides Divina *Catholica*, though by Fides Divina.

The question follows, is another channel of revelation, another guarantee of truth revealed by God and capable of being known as revealed, to be found in the doctrinae in the Allocutions of the Popes or, in the Decreta etc (in opposition to Anathematizing Canons) of Ecumenical Councils? And if so, is this channel public or private?

These teachings (doctrinae) do not admit of being believed by Divine Faith unless they are revelations; if they are revelations, they are public revelations or private. If they are public revelations, they are received by Divina Fides Catholica; if they are private, by Fides divina in the case of those minds to whom they are brought home.

It is a received principle that there has been no revelation made since the time of the Apostles; that is, none but private revelations, made to individuals. If then the doctrinæ of Allocutions are the object of Fides Divina Catholica, if they are binding on the faith of the whole Church, if they are more than matter of private revelation, if they are correlative with heresy and invincible ignorance, they must have been revealed to the whole Church by Christ and His Apostles, and received by the whole Church as such.

This I do not think any one says — neither Popes, nor Councils, nor Divines, say it — and therefore I do not see that these doctrinae can be the object of Fides Divina Catholica, nor those persons in mortal sin, and heretics, etc etc who do not receive them as such.

But still they are not proved *not* to be private revelations, (in that large sense of the word in which I have used it above.) As the Catholic who sees what seems to him a necessary conclusion in a revealed premise, whether he be right in his view of it or not, is bound to receive that conclusion as revealed, and if he is right, receives it by fides divina (not catholica) and, if he is wrong and it is *not* revealed, receives it by fides humana, but in neither case can make the reception of it obligatory on others, who do not see that conclusion ⟨inference⟩, so, if a man believes ever so much that the doctrinae of a Pope's Allocution is true, as believing it revealed, at most he believes it with a fides divina not catholica, (whereas, if he is wrong in his belief that it is revealed, his faith is but humana) and cannot make his own faith obligatory upon others.

Next let me consider what is the duty of those who do *not* believe that the doctrinae Pontificum are revealed truths, and think such a notion new and dangerous, when they find themselves confronted by a set of theologians who do believe it. I do not inquire into what is the duty of the latter (who *do* believe it) — though, if asked about it, I should say that they ought to take pretty good care not to be so sure that they are right as not to scatter their anathemas on those who take the contrary view — but I ask myself what is the duty of those who take that contrary view, because it is my own case, and I wish to investigate therefore what such as I ought to do.

It does not seem to me difficult to determine, for the difficulty is a common one. Why do we, whenever we write on theological topics, say, 'I submit what I have said to the judgment of the Church'? We mean 'I believe *whatever* the Church teaches as revealed, *and* on these particular points I *believe implicitly what* the Church teaches, whether it be *as I think*, or as *others* think it'.

We ever have to flee for refuge to that implicit faith. We exercise fides divina Catholica *implicitly* — we exercise faith directly on the Church (as the objectum materiale) as the instrument of revelation, and indirectly on the *unknown* truth in question, whether it be this way or that way, whether as I think or as others think.

Therefore, when you ask me, as you did last night, whether I believe on fides divina or humana what the Pope said about the 'Minister' in marriage, I answer I believe the word of the Church, as the word of God, and the word of the Pope, *implicitly*, *if* his word in this Brief of his *is* the word of the Church and so the word of God. Whether I believe by Fides divina or humana, depends on the solution of this 'if', which question at present is not solved any more than many other questions. Any how, it is Fides Divina so far as the object is *the Church* and to a penitent (to go on to J. S. F[lanagan]'s case), I should say 'You must believe *all* that God has revealed through His Church, and conditionally *this doctrine if* it is among the things revealed.'

JHN.

Chapter iii
§1
April 26, 1868
again May 5, 1868
again September 7, 1868

On apprehension and assent through the imagination, considered in reference to the being of a God. ⟨On concrete apprehension and real assent in relation to it⟩.

The conclusions, at which I have arrived, about assent given to propositions, are these:-

1. An act of Inference, explicit or implicit, ordinarily precedes, but does not compel, an act of Assent.

2. While Inference, as such, admitting as it does of analysis, and being one and the same in all reasonings, is neither dependent on, nor reaches to the concrete, Assent on the contrary, admits of being in concrete matter.

3. Inference, as not reaching as far as the concrete, is but accommodated to it with greater and less accuracy, and accordingly is only able to arrive at conclusions conditional, and more or less probable; but Assent to a proposition does not admit of more or less, but is always absolute and simple.

4. Inference, as being independent of the concrete, has no need, as a condition of its act, of the ⟨an⟩ intelligent apprehension, either of the proposition inferred, or of its subject-matter, nay nor of any subject-matter whatever, being only concerned with the correlation of propositions; but on the contrary an act of Assent cannot be made without a given subject-matter nor without some direct intelligent apprehension of the proposition to which assent is given.

5. The apprehension, which is thus a condition of Assent to a proposition, is of two kinds, apprehension of its meaning and of its object; the former of these is mainly an act of pure intellect, the latter an act of experience, present or past and in memory in aid of experience; and according, and so far as, the apprehension is of the former or the latter kind, so is the assent languid or energetic.

6. If the faculty of imagination may be taken to stand, not for an inventive power, but for the power, which attends on memory, of recalling to the mind and making present the absent, then, while the former kind of apprehension by the pure intellect may be fitly called notional, the latter may be called by way of contrast imaginative.

7. According as the apprehension is notional or imaginative, so may the assent be called one or the other, the notional assent being languid, and the imaginative energetic. At the same time, though there are two kinds of apprehension, there are not two kinds of assent; but in both cases it is one and the same assent in its nature given to different subject matters, in one case to notions, in the other to imaginations.

If abstract truths, (or what nominalists call 'generalizations' from experience) are objective, (as realists would hold,) therefore they are objects — what *is* the *object*? Beautifulness, for instance — *what* does the mind see when it contemplates this abstraction? — is it God? If not, is it one of the Platonic everlasting ideas external to God? if not, can it be any thing at all, and are we not driven to agreement with the school of Locke and of sensible experiences?

I dare say there is some simple refutation at once to the following answer, which has this only recommendation, that I have held it these forty years strenuously — on the other hand I am so little versed in the controversy, in that I am not sure that it is not inconsistent with the elementary conditions to which both parties in it agree before engaging in it, or resolvable at once into some perfectly known doctrine belonging to one party or the other.

I do not allow the existence of these abstract ideas corresponding to objective realities with Locke — but then, I do not pass over the experiences gained from the phenomena of mind so lightly, as I fancy the school of Locke is apt to do. I should argue as follows:-

There is a right and a wrong — a true and a false — a better and a worse — we have a sense of these as realities. We have a sense of duty, of virtue, of justice, of beautifulness; — Have we (what is often called) an *intuition* of these? do we see them with the mind's eye as objects, as we see with the bodily eye colours and forms and the phenomena of material things generally?

What I think our mind really has as parts of its nature is certain sensations, that is, a property of being affected in a certain way by certain concrete sensible objects or experiences — a certain class of sensible objects produce on our palate an effect which to the sentient mind is what it calls sweetness — and other certain things, individual and sensible, create the feeling of pain, when they are applied to the nerve. Thus I get the idea of sweetness or of painfulness — it is the quality ⟨cause⟩ of a feeling. I do not need, nor do I believe there is, any object which my mind sees and calls sweetness or painfulness. The idea conveyed in those words are ⟨is⟩ my mode of apprehending a quality.

Now to proceed to experiences not sensible. A danger is impending over me; it continues days and months; in consequence I have a sensation of mental pain, continual and wearing, sui generis. It is a pain perfectly distinct from other pain — e.g. from the pain of bereavement, of disgrace, of self discipline. I give it a name. I call it 'anxiety'. I have a clear idea of what I mean by anxiety. It is an abstract word — it denotes a *mode* of mind. It does not denote a generalization or universal on the one hand, or an intuition of some extra-mental object on the other. I contemplate anxiety, not as a thing, yet it has its *root* in that which is a thing.

So as to beautifulness. Brown says, Lecture LVI,[1]

The word *man* may be used in two ways — for an idea and for a thing. When it stands for an idea, it is an abstract — when for a thing, it denotes an individual. Or the word *sweet* may denote an abstract quality which applies to and is gained from many substances, or a particular quality of a lump of sugar which is in my mouth.

In the first way of using it, it is a coinage of the intellect — in the second it is an experience, brought home to us through the senses.

The instrument by which it is present to us in the first case, is the power of abstraction — the instrument in the latter case (if the thing is not sensibly

---

[1] In Lecture LVI Thomas Brown adopted the view that the emotion of beauty seemed to be an original feeling of the mind. *Lectures on the Philosophy of the Human Mind*, Edinburgh 1851, pp. 367–75.

present) is the memory. And as abstraction gives us an idea, so memory gives an image.

Man then in the first case excites in the mind an idea, in the second an image.

The first way of using words is so intellectual, that it does not require the senses — e.g. a blind man might have tigers, lions, leopards, cats, so described to him, as to form an abstract idea of the genus *cattus*. On the other hand, the second way so depends on the senses, that a brute possesses it as well as man — I do not mean he has a meaning of words, but of that thing which the word stands for, viz. in memory; or at least we can conceive his having it. When he pines for an absent master, when he sets out across country for the place he has been used to, he may be conceived to have through memory an image of what is not before him.

These two ways of using words, I call two apprehensions of them — and I say that, according as we apprehend them in one or the other way, so is the assent that we give to a proposition of this or that quality. Hagar said in the desert 'Thou, God, seest me.'[1] She spoke of a fact, which she contemplated by a quasi-image — it was not a mere intellectual idea — but in a philosopher or a child 'the Omniscience of God' stands for a notion which he has formed in his mind from many other notions, and which he could hold quite as well, if he had no experience of God's omniscience, as if he had.

Chapter iii §2. (not 'weak assent', but always 'notional assent?') finished July 15, 1868

On notional apprehension and assent in respect to the Being and attributes of God.

In the line of investigation pursued in the foregoing Section, the characteristic of the propositions concerning the Supreme Being, arrived at and laid down, was this, that they were subjects of real, not merely notional, apprehension and assent, that is, they were what I have called beliefs. They suggested objects to the mind by means of images, in that large sense of the word 'image' or experience which I have already explained. For instance, we have been hearing a tune, and cannot get rid of it, after the organ-grinder has passed on; we recall at will, or at particular times, the scent of a rose or a clematis; we shut our eyes and eat an apple and are sure, from the taste, it is not a pear. The experience of what we heard, smelt, and tasted remains on the memory by a certain impression or semblance, which I called an image, though the word properly belongs to the sense of sight. Descriptions, which are such, as appealing ultimately though indirectly to combined experiences, also supply us with images parallel to the images which come directly from the memory of definite facts. Thus without having seen Abyssinia or any views of the country, I may, if I am acquainted with Scotland, Switzerland, or Norway, have a vivid picture of its mountainous wilds from the letters of the correspondents of English Newspapers; and so the pictures remaining after direct

[1] *Genesis* 16: 13.

experience or suggested by description or gathered from indications may be of purely mental objects [Four words illegible]. Thus a peculiar sensation not to be put into words attends on many of our childhood, of our nursery, or our first year at school, or of past moments of grief or joy, when it accidentally renews within us, a sensation which is the representation of our mental state in that past time, and is sometimes so vivid and fresh, that it is like a scent or a colour. Sometimes from the force of association a single word or scent may kindle a whole scene. Such too is the image I obtain of an author's mind from his published letters and table talk. And such is the mental embodiment which I am able to make for myself of an author's style, an embodiment not consisting in its peculiarities of grammar, idiom, construction, or in other visible tokens, which are the result of an intellectual analysis, but in a concrete whole, in a certain characteristic taste, temper, tone, and sentiment, impressed upon my mind by his writings. Thus I speak of the feelings and sweetness of Herodotus and the majesty of Virgil. And in like manner, from the method of knowledge concerning the Almighty delineated [?] in the foregoing section, by means of conscience and our reflections on the teaching of conscience, by the wonders of creation, by catechetical instruction, from the Scriptures, by religious books we read and by conversation with devout people, we gain, not a mere intellectual notion, but an image of the unseen God, a mental image of a loving Father, a great Lord, and a[1]

January 5, 1869

Arguments against Mill's doctrine of association
1. conscience is too *early* to enable us to account for it by association
2. the principle of association itself is to be accounted for
3. The Greek ethics is too like to the Christian to suppose it to be from accidental association
4. *Why* has punishments always attached to the *same* act, so as to create an association
5. Is not association, as Mill uses it, an unknown cause [?]
[On the reverse side of the above paper, without date.]
1. The true 'real Inference' ⟨a faculty⟩ depends on apprehension, *at once* real and notional.
2. The system of 'real Inference' exalts the *aristocracy of the Intellect*. It makes certain.
3. And it is in *all* subject matters, though some allow of science more than others.
4. The *state of mind*, even the moral state, will come in, for from [therefore?] moral *sentiments*, *principles* are deduced, as I have said about notional assents.

[1] The page ends here. Cf. *A Grammar of Assent*, p. 103.

June 26, 1869

For *design* ⟨assumption of the One premiss⟩ in the physical world is an assumption, and must not be made the basis of an argument in behalf of mind, it is the very thing to be proved, but the order of the world is no assumption, but a fact.[1] Again, every effect implies an efficient cause, but design is not a cause of this kind, and therefore does not answer to our question.

A second argument in collateral to this is the argument from the human mind. It must have a cause. *Whence* come its powers — and they are on the whole the same in one man as in another — here again is what is called Law, and argues an extra-human intellect as its cause, and that cause cannot impart qualities which it cannot have itself — (i.e. therefore it ought to have *physical* qualities, since it imparts them?) therefore it has goodness, wisdom etc etc which man has. But then why not weakness and evil?

June 26, 1869

Begin again

I am not to draw *out a proof* of the being of God, but the mode in which practically an individual believes in it. This notoriously is partly from teaching and authority, but, *assuming* as I do, the being of a God to be true, it is no matter *how a person* gets to it, so that he does his best, is as candid and logical as he can be, and does hold it.

April 20, 1877

The only assent which is of the same kind as that of faith is assent to sight ⟨physica evidentia⟩ and assent to a logical deduction ⟨metaphysica⟩.

Assent to what is called moral evidence 'ut nemo possit *prudenter* dubitare' Viva, p. 65[2] are not made strictly speaking to the truth of the object of the assent but to its credibility.

Such is the assent of the mind as given to the *conclusion* of the motiva which lead to faith — it is an assent to its credibility; and on this the mind, when that conclusion assumes its new and material object, acting upon this conclusion thus recognized, goes on to view the conclusion in a new aspect and makes a direct assent to it as its formal [object] viz — as the revelation with its contents.

Perhaps it is not a subtlety, to say, as Viva seems to do, that the conclusion drawn from the motiva or reasonings is the *fact* of the revelation or revelation as the *subject* of the proposition, 'There is a revelation'; and ⟨but⟩ the object of the assent of faith ⟨faith⟩ is not the mere fact that there is a revelation, [but] is the revelation itself with its contents.[3]

[1] See below, p. 156 from *Stray Essays*, p. 105. See also A. J. Boekraad, *Argument from Conscience* pp. 156–8; *Philosophical Notebook*, II, pp. 60, 131.
[2] *Cursus Theologicus*, I, Padua 1755, IV, *De Fide, Spe, et Charitate*.
[3] There follow a series of quotations from Viva, *De Fide, Spe, et Charitate*.

VIII   Revelation in its Relation to Faith, 1885

§ I

The Author's view of 'Reason.'

It would be easy to expose the errors about me, both in fact and in logic, for which Principal Fairbairn has made himself responsible in his May [1885] article in *The Contemporary Review*, but that would not answer the purpose which leads me to write.[1] Such an outlay of time and trouble is not what those who take an interest in me would thank me for. They would rather wish me to say what I myself think upon the subject he has opened, and whether there are any points for explanation lying about in the vehement rhetoric he has directed against me. Certainly they will not think there is any call for my assuring them that I am not a hidden sceptic; and I can meet them with the thankful recognition that for a long seventy years, amid mental trials sharp and heavy, I can, in my place and in my measure, adopt the words of St. Polycarp before his martyrdom: 'For fourscore years and six I have served my Lord, and He never did me harm, but much good; and can I leave Him now?' But this immunity neither has nor ought to have hindered me from entering with sympathy in what I have written into the anxieties of those who are in this respect less happy than myself; and be it a crime or not, I confess to have tried to aid them according to my ability. Not that I can pretend to be well read in mental science, but I have employed such arguments and views as are congenial to my own mind, and I have not been unsuccessful in my use of them.

As I have said in print: 'A man's experiences are enough for himself, but he cannot speak for others. . . . He brings together his reasons and relies on them, because they are his own, and this is his primary evidence; and he has a second ground of evidence in the testimony of those who agree with him. But his best evidence is in the former, which is derived from his own thoughts. . . . He states what are personally his own grounds in natural and revealed religion, holding them to be so sufficient that he thinks that others also do hold them implicitly or in substance, or would hold them, if they inquired fairly, or will hold if they listen to him, or do not hold from impediments, invincible or not as it may be, into which he has no call to inquire.' (*Gram. of Assent*, pp. 385–6.)

---

[1] [This is the revised version of Newman's article in the *Contemorary Reveiw*, Oct. 1885, in reply to the accusation of scepticism made by A. M. Fairbairn. It was privately printed by Newman in *Stray Essays*, Birmingham 1890, together with a few pages altogether unpublished, in answer to Fairbairn's further article of Dec. 1885. See W. Ward, *Life of John Henry Newman*, II, pp. 505 ff.]

§ 2

The meaning of the word 'Reason' continued.

Enough of introduction: I begin with what is of prime importance in Dr. Fairbairn's charges against me — the sense in which I use the word 'Reason,' against which Reason I have made so many and such strong protests. It is a misleading word, as having various meanings. It is sometimes used to signify the gift which distinguishes man from brute; I have not so used it. In this sense it is mainly a popular word, not a scientific. When so taken it is not a faculty of the mind, rather it is the mind itself; or it is a generalization; or it stands for the seat of all the mental powers together. For myself, I have taken it to mean the faculty of Reasoning in a large sense, nor do I know what other English word can be used to express that faculty. Besides, 'Reason' is of a family of words all expressive of Reasoning. I may add that it is the meaning which Dr. Johnson puts upon the word, and the meaning which he traces through its derivative senses, corroborating his account of it by passages from English authors. 'Reason,' he says, is 'the power by which man deduces one proposition from another, or proceeds from premisses to consequences; the rational faculty; discursive power.' Also it is the sense, I suppose, which Principal Fairbairn himself gives to the word, for he speaks of 'the region of reason and reasoning' (p. 667).

§ 3

The sense of 'Reason' as used in the 'Apologia.'

This being the recognised sense of the word, it is quite as important for my present purpose to show it to be the sense in which I have myself used 'Reason' in what I have written at various times; though Dr. Fairbairn, as having 'studied' all my books (p. 663), must be well aware of it already. For instance:

First, I discard the vague popular sense of it as the distinguishing gift of man in contrast with the brute creation. 'Sometimes,' I say, 'it stands for all in which man differs from the brutes; and so it includes in its signification the faculty of distinguishing between right and wrong and the directing principle of conduct. In this sense certainly I do not here use it.' (*Univ. Serm.*, p. 58.)

This is but a negative account of it, but in another Sermon I speak more distinctly. 'By the exercise of reason is properly meant any process or act of the mind, by which, from knowing one thing, it advances on to know another.' (*Ibid*, p. 223.)

Again: 'It is obvious that even our senses convey us but a little way out of ourselves, and introduce us to the external world only under circumstances, under conditions of time and place, and of certain media through which they act. We must be near things to touch them; we must be interrupted by no simultaneous sounds in order to hear them; we must have light to see them; we can neither see, hear, nor touch things past or future. Now, Reason is that faculty of the mind by which this deficiency is supplied; by which knowledge of things external to us — of beings, facts, and events — is attained beyond the range of sense; . . . it brings us knowledge, whether clear or uncertain, still knowledge, in whatever degree of perfection, from every side; but, at the same time, with this characteristic, that it obtains it indirectly, not directly, . . . on the hypothesis of something else . . . being assumed to be true.' (*Ibid*, p. 206)

And again: 'Reason, according to the simplest view of it, is the faculty of gaining knowledge without direct perception, or of ascertaining one thing by means of another. In this way it is able, from small beginnings, to create to itself a world of ideas, which do or do not correspond to the things themselves for which they stand, or are true or not according as it is exercised soundly or otherwise.' (Vide *Serm.* xiii, p. 256).

§ 4

The result of this use of 'Reason.'

These passages of mine are on subjects of their own; but they will serve the purpose of making clear the account which in times past, as now, I have given of the reasoning faculty; and, in doing so, I have implied how great a faculty it is. In its versatility, its illimitable range, its subtlety, its power of concentrating many ideas on one point, it is for the acquisition of knowledge all-important or rather necessary, with this drawback, however, in its ordinary use, that in every exercise of it, it depends for success upon the assumption of prior acts similar to that which it has itself involved, and therefore is reliable only conditionally. Its process is a passing from an antecedent to a consequent, and according as the start so is the issue. In the province of religion, if it be under the happy guidance of the moral sense,[1] and with teachings which are not only assumptions in form but certainties in fact, it will arrive at indisputable truth, and then the house is at peace; but if it be in the hands of enemies, who are under the delusion that their arbitrary assumptions are self-evident axioms, the reasoning will start from false premises, and the mind will be in a state of melancholy disorder. But in no case need the reasoning faculty itself be to blame or responsible, except when identified with the assumptions of which it is the instrument. I repeat, it is but an instrument; as such I have viewed it, and no one but Dr. Fairbairn would say as he does — that the bad employment of a faculty was a 'division,' a 'contradiction,' and 'a radical antagonism of nature,' and 'the death of the natural proof' of a God. The eyes, and the hands, and the tongue, are instruments in their very nature. We may speak of a wanton eye, and a murderous hand, and a blaspheming tongue, without denying that they can be used for good purposes as well as for bad.

---

[1] Vide *Art.* III, §§ 2 and 4. [In a reprint of the article 'The Development of Religious Error', *Contemporary Review* (October 1885), reprinted by Burns Oates 1886, there is no reference as in *Stray Essays* and the note reads: 'I believe that some philosophers, as Kant, would speak of the Moral Sense as a Divine Reason. Of course I have no difficulty in accepting "Reason" in this sense: but I have not so used it myself.']

§ 5

Its use as recognised by other writers.

Such, in accordance with received English literature, is the sense in which I have used the word 'Reason,' and not in the sense of foreign writers. It must by no means then be supposed that I think a natural faculty of man to have been revolutionized, because an enemy of truth has availed itself of it for evil purposes. This is what Dr. Fairbairn imputes to me, for I hold, it seems, that 'in spite of the conscience there is' not a little 'latent atheism in the nature, and especially in the reason, of man' (p. 665). Here he has been misled by the epithets which I attached in the *Apologia* to the Reason, as viewed in its continuous strenuous action against religious truth, both in and outside the Catholic body. I will explain why I did so. I had been referring to the fall of man, and our Catechisms tell us that the Fall opened upon him three great spiritual enemies, the World, the Flesh, and the Devil, which need to be resisted by means natural and supernatural. I was led by my general subject to select one of the three for my remarks, and to ask how it acted, and by what instruments? The instruments of the Evil One are best known to himself; the Flesh needs no instruments; the Reasoning Faculty is the instrument of the World. The World is that vast community impregnated by religious error which mocks and rivals the Church by claiming to be its own witness, and to be infallible. Such is the World, the False Prophet (as I called it fifty years ago), and Reasoning is its voice. I had in my mind such Apostolic sayings as 'Love not the world, neither the things of the world,' and 'A friend of the world is the enemy of God;' but I was very loth, as indeed I am also now on the present occasion, to *preach*. Instead then of saying 'the World's Reason,' I said 'Reason actually and historically,' 'Reason in fact and concretely in fallen man,' 'Reason in the educated intellect of England, France, and Germany,' Reason in 'every Government and every civilization through the world which is under the influence of the European mind,' Reason in the 'wild living intellect of man,' which needs (to have) 'its stiff neck bent,' that ultra 'freedom of thought, which is in itself one of the greatest of our natural gifts,' 'that deep, plausible scepticism' which is 'the development of human reason as practically exercised by the natural man.' That is, Reason as wielded by the Living World, against the teaching of the Infallible Church.

And I was sanctioned in thus speaking by St. Paul's parallel use of the word 'Wisdom,' which is one of the highest gifts given to man, and which, nevertheless, he condemns, considered as the World's Wisdom, pronouncing that 'the World by Wisdom knew not God.'

§ 6

The sense of 'Reason' as superseded and perverted by other writers.

In thus shifting the blame of hostility to religion from man reasoning to man collective, I may seem to be imputing to a divine ordinance (for such human society is) what I have disclaimed to be imputing to man's gift of reason; but this is to mistake my meaning. The World is a collection of individual men, and any one of them may hold and take on himself to profess unchristian doctrine, and do his best to propagate it; but few have the power for such a work, or the opportunity. It is by their union into one body, by the intercourse of man with man and the sympathy thence arising, that error spreads and becomes an authority. Its separate units which make up the body rely upon each other, and upon the whole, for the truth of their assertions; and thus assumptions and false reasonings are received without question as certain truths, on the credit of alternate appeals and mutual cheers and *imprimaturs*.

I should like, if I could, to give a specimen of these assumptions, and the reasonings founded on them, which in my *Apologia* I considered to be 'corrosive' of all religion; but before doing so, I must guard against misconstruction of what I am proposing. First, I am not proposing to carry on an argument against Dr. Fairbairn, whose own opinions, to tell the truth, I have not a dream of; but I would gladly explain, or rather complete on particular points, the statements I have before now made in several works about Faith and Reason. Next, I can truly say that, neither in those former writings nor now, have I particular authors in mind who are or are said to be prominent teachers in what I should call the school of the World. Such an undertaking would require a volume, instead of half a dozen pages such as these, and the study too of many hard questions; and I repeat, here I am attempting little more than to fill up a few of the *lacunæ* to be found in a chapter of the *Apologia*, which, like the rest of the book, had to be written *extempore*; certainly I have no intention here of entering into controversy. And further, I wish to call attention to a passage in one of my St. Mary's Sermons,[1] headed, 'The World our Enemy,' which is not directly on the subject of religious error, but still is applicable when I would fain clear myself in what I am saying of falling unintentionally into any harsh and extreme judgments. A few sentences will be enough to show the drift with which I quote it.

'There is a question,' I say, 'which it will be well to consider, viz., how far the world is a separate body from the Church of God. The two are certainly contrasted in Scripture, but the Church, so far from being literally and in fact separate from the world, is within it. The Church is a body, gathered together indeed in the world, but only in a process of separation from it. The world's power is over the Church, because the Church has gone forth into the world to save the world. All Christians are in the world and of the world, so far as Evil still has dominion over them, and not even the best of us is clean every whit from sin. Though then, in our idea of the one and the other, and in their principles and in their future prospects, the Church is one thing and the World is another, yet in present matter of fact the Church is of the World, not separate from it; for the grace of God has but partial possession even of religious men, and the best that can be said of us is that we have two sides, a

---

[1] [*Parochial and Plain Sermons*, VII, pp. 25 ff.]

light side and a dark, and that the dark happens to be the outermost. Thus we form part of the world to each other, though we be not *of* the world. Even supposing there were a society of men influenced individually by Christian motives, still, this society, viewed as a whole, would be a worldly one; I mean a society holding and maintaining many errors, and countenancing many bad practices. Evil ever floats on the top' (*Sermons*, vol. vii, p. 35–36). In accordance with these cautions I will here avow that good men may imbibe to their great disadvantage the spirit of the world, and, on the contrary, inferior men may keep themselves comparatively clear of it.

§ 7

Illustrations in point.

These explanations being made, I take up the serious protest which I began in the *Apologia*. I say then that if, as I believe, the world, which the Apostles speak of so severely as a False Prophet,[1] is identical with what we call human Society now, then there never was a time since Christianity was, when, together with the superabundant temporal advantages which by it may come to us, it had the opportunity of being a worse enemy to religion and religious truth than it is likely to be in the years now opening upon mankind. I say so, because in its width and breadth it is so much better educated and informed than it ever was before, and because of its extent, so multiform and almost ubiquitous. Its conquests in the field of physical science, and its intercommunion of place with place, are a source to it both of pride and of enthusiasm. It has triumphed over time and space; knowledge it has proved to be emphatically power; no problems of the universe — material, moral, or religious — are too great for its ambitious essay and its high will to master. There is one obstacle in its path, I mean the province of religion. But can religion hope to be successful? It is thought to be already giving way before the presence of what the world considers a new era in the history of man.

§ 8

As proved in argument.

With these thoughts in my mind, I understand how it has come to pass, what has struck me as remarkable, that the partizans and spokesmen of Society, when they come to the question of religion, seem to care so little about proving what they maintain, and, on the warrant of their philosophy, are content silently and serenely to take by implication their first principles for granted, as if, like the teachers of Christianity, they were inspired and infallible. To the World, indeed, its own principles are infallible, and need no proof. Now if its representatives would but be candid, and say that their assumptions, as ours, are infallible, we should know where they stand; there

---

[1] Vide *University Sermons*, "Contrast between Faith and Sight." [i.e. "*Contest* . . ." pp. 120 ff.]

would be an end of controversy. As I have said before now, 'Half the controversies in the world, could they be brought to a plain issue, would be brought to a prompt termination. Parties engaged in them would then perceive . . . that in substance . . . their difference was of first principles. . . . When men understand what each other means, they see for the most part that controversy is either superfluous or hopeless' (*Univ. Serm.*, p. 200–1). The World, then, has its first principles of religion, and so have we. If this were understood, I should not have any present cause of protest against its Reason as corrosive of our faith. I do not grudge the World its gods, its principles, and its worship; but I protest against its sending them into Christian lecture rooms, libraries, societies, and companies, as if they were Christian — criticising, modelling, measuring, altering, improving, as it thinks, our doctrines, principles, and methods of thought, which we refer to divine informants. One of my *University Sermons*, in 1831, is on this subject; it is called 'The Usurpations of Reason,' and I have nothing to change in the substance of it. I was very jealous of 'the British Association' at its commencement, not as if science were not a divine gift, but because its first members seemed to begin with a profession of Theism, when I said their business was to keep to their own range of subjects. I argued that if they began with Theism, they would end with Atheism. At the end of half a century I have still more reason to be suspicious of the upshot of secular schools. Not, of course, that I suppose that the flood of unbelief will pour over us in its fulness at once. A large inundation requires a sufficient time, and there are always in the worst times witnesses for the Truth to stay the plague.[1] Above all things there is the Infallible Church, of which I spoke so much in the *Apologia*.[2] With this remark I am led on to another subject.

§ 9

Its bearing on dogmatic fact.

I will take an illustration of the prospect before us in the instance of a doctrine which is more than most the subject of dispute just now. Lest I should be mistaken, I avow myself, while holding it, to do so, not because of the disintegrating consequences of letting it go, but on the simple word of the Divine Informant; yet I want to show the prospective development of error where Faith is not. A hundred years ago the God of Christianity was called a God of mere benevolence. That could not long be maintained, first, because He was the God of the Old Testament as well as of the New, and next and specially because the New Testament opened upon us the Woe thrice uttered by the Judge himself, the Woe unquenchable which is denounced upon transgressors.[3] But the instinct of modern civilization denies the very idea of such a doom in the face of a progressive future. As to the Old Testament, it has

---

[1] Vide one of my *University Sermons*, "Personal Influence the means of propagating the Truth."

[2] [Chapter V, pp. 245 ff.]

[3] Vide *S. Marc*, ix, 43, 45, 47, Vulg.

been comparatively easy to loosen its connection with Christianity; but how shall we release ourselves from the strong unequivocal teaching of the New? And, before we consider it, let me ask, is there nothing in the history of mankind to bring home to us that there exists a world of evil as well as a world of good? Is there not now — has there not ever been — a vast aggregate of sin and suffering, of intense weary pain, bodily and mental, of wicked self-consuming passions and their widespread destructiveness, occupying the earth for an unknown succession of centuries? Consider only the long pain and anguish, which are the ordinary accompaniments of death. Supposing mankind to have lasted many thousand years, the suffering has been just as long; there has been no interval of rest.

This for the past and present; but you will say that to each who suffers here suffering has an end and is comparatively brief, and that this is not a difficulty to be compared to that of suffering which is to be for ever, and that you cannot receive the teaching of Scripture, if the word 'eternal' there used of future punishment must be taken to mean everlasting: — Indeed? would you really then be content if such an interpretation of the word 'eternal' as you desire were conceded to you? Do you want nothing more? What is the nature of the punishment as defined in Scripture? Fire. You will say this is a figure of speech; even granting it, still, figures are representations of fact, and must not be explained away. Besides, Dives speaks of 'torments,' and more than once or twice we read of 'wailing and gnashing of teeth.' This being considered, what time do you contemplate as being represented by the word 'eternal?' an aeon? a thousand years? I do not believe it — you would not be satisfied, though the period was contracted to a hundred, nay to fifty, or to twenty, or to a dozen; not satisfied, though it be granted, or rather explained, that the degrees of punishment are numberless. In spite of the word of Scripture, your imagination would carry you away; it is a subject beyond you; it is not duration that is your supreme difficulty, rather it is pain. We have no positive notion of suffering in relation to simple duration. Time and eternity are not qualities of suffering; nor is punishment *therefore* infinite, because it is without end. What we know about the eternal state is negative, that there is no future when it will not be. All that is necessary for us to be told is that the state of good and evil is irreversible. We know there will be a judgment and a final decision. 'After death, judgment,' and before it a trial in order to it. Such a dispensation of things is revealed as definite, as once for all. If this, too, is denied, as it probably will be, then another Christian doctrine goes.

§ 10

Digressions in consequence.

But again, the Scripture announcement of the Last Judgment may be viewed in another aspect: — what do we know of the obstacles to a reconciliation between God and man? Suppose the punishment is self-inflicted;

suppose it is the will, the proud determination of the lost to breathe defiance to his Maker, or the utter loathing of His Presence or His Court, which makes a reconciliation with Him impossible. To change such a one may be to destroy his identity. Moreover, what do we know of the rules necessary for the moral government of the universe? What acts of judgment are or are not compatible or accordant with the bearing of a Just Judge? and by what self-evident process do we ascertain this? What of His knowledge who is able to 'search the heart?' We are told He is one who 'overcomes when He is judged;' ought we not to have the whole case spread out for us, as it will be at the Last Day, before we venture to pronounce upon its details? they are parts of a whole. Go to what is the root of the mystery, and tell us what is the Origin of Evil. Solve this, and you may see your way to dispose of other difficulties. Does not this greatest of mysteries, the 'Origin and prevalence of Evil,' fall as heavily upon Natural Religion as future punishment upon Revelation? After all, the Theist needs Faith as well as the Christian. All religion has its mysteries, and all mysteries are correlative with faith; and, where faith is absent, the action of relentless 'reason,' under the assumptions of educated society, passes on (as I have given offence by asserting) from Catholicity to Theism, and from Theism to a materialistic cause of all things. Dr. Fairbairn calls it sceptical to preach Faith, and to practise it.

§ 11

'The Atonement' or 'Divine Reconciliation.'

I have confined myself to the Divine Judgment; but this is only one of the doctrines which the abolition of the Woe to come is made to compromise. Here again modern philosophy acts to the injury of religion, natural and revealed. Those solemn warnings of Scripture against disobedience to the law of right and wrong are but fellows of the upbraidings and menaces of the human Conscience. The belief in future punishment will not pass away without grave prejudice to that high Monitor. Are you, in weakening its warning voice, to lose an ever-present reminder of an Unseen God? It is a bad time to lose that voice when efforts so serious have so long been making to resolve it into some intellectual principle or secular motive. But there is another doctrine, too, that suffers when future punishment is tampered with, namely, what is commonly called the 'Atonement.' The Divine Victim took the place of man: how will this doctrine stand, if the final doom of the wicked is denied? Every one who escapes the penalty of pain, escapes it by virtue of the Atonement made instead of it; but so great a price as was paid for the remission supposes an unimaginable debt. If the need was not immense, would such a Sacrifice have been called for? Does not that Sacrifice throw a fearful light upon the need of it? And if the need be denied, will not the Sacrifice be unintelligible? The early martyrs give us their sense of it; they considered their torments as a deliverance from their full deserts, and felt that, had they recanted, it would have been at the risk of their eternal welfare. The Great Apostle is in his writings full of gratitude to the Power who has 'delivered us from the wrath to come.' It is a foundation of the whole spiritual fabric on which his life is built. What remains of his Christianity if he is no longer to be penetrated by the thought of that second death from which he had been now delivered? Further, what becomes of the doctrine of the Incarnation? Can the religion with which Society at present threatens us be the same as the Apostle's, if these solemn doctrines are in this Religion and not in that?

§ 12

The need of dogma.

Shall I be answered that it is only dogma that is left out in modern Christianity? I understand; dogma is unnecessary for faith, because faith is but a sentiment; vicarious suffering is an injustice; spiritual benefits cannot be wrought by material instruments; sin is but a weakness or an ignorance; this life has nearer claims on us than the next; the nature of man is sufficient for itself; the rule of law admits no miracles; and so on. There is any number of these assumptions ready for the nonce, and there is Micio's axiom in the Play, soon, perhaps, to come upon us, 'Non est flagitium, mihi crede, adolescentulum scortari.'[1] When Reason starts from assumptions such as these, its corrosive quality ought to be sufficient to satisfy Dr. Fairbairn.

This is all I think it necessary to set down in explanation of passages in my *Apologia*. As to my other writings, I can safely leave them to take care of themselves. Anyone that looks into them will see how strangely Principal Fairbairn has misrepresented them

N.B.—*The paging, inquotations made, as above, from 'The Contemporary Review,' May, 1885, follows the paging of that work, viz., pp. 665, 667.*

The following Sections are appended to the Article from 'The Contemporary Review.'

§ 13

On Philosophical Scepticism.

Principal Fairbairn, in his Article in the *Contemporary* of December, 1885, as an answer to my explanation in October, has repeated his charges against me with much vehemence, but, as I hope to show, with small success. He still considers me as thinking and writing on a foundation of 'underlying scepticism:' he calls it however philosophical scepticism, by which I understand him to mean a sort of scepticism which I am not aware of myself; at least I can only suppose that he contrasts philosophical with personal. Though I do not understand the distinction, I am glad to receive from him a token of good feeling and courtesy such as I believe this to be.

[1] [Terence, *Adelphi*, I. ii. 22.]

He says that I am only a philosophic sceptic, and that he has taken considerable pains to bring this home to me. He says, 'What he (the Cardinal) was charged with, and in terms so careful and guarded as ought to have excluded all possible misconceptions, was 'metaphysical or philosophical' scepticism.' This sort of scepticism he proceeds to define, but I fear I cannot call him happy in his attempt. He defines it as 'a system which . . . subjectively affirms the impotence of human reason for the discovery of truth.'[1] Such a definition (in religious questions, as in the case before us) is seriously incomplete. If it be taken in its letter, I certainly cannot deny that it has proved me to be a sceptic, for I do affirm the impotence of human reason for the discovery of a great many truths; but then it has done so at the expense of convicting of scepticism all Catholics, besides all theologians of the Greek Church and all orthodox Anglicans. Dr. Fairbairn's definition tells against all whosoever hold on faith the great truths of Revelation, such as the Holy Trinity and the Incarnation, and beyond all mistake includes in its imputation the Vatican Council itself, which expressly anathematises any one who shall say 'that in Divine Revelation there are contained no true and properly so called mysteries, but that all the dogmas of faith can be understood and demonstrated from natural principles by means of Reason properly cultivated.' If to deny the omnipotence of reason in the discovery of truth is scepticism, I am in good company.

Let me take a more exact and adequate definition of scepticism, and see if I fall under it. The definition of scepticism to which I am myself accustomed is such as this: 'Scepticism is the system which holds that no certainty is attainable, as not in other things so not in questions of religious truth and error.' How have I incurred this reproach? On the contrary, I have not only asserted, with a strength of words which has sometimes incurred censure, my belief in religious truth, but have insisted on the certainty of such truth, and on Certitude as having a place among the constituents of human thought; — analysing it, discriminating it, and giving tests of it, with a direct apprehension and manipulation quite incompatible with my never asking myself whether intellectually I was in any sense a sceptic or not. It seems to me that the charge of scepticism which has been used against me elsewhere, as well as in England, is a mere idle word, serviceable in an intellectual combat; and I think it would be more charitable in opponents if, instead of imputing it to any dissatisfaction which I have at any time expressed with certain arguments used in Catholic controversy, they ascribed it, not to an underlying scepticism as to the truths in dispute, but rather to an unmeasured and even reckless confidence in them, or, again, to an attempt to test the availableness at the present time of certain conventional proofs used for polemical purposes.

---

[1] Dr Fairbairn's words are, 'Scepticism in philosophy means a system which affirms either subjectively, the impotence of the reason for the discovery of the truth, or objectively, the inaccessibility of truth to the reason.'

§ 14

On the Meaning of the word 'Reason.'

So much on Dr. Fairbairn's definition of what he considers the 'philosophical' scepticism which runs through all my writings. And now I come to what seems to him a main instance of it — my account of Reason considered as the faculty of reasoning. Here he drops his unfortunate attempt at defining; at least he does not tell us what Reason is, as far as I can make out, but he is severe in pronouncing it to be constitutive, architectonic, true, and religious; whereas, in my idea of it, it is a mere instrument, 'an inferential instrument,' from which nothing great can come. He says, 'What works as a mere instrument never handles what it works in, the things remain outside it, and have no place or standing within its being . . . To a reason without religious character . . . truth is inaccessible. . . This is philosophical scepticism.' I am quite ready to meet him on this new ground of argument. He says that Reason, as I consider it, is necessarily sceptical; let us see.

Here, first, I must protest against its being magisterially ruled by Dr. Fairbairn that the word Reason has one and one only definite scientific meaning, accepted by all authorities in metaphysics, and incapable of any other; whereas, before coming to the question of particular words and phrases, I really wish it settled whether there is a recognised science of metaphysics at all. Certainly in 1831 and the following years the terminology which he takes for granted was little known in Oxford,[1] nor indeed any terminology but Aristotle's; much less were any words or definitions taken for stereotyped truths. I have no great remorse that for fifty years I have used my native tongue as a vehicle for religious and ethical discussions; in this instance, indeed, with the sanction of a writer who is commonly called *par excellence* our lexicographer. Provided I am careful to record the senses in which I use words, it is not the part of a fair critic to take them in another sense, and in that sense to be tragic in his reprobation of them. My turn of mind has never led me towards metaphysics; rather it has been logical, ethical, practical. As to the word 'Reason,' it would have been a strange digression had I, in speaking of the religious state of Europe, entered into an account of the faculties of the human mind and the analysis which has been made of them by various metaphysicians.

Here it is very pertinent to quote in my favour the remarks of Sir William Hamilton; they will protect me in the acts of private judgment which are so offensive to Dr. Fairbairn.

'"Reason,"' he says, 'is a very vague, vacillating, and equivocal word. . . . Throwing aside its employment in most languages for *cause, motive, argument,*

---

[1] I am not forgetful of Mr. Johnson's translation of Tennemann, in 1832, but I doubt if it was much read. [*A Manual of the History of Philosophy*, translated from the German of Ternemann, by Arthur Johnson, Oxford 1832.]

etc., considering it only as a philosophical word, denoting a faculty or complement of faculties, in this relation it is found employed in the following meanings, not only by different individuals, but frequently to a greater or less extent by the same philosopher. . . . Nothing can be more vague and various than his (Kant's) employment of the word (Reason) . . . but even in his (Kant's) abusive employment of the term, . . . no consistency was maintained.' (*Hamilton on Reid*, Note A, § v. 7.)

In this latitude and confusion of the terminology found among professed metaphysicians I think I have a right to my own way of regarding the faculty of Reason, whether I fail in it or not; and that the more because, while I am following the English use of the word, it is a personal satisfaction to me to be able also to believe that I am adhering to the ecclesiastical. At least Gregory the 16th, Pius the 9th, and the Vatican Council, when they would speak of 'proving' and of 'demonstrating,' refer the act of the mind to 'human reason.'[1]

§ 15

On the Faculty of Reason.

When, then, in times past I have wished to express my anxiety lest serious dangers might be in store for educated society, my first business was to determine what sense I ought to give to the word 'Reason,' claimed by Rationalists as if specially belonging to themselves. The only senses of it which I knew — nay, which I know of it now — are two: in one of the two senses it seems to be a synonyme for 'Mind,' as used in contrast with the condition of brutes. This is far too broad an account of it to be of service in such a purpose as my own, and in consequence I have been thrown of necessity on the sense which is its alternative, viz., that reason is the faculty of reasoning; and though such a view of it does not suggest that venerable and sovereign idea which we usually attach to 'Reason,' still, as I was not writing metaphysics, but with an ethical and social view, I did not find any great inconvenience in taking the word in its popular, etymological, and, as I hope, ecclesiastical acceptation.

To such a view of Reason however Dr. Fairbairn objects, as leading to scepticism; but I have never thought, as he supposes, of leaving truth to so untrustworthy a protection as reasoning by itself would be to it. The mind without any doubt is made for truth. Still, it does not therefore follow that truth is its object in all its powers. The imagination is a wonderful faculty in the cause of truth, but it often subserves the purposes of error — so do our most innocent affections. Every faculty has its place. There is a faculty in the mind which acts as a complement to reasoning, and as having truth for its direct object thereby secures its use for rightful purposes. This faculty,

---

[1] Gregor. XVI. In causa Bautain, 1840; 'Ratio cum certitudine authenticitatem Revelationis *probat*.' Pius Encyc., 1846: '*Recta* ratio fidei veritatem *demonstrat*.' Concil. Vatican., 1870: '*Recta* ratio fidei fundamenta *demonstrat*.' And it speaks of 'argumenta humanae rationis.' The 'lumen rationis' I will notice presently. Vide also contrast between antecedent opinion and pre-existent truth in my *University Sermons*. [pp. 197–201].

viewed in its relation to religion, is, as I have before said, the moral sense; but it has a wider subject-matter than religion, and a more comprehensive office and scope, as being 'the apprehension of first principles,' and Aristotle has taught me to call it νοῦς, or the *noetic* faculty.[1]

§ 16

On the Action of Reason as determined and regulated by other Faculties.

How this faculty of νοῦς bears upon the action of reasoning scarcely requires many words. I have considered Reasoning as an instrument — that is, an instrument for the use of other faculties, for who ever heard of an instrument without there being, as I have taken for granted, some distinct power to make use of it? Now to know what the reasoning faculty needs for the purposes of religion we must consider it, not in its abstract idea, but in the concrete. When so viewed, it includes an antecedent and a consequent, and it is at once plain what is the connecting link between it and (for instance) the noetic faculty. The antecedent of the reasoning is that link; for the matter (as it is called) of the antecedent belongs both to the reasoning and also to those other faculties, many or few, which have for their object the antecedent.[2] Great faculty as reasoning certainly is, it is from its very nature in all subjects dependent upon other faculties. It receives from them the antecedent with which its action starts; and when this antecedent is true, there is no longer in religious matters room for any accusation against it of scepticism. In such matters the independent faculty which is mainly necessary for its healthy working and the ultimate warrant of the reasoning act, I have hitherto spoken of as the moral sense; but, as I have already said, it has a wider subject-matter than religion, and a larger name than moral sense, as including intuitions, and this is what Aristotle calls νοῦς.

Here I am struck by what I must call the aridity of Dr. Fairbairn's polemic. What could be more natural, what more congruous, than that there should be a faculty which was concerned with the antecedent of the reasoning, as the reasoning itself is concerned with the consequent, so that the two faculties unite in a joint act, each of the two having need of the other? But instead of accepting this division and arrangement of work, Dr. Fairbairn, I must insist, ungraciously refuses to see a harmony in such an association of two great faculties, and makes them enemies and rivals, as if I inordinately exalted the moral sense and crushed the reason.

---

[1] ἐπιστήμη, Aristotle's second faculty, conversant with necessary truth, answers well (analogically) to Reason, as I am considering it. (Vide Chase on Aristotle's ἐπιστήμη, p. 201). [D. P. Chase, *A First Logic Book*, Oxford 1875.]

[2] *E.g.*, we may *hope* for a revelation by reason of the *divine goodness*. Here the 'hope,' which is the consequent of the reasoning, is arrived at by the antecedent the 'divine goodness,' which antecedent not only belongs to the reasoning but to the faculty of theology also, being a truth belonging to its subject-matter. To put it otherwise, (1) the *hope* of a revelation (2) depends on the *divine goodness*, (3) and the divine goodness depends on theology, therefore the reasoning is regulated by theology.

I have been speaking of antecedents which are true; other antecedents may be founded on error. Dr. Fairbairn speaks as if the fact that the faculty of reason can be exercised on false antecedents as well as on true, opens a way to scepticism. That depends on what is meant by reason; my own account of the faculty may be wrong, but at least it has no such tendency. If it has, then all I need say is that since writers in general speak of a right and a wrong use of reason, Dr. Fairbairn, I suppose, would consider them sceptics too. Still, what else can a man mean by speaking of a right use but that there is a wrong? — right, because its antecedents are chosen rightly by the divinely enlightened mind, being such as intuitions, dictates of conscience, the inspired Word, the decisions of the Church, and the like; whereas we call it false reason or sophistry when its antecedents are determined by pride, self-trust, unbelief, human affection, narrow self-interest, bad education, or other mental agencies, which are found in the world and in the individual. It corroborates my doctrine of these two aspects of reason that, as if with the same drift of marking the broad difference between one aspect of the reasoning faculty and the other, ecclesiastical treatises speak of the '*lumen* rationis,' as they speak of the '*recta* ratio,' as if there was a use of reason which was really darkness.

§ 17

On the Mind's Faculties existing, not 're,' but 'ratione,' and therefore only abstract names for its operations.

I have tried in the above pages, as in my original article, to explain with all necessary precision and clearness what I understand, whether rightly or wrongly, by the faculty of Reason, and what is the office which I attribute to it. I wonder whether it is a fault of mine that I do not find myself able to discern a like frankness on the part of Principal Fairbairn. Perhaps if he had informed me what he meant by 'Reason,' as I have myself freely expressed my own account of it, it would be easier to me to understand his logic; but he seems to me to heap up epithets of praise upon what he calls Reason without telling us what Reason is. In this he is unfair to himself; for how can a disputant hope to recommend to others what he has not yet himself taken the pains to master? I will give a few instances out of many of this mistake in him.

He arrays against me a sufficient number of *dicta*, which in their form seem to be meant for axioms, but which I must call unintelligible. Here are specimens of them:

1. 'The reasoning process, to be valid, must proceed from principles valid to the *reason*.' In what sense does he here use the word Reason? Does he mean the reasoning faculty or the noetic? — though as an argument against me it does not matter to me which. If he means the reasoning, I do not admit what is simply an assumption; if the noetic, since in that case I agree with him, it does me no harm.

2. 'To use principles truly, one must be able to judge concerning their

truth.' Certainly; just as to use scientific terms rightly we must first give their definitions; but we judge of the truth of principles by the appropriate faculty, and not by a faculty which is not concerned with them. We cannot speak of Reason — that is, Reasoning — as *judging* truth; it does but *treat* of it. The judgment lies in the antecedent, and in the particular faculty to which the antecedent belongs.

3. 'How can Reason truly and justly act, even as a mere instrument of inference, on the basis of premises which it neither found, nor framed, nor verified, being indeed so constituted as not to be able to do any one of these things?' How? By looking for means of doing so in the right direction. There cannot be an act of reasoning without an antecedent, and to determine the antecedent we must use the particular faculty to which the antecedent's subject-matter belongs. In questions of religion it is mainly the noetic, sometimes another; in mathematics, the noetic faculty only. That particular faculty would be able to 'find, frame, and verify,' which was 'so constituted' as to be able 'to do any one of these things.' Why will Dr. Fairbairn persist in proving that the reasoning faculty cannot do its own work because it cannot do the work of another faculty?

4. Here is another instance of Dr. Fairbairn's finding it easier to attack my account of 'Reason' than to state his own. He says I make it 'a deductive instrument, void of God, and never able to know Him directly or for itself,' p. 850. The answer to this depends upon what he means by Reason: it is the same fallacy all through. He argues with two contrary views of Reason in his hands at the same time, and uses one of them to refute the other. But this is not all; he speaks as if faculties were something real and substantive; whereas they are no more than simple powers. Void of God — that is, I suppose, of religion! Why every faculty may be said to be void of the objects of every other faculty: imagination is void of memory, memory of sense, and so on. A faculty is as little capable of being 'emptied' and made 'void' as the act of reading or writing. It is the exercise of a power of the mind itself, and that *pro re nata*; and, when the mind ceases to use it, we may almost say that it is nowhere. Of course, for convenience, we speak of the mind as possessing faculties instead of saying that it acts in a certain way and on a definite subject-matter; but we must not turn a figure of speech into a fact.

§ 18

On Final Causes.

I consider I have said enough to show that whatever criticisms may fairly be made on the view I have taken of the faculty of reason, they do not bear out Dr. Fairbairn's charge that the view itself is in its nature sceptical, and is used by me with a purpose. But he has a more serious charge in store, very different from anything that has gone before, to which I must now call attention; it is that in this same sceptical spirit I weaken the force of arguments for religion, pronouncing (for instance) that atheism is an hypothesis equally consistent with the phenomena of the physical universe as the hypothesis of a creative intelligence. And, further still, though it is not a subject that I have now immediately before me, that I have wished by such depreciation of the arguments for religion to magnify the teaching of the Catholic Church. I observe as follows:

(1) From the time that I began to occupy my mind with theological subjects I have been troubled at the prospect, which I considered to lie before us, of an intellectual movement against religion, so special as to have a claim upon the attention of all educated Christians. As early as 1826 I wrote, 'As the principles of science are in process of time more fully developed, and become more independent of the religious system, there is much danger lest the philosophical school should be found to separate from the Christian Church, and at length disown the parent to whom it has been so greatly indebted. And this evil has in a measure befallen us,' etc., etc. (*Univ. Serm.*, p. 14). This grave apprehension led me to consider the evidences, as they are called, of Religion generally, and the intellectual theory on which they are based. This I attempted with the purpose, as far as lay in my power, not certainly of starting doubts about religion, but of testing and perfecting the proofs in its behalf. In literal warfare, weapons are tested before they are brought into use, and the men are not called traitors who test them. I am far indeed from being satisfied with my own performances; in my *Apologia* I call them tentative.[1] They might be rash, but they were not sceptical, nor had I in my mind any thought, when thus engaged, of substituting for Christian evidences the word of the 'Infallible Church,' which appears to be Dr. Fairbairn's strange imagination.

(2) Thus I was brought to the popular argument for a Creator drawn from the marks of what is commonly called Design in the physical world. Led on by Lord Bacon, I found I could not give it that high place among the arguments for religion which is almost instinctively accorded to it by a religious mind. Such a mind starts with an assumption which a man who is not religious requires in the first instance to be proved. A believer in God recognises at once, and justly recognises, the marks of design which are innumerable in the structure of the universe, and has his faith and love invigorated and enlarged by the sight of so minute and tender a Providence. But how is an objector to be met who insists that the problem before us is, when viewed in itself, simply which of two hypotheses is the best key to the phenomena of nature — a system founded on cause and effect, or one founded on a purpose and its fulfilment? It is a controversial question, — not as to what is true to hold, but as to what is safe to maintain. Many things are true in fact which cannot be maintained in argument. What is true to one man is not always true to another. Final causes, says Lord Bacon, 'are properly alleged in metaphysics; but in physics are impertinent, and as *remoras* to the ship, that hinder the sciences from holding on their course of improvement, and as introducing a neglect of

[1] [pp. 241 ff., esp. 262-3.]

searching after physical causes.'[1] (Vide my *Idea of a University*, p. 222.) Was Bacon an infidel or a sceptic?

(3) Another point may be urged against Dr. Fairbairn. He argues as if the finding difficulty in the argument from final causes is to be sceptical to the full extent of invalidating the proofs of the being of a God gained from the existence of physical nature. This is far from being the fact; those proofs are not at all affected by any difficulty which may attach to the argument from final causes. The very fact of the universe is quite independent of final causes, and leads to the recognition of a First Cause. Again, it must be recollected that the argument from Design remains, in the large sense of design, as forcible as ever, even though Final Causes are not included in the sense of the word. I will quote a passage to this effect of my own: 'Did we see flint celts, in their various receptacles all over Europe, scored always with certain special and characteristic marks, even though those marks had no assignable meaning or final cause whatever, we should take that very repetition, which indeed is the principle of order, to be a proof of intelligence. The agency, then, which has kept up and keeps up the general laws of nature, energising at once in Sirius and on earth, and on the earth in its primary period as well as in the nineteenth century, must be Mind, and nothing else, and Mind at least as wide and as enduring in its living action as the immeasurable ages and spaces of the universe on which that agency has left its traces.' (Vide *The Grammar of Assent*, p. 72.)

This passage Dr. J. W. Ogle has introduced into his learned *Harveian Oration* of 1880, p. 161, where he also quotes from a letter of mine — 1. 'By design in Creation is generally meant the application of definite means for the attainment of a definite end, or the aim at a final cause. There is a difficulty I consider, in accepting, in this sense, the "argument from design" as a strictly logical proof of a creative Mind in the universe.' 2. 'But design also means *order*, as when we speak of beautiful *designs*, in decorative patterns, in architecture, mosaic, needlework, etc. In this sense of *order*, Design is in every part of the universe, and a proof of an intelligent mind.'[2]

And now, if I come to an abrupt conclusion, it is because I have said all that I have felt it a duty to say in answer to Dr. Fairbairn's criticisms. Perhaps I should not have noticed them at all, had I known that I was to have the advantage of Dr. Barry's able, and, as I consider, successful defence of me, last November[3], though he has taken a larger field for remark than I have felt reason to do.

J.H.N.

---

[1] *De Augment.*, 5.
[2] [See also A. J. Boekraad, *Argument from Conscience.* p. 158.]
[3] ['Catholicism and Reason', the *Contemporary Review*, Nov. 1885.]

Works and Editions Cited in Newman's Papers on Faith and Certainty

ALDRICH, M. *Artis Logicae Rudimenta*, see Mansel, H. L.
ALISON, A., *History of Europe*. 12 vols. Edinburgh 1853–6
ALPHONSUS LIGUORI, ST. *Homo Apostolicus*. 3 vols. Malines 1842
ARISTOTLE. *Nicomachean Ethics*.
BACON, F. *Works*. 12 vols. London 1824
BALMES, JAMES, *Fundamental Philosophy*, translated from the Spanish by Henry F. Brownson, 2 vols. New York 1856
BILLUART, C. R. *Cursus Theologiae*. 3 vols. Brescia 1836–8
BONELLI, A. *Institutiones Logico-Metaphysicae*. 2 vols. Rome 1846
BREWSTER, SIR, D. *Memoirs of the Life, Writings and Discoveries of Sir Isaac Newton* Edinburgh 1855
BROWN, T. *Lectures on the Philosophy of the Human Mind*. Edinburgh 1851
Buckingham and Chandos, Duke of *Memoirs of the Court and Cabinets of George the third*. London 1855
    Memoirs of the Courts and Cabinets of William the fourth and Victoria. London 1861
BUTLER, Joseph *Works*. 2 vols. Edinburgh 1813
CARLYLE, T. *History of the French Revolution*. 2 vols. London 1857
CLARKE, SAMUEL. *Works*. 4 vols. London 1738
COOK, JAMES. *An Account of the Voyages undertaken by the Order of His Present Majesty for making Discoveries in the Southern Hemisphere*. London 1773
COPLESTON, E. *Praelectiones Academicae Oxonii Habitae*. Oxford 1813
DMOWSKI, J. A. *Institutiones Philosophicae*. 2 vols. Rome 1843
FRANKLIN, B. *Works*. London 1835
GERDIL, G. S. *Opere, edite et inedite*. 20 vols. Rome 1806–21
HAMILTON, W. *Lectures on Metaphysics*. London 1853
KANT, I. *Critique of Pure Reason*. London 1855
LUGO, J. de *Theologia Scholastica*. Lyons 1647
MACAULAY, T. B. *Essays*. London 1851
MANSEL, H. L. *Artis Logicae Rudimenta from the Text of Aldrich, with Notes and Marginal References*. Oxford 1862
MAX MULLER, F. *Lectures on the Science of Language*. London 1861
MILL, J. S. *A System of Logic, Ratiocinative and Inductive*, 2 vols. London 1851
NICOLAS, A. *Etudes philosophiques sur le Christianisme*. Brussels 1849
PASCAL, B. *Thoughts on Religion and Philosophy*. Glasgow 1838
PERRONE, G. *Praelectiones Theologicae*. 9 vols. Rome 1840–4
PORT ROYAL. *Logique ou l'art de penser*. Paris 1724
    Logic, or the Art of Thinking: being the Port Royal Logic, translated by T. S Baynes. Edinburgh 1850
REID, T. *Collected Writings*, edited by Sir William Hamilton. Edinburgh 1858
SCARAMELLI, J. J. *Direttorio ascetico*. Venice 1784
S. SULPITII PRESBYTER. *Compendium Philosophiae ad usum Seminariorum*, 3 vols Paris 1856
TANDEL, E. *Cours de Logique*. Liège 1844
UBAGHS, G. C. *Logicae seu Philosophiae Rationalis Elementa*. Louvain 1844
VALENTIA, G. de *Commentariorum Theologicorum*. 4 vols. Ingolstadt 1592
VIVA, D. *Cursus Theologicus*. 2 vols. Padua 1755
WALENBURCH, AD. and P. *Tractatus generales de controversiis Fidei*. Cologne 1670
WHATELY, R. *Elements of Logic*. London 1826
WHEWELL, W. *Philosophy of the Inductive Sciences*. 2 vols. London 1847
WOOD, JAMES. *The Principles of Mechanics*. Cambridge 1795

Appendix

LETTER OF DECEMBER 1859 TO CHARLES MEYNELL ON ECONOMY AND RESERVE[1]

not sent

My dear Dr Meynell,

... Mr Mansell's doctrine has met with sufficient opposition among Protestant divines, to make me look narrowly to what I have myself before now said upon the subject which he treats, especially since he actually quotes a passage from me.[2] Now, it is my misfortune that I never have had opportunity to study the question thoroughly, and with the aid of Catholic treatises, and therefore, if I am going to say any thing rash, I wish it unsaid, and what the Church would have me say said instead of it. With this preface I remark as follows:—

St Paul says, 'Videmus nunc per speculum in aenigmate'; commenting on this in loc. St Thomas, if I rightly understand his Latin, says, that there are three ways in which a thing may be seen: 1. per *sui* praesentiam in re vidente, as Almighty God sees Himself, or as the eye sees light: 2. per praesentiam suae *similitudinis*, as perhaps the Angels see God, or as the eye sees the whiteness of a wall (i.e. I suppose by the image of that whiteness in one organ of sense:) 3. by a similitude in the eye, of that similitude which arises by reflexion: as we see God in his works, or a landscape in a mirror, where the image presented to the mind is a similitude of the image in the glass which is a similitude of the thing itself.[3] The first (I suppose) is immediate vision, the second direct, the third indirect. The third is the 'videmus nunc in *speculo*.' Further there are two kinds of vision in speculo viz. clara et aperta, and obscura et occulta, or as it is also called enigmatical. The latter is St Paul's in aenigmate. Now for an instance of the enigmatical knowledge. Supposing ice was revealed, (we will say to the King of Siam, who had never seen it) thus: mother bore it, and its mother is born of it ⟨it bears its mother⟩; but what is the explanation of this is not given. How is a truth revealed enigmatically: the communication is true, but the mind receiving it does not understand more than the enunciation, not the thing, viz that it is frozen from water, and melts into water again.

Such is the knowledge, according to St Thomas, which we have of the

---

[1] See *Letters and Diaries*, XIX, p. 256, and Robin C. Selby *The Principle of Reserve in the Writings of John Henry Cardinal Newman*, Oxford 1975, pp. 63–4.

[2] In the preface to the fourth edition of *The Limits of Religious Thought*, London 1859, pp. xxxix–xl, H. L. Mansel wrote that a better acquaintance with Newman's works might have led him to express his arguments better, and then quoted from *Oxford University Sermons*, pp. 348–9.

[3] *In Epist 1 ad Cor.*, Cap. XIII, Lectio iv.

invisible world and its Almighty Creator. And such in whatever I have written I have considered it to be. And next what words as [are] to be used in describing it. 1. It is more than mere *relative* knowledge, and I don't think I have ever so called it, though I dare say Mr Mansell does. I have not, from being at a very early date warned off the world [sic] by Dr Whately's adoption of it, in order to convey his Sabellianizing notion of the Holy Trinity; the word Person, in his teaching, being not an absolute fact in the Divine Nature, but a relation of the Divine Nature towards us, God acting towards us as Father, as Redeemer, as Sanctifier. 2. It conveys speculative, and not merely practical truth. I have not been equally careful here, and I believe from the circumstance that those words, are not used by Protestants in the Catholic sense of them; speculative meaning not absolute, but disjoined from practical utility or human needs, and practical meaning, not what is not absolute but what has a bearing on those needs. I do not recollect I have ever said the revealed doctrine was not speculatively true, but I have said it was practically true. 3. Mr Mansell uses the word *regulative* instead of practical.[4] This is a word of his own. If it means truth which, while speculative, has a bearing upon practice, or absolute truth revealed so far forth as is practically useful to us, I accept it, but not in another sense. 4. Whether the word *allegorical* can be used, I do not know; St Thomas, if I understand him, seems to do so. 5 My own word from first to last has been *economical*, as I have explained it especially in my work on the Arians. Now to give some instances of it, which after all will fall short of St Thomas's own illustration cited above, or in other words do not go so far in boldness, I think as St Thomas (Sensibilia ad hoc ducere intellectum nostrum non possunt, ut in iis divina substantia videatur *quid sit*, quum sint effectus, causae virtutem non aequantes; sed *quia est*. S. Thom Contr. Gentes p 4 [I, iii]) 1. instances of *partial* truth, i.e. truth, as far as it goes, and not the whole truth. Theologians e.g. Viva allow that ⟨speak of⟩ our enigmatica cognitio Dei, being praecisiva; and as instances he gives the knowledge of the essence of God without His attributes, one attribute without another, the essence without the Personalities, and one Person without the other two.

The above instance of the ice is of the same kind; true as far as it goes but inadequate.

Parable   Shadow for
Scarlet   substance

The best instance that occurs to me of this partial truth is one almost too familiar to mention, though it conveys better than most in what way revelation deals with us. I mean, the answer given to a child who asks what an ox is — The father is represented as answering 'The ox is the calf's *uncle*'.

I recollect a child during the wars at the beginning of this century asking about Bonaparte and being answered that 'he was a naughty man, who took all the toys of little boys' – which was quite true. (Holland being closed as a

[4] Op. cit., p. 127.

toymarket) 2. Instances of undefined or indistinct truth viz. when by means of figures which do not supply the means to determine how far and to what limit the images employed represent the truth revealed to us. The most obvious instance of this is the case of parables; in which it is debated by commentators how far we may pursue the meaning of the figure or interpret the figure into unseen realities. In such cases the task is often quite beyond us of drawing the line between shadow and substance. E.g. in the parable of the Paterfamilias what is meant, or is any thing meant by the torcular and the turris by the first servants, and by the second servants?[5] In the parable of the talents what is meant, or is any thing, by the unicuique secundum propriam virtutem, by the two talents and the five. In the miracle of the loaves is any thing meant by the five loaves, the 5000 and the seven loaves and the 4000, the two fishes and the few small fishes which are not numbered, the 12 baskets of fragments and the 7?

On the other hand when we are read the parable of the Unjust Steward, we are obliged by the analogy of faith and morals to deny that he is put before us as a pattern to us of fidelity and honesty, but of prudence. Again the widow not the unjust judge is the part of the parable which has a fulfilment and our Lord does not come as thief in the night, except in his suddenness.

3 Instances of approximation to the truth by various images correcting each other. We cannot imagine heavenly truths, we cannot express them, Scripture cannot reveal them — except under the terms of sense and of experience. Scripture calls the Second Person of the Blessed Trinity Reason or the Word; this image taken by itself has led to Sabellianism, as if He were impersonal. It calls Him the Son; this taken by itself as [sic] lead to Arianism, as if a Son must have a beginning posterior to his Father. Taken together they limit each other; he is as intimately one with the Father as our reason is with ourselves, He is as distant for Him as a Son from a Father; He is the same God as the Father, yet without ceasing to be Himself; he can undertake an office of ministration and of dependence, without ceasing to be God. The limitation which these separate figures place upon the meaning of each other, plainly does not exhaust all possible limitations. They do not finish ⟨complete⟩ ⟨present a complete portrait⟩ an exhibition of the divine fact; they do but suggest certain portions of the whole. Though we speak of the 'Son and Word' we have not thereby a clear or perfect picture of the second person of the Divine Trinity, but a broken outline and a faintly coloured ⟨tinted⟩ picture.

4. Sometimes only one definite image is taken, and we have to discover by reason or by external teaching the point of the analogy. Thus when if a blind man were told, to take the common image, that scarlet was like the sound of a trumpet, it would give him a certain vague notion of the colour, as good as he could receive, and a real true notion, though vague, and though

[5] *Matthew* 21:33–31.

he included in it ideas which did not belong to it. For instance, it is said that Mozart fainted when a boy on hearing the sound, from its imperfection and dissonance which accompanies it. If the blind attached in consequence to the idea of scarlet that of harshness and heterogeneity, he would be introducing an idea never intended. Yet if we attempted to set him right he might answer 'Well, I cannot for the life of me separate the sound of the trumpet from that crash frightening the air out of its proprieties; in it consists its characteristic effect.' And if we persisted, he would say, 'Well, if in spite of this scarlet is analogous to the sound of a trumpet, it is a mystery; I must take it on faith.'

Parallel to this is the Scripture language concerning God's wrath, jealousy, and repentance. They convey to us ideas of states of mind which we cannot possibly dissociate from human imperfection — but we believe, without knowing how, that they stand in Him for nothing but what is perfect.

4 [5] Instances of deduction. The view of nature irresistiblly leads us to the notion of design — You may call it anthropomorphism or fetism, but it does. Who can read a work like Paley's Natural Theology without having his imagination powerfully affected towards that conclusion? Yet is is most difficult to support these deductions on strictly philosophical grounds, and it would seem as if the bulk of men in consequence who believe in God argumentatively, believe on a wrong basis. For argument's sake I grant it ⟨this⟩. But let us suppose there *is* a God — Then, it is that an uncertain or unsound ⟨imperfect⟩ argument leads to a right conclusion. Now is it impossible that God should have chosen an argument ⟨deals with men according to their powers⟩, which though not logically impregnable, is higher [highly?] impressive, and *the fact*, to bright [bring?] the multitude, as by the imagination, to a truth which logic and metaphysics cannot reach, but which they could know in no other way?

In this way of viewing the subject, the Almighty may be considered to *try* men according to the constitution of their intellect, in order to manifest their secret moral tendencies. We are so constituted that we do naturally argue from ourselves to God, and Scripture encourages and sanctions the process. He is represented there as a sovereign, on a throne, delighting in the praises paid Him etc. This is the popular view of religion, and it comes to us by inspiration.

And it is intended to try the separate hearts to which it is presented. For as regards the multitude none but hard and irreligious hearts will or can reject it. Hence it does not go so far as the remarkable instance in the gospel in which our Lord feigns making as though He would have gone further — or His repelling the Syrophoenician woman — trials of faith arising out of a representation which was short of the absolute ⟨simple⟩ truth; at the same time they are true as far as they go, while these instance alluded to are only indirectly and interpretatively true.

Theology on the other hand takes the more philosphical view, and explains these things. It tells us that the Almighty delights in our praises for our own sake, not for His own — that He is not angry, or repentant in the way of human passion, as I have already said. Nay that He is not good in the sense in which we are good, but in an analogous ⟨?⟩ and higher sense; that all the words we use of God must be taken in a transcendant sense; that we talk, for instance, of God as one and three, but strictly speaking number does not enter into His essence; without beginning and ending, as if necessary existence had more to do with duration, than the mathematical truth that the 3 angles of a triangle equal 2 right angles and so on. Nay that what is told us is not true, but it is not true in that nearest approach to truth which our intellect, whose object is truth, can arrive at, and which after all is rather negative than positive — but a religious truth, i.e. truth in that form in which force and the positive are gained by clothing it in human forms.

It must be considered in this point of view that the very notion of a variety of attributes instead of one infinitely simple perfection is but a mode of speech by which we convey to our minds in some faint degree what God is — not as if those attributes were not real and absolute but they are such not in the form of attributes but as existing incomprehensibly in the ineffable unity of the Divine Essence.

Nay it would seem as [if] the same thing may in some sense be said even of the creation, and of matter, and of material and as it will throw light upon the doctrine which I am illustrating I will enlarge upon it.

Now nothing I am going to say is intended to give any sanction to the doctrine of Berkeley who denied the existence of matter. I begin by laying it down that it is a real substance as much so as the soul or an angelic nature, or the Supreme Being, but it is one thing to say that it really exists, quite another to identify it with the nature under which it presents itself to our minds — and on this point I should like under correction to hold as follows:—

The ideas under which we conceive of matter through the instrumentality of one sense are very different from those which we derive through another; a man who had only the sense of taste or hearing and no other, would [have] extremely vague or (I may say) erroneous, because partial notions of what matter was. In like manner a man who had only the sense of taste would hardly have any idea about matter in common with a man who had only the sense of touch. Moreover, a man who had only one or two senses, as smell and hearing, would be utterly unable to conceive the existing of other senses, till he was told of their existence, and would think that two senses were all that could be and that matter had the attributes of sound and scent and no other. How then do we know but that there may be a sixth sense and a seventh sense possible, which would throw our idea of matter into a sphere of thought, at present utterly unsuspected and beyond imagination? Further may we not suppose our present senses being simpy annihilated, and five new senses given us which would make us take a view of matter utterly distinct from our present notion

This reflection shows us that we cannot rely on the senses for giving us any kind of idea of what matter is in itself or absolutely, since a being who had our five senses would have an idea of it simply heterogeneous to that which would be possessed by a being who had other five senses. Now it may be said, of course, that such informants though altogether independent of each other, are not inconsistent with each other; that their separate informations may be true together; that each fresh sense *adds* knowledge as far as it goes of properties of matter which was otherwise unknown, and not *undoes* what another sense seemed to teach; that it does not follow that colour is not a real thing, because it is not brought to our knowledge by any other of the senses. But this representation is not fully borne out; for the senses certainly do *correct* each other, that is, we are forced to unlearn our trust in some of their announcements as real by means of announcements through others.

Now every thing depends on proving this. The various images which we have about unseen things in theology carry with them their economical nature from the fact that one contradicts or modifies each other — as our Lord is both Pastor and Agnus — priest and sacrifice etc. He is the Word in one portion of the sense of the word Word, and Son in one portion of the sense of the word Son. If then one sense in the fullest of its ⟨its direct⟩ manifestations brings an idea about matter which another sense contradicts, it is plain that the senses too are economical, or only tell us the absolute truth to a certain point. Without then determining that there is no other way besides this of proving that the senses are in the category of figures, it is of great importance to prove that they are, if they are.

Here, in the first place, it is not necessary that one sense which directly profess its contradict to another [sic], for that is impossible — by the hypothesis each sense being confined to its own limits, and knowing nothing of the existence of another or of its teaching. It cannot contradict that (e.g. solidity, or inertia) of which it does not know the existence. But what is to be sought is some *positive teaching* of a sense which contradicts the positive teaching of another sense —

Such I consider smell to supply as contrasted with sight. Sight gives us the idea of extension and of a whole and parts; and of matter being divisible. On the other hand smell, I conceive, gives us an idea of matter as indivisible — scents being perfect at once without reference to time, as indivisible as thought, yet as perfectly distinct from each other as one thought from another. It would seem then as if the teaching of smell is not true in its fulness, if the teaching of the sight is true — for the smell impresses upon one the idea that matter is indivisible — but if one or other cannot be true as regards this popular attribute of matter, perhaps smell is true and not sight — or in other words, extension ⟨duration⟩ and divisibility are not essential attributes of matter — or that, though matter is one thing and spirit another, extension or divisibility is not that in which they essentially differ.

To take other instances . . .

So different are the senses from each other, that we can conceive ⟨(Has not Whately — thoughts of this kind somewhere?)⟩ the possibility, of a new sense being granted us utterly different from any of the existing senses, and again equal for all practical uses to the whole five together and such as to bring in new ideas, as specific, important, and vast, as *space* is, an idea which we should not gain e.g. from the smell — or (if it be objected that space is not conceived by the senses but is an original form of the intellect, then I say) as straight lines, curves, figures etc. Let us suppose a race of men with this new sense, and the original five senses wanting to them, and this new sense supplying their loss. Such men by the hypothesis would ⟨might⟩ be responsible beings on their trial, they could ⟨would⟩ hold intercourse with each other, they could form society, they would have a history — they would have records — yet all in a sphere as different as heaven is from earth.

Index of Persons

Index of Subjects

169